Personal Investment:

financial planning in an uncertain world

Personal Investment:

financial planning in an uncertain world

Mariana Mazzucato, Jonquil Lowe, Alan Shipman and Andrew Trigg

The Open University

palgrave
macmillan

Published by

PALGRAVE MACMILLAN

Palgrave Macmillan in the UK is an imprint of Macmillan Publishers Limited, registered in England, company number 785998, of Houndmills, Basingstoke, Hampshire RG21 6XS

Palgrave Macmillan in the US is a division of St Martin's Press LLC, 175 Fifth Avenue, New York, NY l0010

in association with

The Open University, Walton Hall, Milton Keynes, MK7 6AA

First published 2010.

Edited, designed and typeset by The Open University.

Printed in Malta by Gutenberg Press Ltd.

The paper used in this publication is procured from forests independently certified to the level of Forest Stewardship Council (FSC) principles and criteria. Chain of custody certification allows the tracing of this paper back to specific forest-management units (see www.fsc.org).

This book forms part of the Open University course DB234 Personal investment in an uncertain world. Details of this and other Open University courses can be obtained from the Student Registration and Enquiry Service, The Open University, PO Box 197, Milton Keynes MK7 6BJ, United Kingdom (tel. +44 (0)845 300 60 90, email general-enquiries@open.ac.uk).

www.open.ac.uk

British Library Cataloguing in Publication Data: applied for

Library of Congress Cataloging in Publication Data: applied for

ISBN-13: 978-0-230-24660-7

1.1

Contents

Contributors

George Callaghan is Senior Lecturer in Economics at The Open University. He is co-editor of *Personal Finance* (Wiley, 2007) and author of *Flexibility, Mobility and the Labour Market* (Ashgate, 1997). His most recent research concerns the economic impact on local economies of communities that have bought their own land.

Jonquil Lowe is a Lecturer in Personal Finance at The Open University and a personal finance practitioner, specialising in consumer research and financial capability resources. Her recent book publications include *The Pension Handbook* (Which?, 2006), *Save and Invest* (Which?, 2008), *The Personal Finance Handbook* (Child Poverty Action Group, 2009) and, with Sara Williams, *The Financial Times Guide to Personal Tax* (Pearson Education, 2009).

Mariana Mazzucato is Professor of Economics of Innovation at The Open University. She is the coordinator of a European Commission collaborative project on Finance, Innovation and Growth, and Director of The Open University's research centre on Innovation, Knowledge and Development. Her work on the relationship between technological innovation and stock price volatility has been published in various journals. She is the author of *Firm Size, Innovation and Market Structure: The Evolution of Market Concentration and Instability* (Edward Elgar, 2000) and co-editor of *Knowledge Accumulation and Industry Evolution: Pharma-Biotech* (Cambridge University Press, 2006).

Janette Rutterford is Professor of Financial Management at The Open University Business School. She is the author of *Introduction to Stock Exchange Investment*, in its third edition (Palgrave Macmillan, 2007) and editor (with Anne Laurence and Josephine Maltby) of *Women and their Money 1700 to 1950* (Routledge, 2009). She is currently researching the identity of small investors in the USA and the UK in the nineteenth and twentieth centuries.

Alan Shipman is a Lecturer in Economics at The Open University. A former emerging-markets analyst and consultant, his publications include *The Market Revolution* (Routledge, 1999), *The Globalization Myth* (Icon, 2002) and *Knowledge Monopolies* (Imprint Academic, 2006).

Andrew Trigg is Senior Lecturer in Economics at The Open University. He is co-editor of *Economics and Changing Economies* (Thomson, 1996) and *Microeconomics: Neoclassical and Institutionalist Perspectives on Economic Behaviour* (Thomson, 2001); and author of *Marxian Reproduction Schema: Money and Aggregate Demand in a Capitalist Economy* (Routledge, 2006).

Preface

It is hard to escape the need for personal investment and financial planning. In many advanced economies, the affordability of state support during periods of unemployment, infirmity or old age is being questioned, driven in large part by the need to adapt to the demographic challenge of ageing populations. At the same time, decades of economic growth have raised societies' expectations about living standards throughout life. As a result, individuals and households are finding that increasingly they must organise their own financial security, and personal investment has become the main route.

The first objective of this book is to raise your understanding and confidence in making personal investment decisions. These will be affected by some factors outside your control (for example, inflation and the setting of interest rates) and others within your control (such as choices about the mix of assets that you hold). All financial planning requires an understanding of how the local context – your own particular situation – is part of a wider context, including the role of the economy and governments. In helping you to better understand both the local and wider context of investment planning, the book will help you to become more knowledgeable and thoughtful about your own investment decisions.

Some of you reading this book will be doing so as part of a university or college course covering personal investment and financial planning, for which this is a core text. You may be following, or preparing for, a career in financial services, an industry in which selling and giving advice about personal investment products plays a key role, and is going to increasingly require higher level study. In the UK, Level 4 of the Qualifications and Credit Framework in England, Wales and Northern Ireland or Level 7 of the Scottish Credit and Qualifications Framework has already been set as the new minimum qualification level for investment advisers from 2012 onwards, with a requirement for ongoing continual professional development. So a second objective of this book is to make a major contribution to that professional development for people working in the financial services industry.

The book explores the landscape of the financial services sector: how financial innovation creates new products and may change the nature of existing ones; how savers interact with providers and other players, such as banks, life companies, fund managers and advisers; the different incentives and conflicts involved; and the role of financial regulation. It will be useful for anyone who wants to know more about ways of planning for the financial future, and what happens to money once it leaves the hands of savers and investors.

Personal investment: financial planning in an uncertain world crosses traditional disciplinary boundaries to bring together economics, finance, statistics, history, business and sociology. It also draws on a wealth of relevant and topical examples from the everyday world around you, including bank runs, asset bubbles and changing pension provision. We hope that this book will not only empower you with a new understanding about how to plan your personal investments, but also give you a passion for understanding the fascinating subject of personal finance.

Acknowledgements

The Editors would like to thank Janette Rutterford of The Open University Business School and George Callaghan, at The Open University in Scotland, who authored Chapters 3 and 7, respectively, of this book. Particular thanks are also extended to Jérôme De Henau for his key role as a member of the project team.

The Editors would also like to acknowledge the substantial contributions to this project from: Leslie Budd, Ian Fribbance, Susan Himmelweit and Martin Upton at The Open University; our External Assessor, Professor Peter Howells of the Centre for Global Finance at Bristol Business School; and John Bloxham, financial services practitioner and Associate Lecturer with The Open University.

The book's production would have been impossible without extensive and generous assistance from the following people: Karen Barboteau, Brenda Barnett, Margrit Bass, Helen Birkbeck, Kathleen Calder, Heather Clarke, Lene Connolly, Jeff Edwards, Richard Golden, Paul Hillery, Shereen Karmali, Joanna Mack, Margaret McManus, Nic Morris, Luke Nolt, Sally O'Brien, Nina Randall, Liz Vidler and Andrew Whitehead, all at The Open University; and Martin Drewe at Palgrave Macmillan.

Disclaimer

This book does not claim to give specific individual financial advice and nothing contained within it should be interpreted as doing so. If you think that you need specific individual financial advice, you should see an authorised financial adviser.

Introduction

Mariana Mazzucato, Jonquil Lowe, Alan Shipman and
Andrew Trigg

Introduction

At some point in our lives most of us will save: for retirement, for a deposit on a home, or just for a rainy day. By not spending our money in the present, saving allows us to put aside resources for the future. Countries around the world differ greatly in the extent to which their citizens save. In Italy, for example, people have higher saving rates than in other large European countries, which means that they are less vulnerable to unexpected changes in personal and economic conditions. By contrast, US and British citizens are better known for their indebtedness than their savings, with the average American having 50 per cent more debt than income (Bucks et al., 2009). Those of us who are reluctant or unable to save are often encouraged by government to do so, usually through tax incentives or other subsidies.

Ensuring that savings will be available in future to meet an individual's or household's goals requires strategic planning and decision making. Investing strategically requires knowledge and understanding about the options available, the significance of the context in which choices are made and the implications of those choices. Consider the issue of inflation. Rising price levels damage the real value (buying power) of most investments. Therefore it is essential that investors understand where inflation comes from, how governments may react and the impact on different investments. For example, back in 1948, £60 would have purchased a new motorbike; 60 years later it could barely buy a pair of wing mirrors – a vivid demonstration of the destructive power of inflation. In comparison, £60 invested in the UK stock market in 1948, with income reinvested (ignoring tax), would have been worth over £50,000 by 2009 (based on data from Barclays Capital, 2009) – enough to buy ten motorbikes. Inflation compels investors to make choices to try to protect the future value of their money and to engage with stock markets. Even when savers put money into bank accounts, they usually expect a return that will beat inflation and this is possible only if banks invest the savings in some way.

This book provides an introduction to the main choices available to personal investors. Four types of assets will be considered as possible vehicles for investment: cash (meaning deposits, such as savings accounts), bonds, shares and property. These assets can be chosen directly, for example, by purchasing the shares of a particular company, or indirectly by investing in financial products, such as investment funds. Personal investment, as we broadly define it, looks at the investment of savings in such assets and their related financial products. (This can be distinguished from real investment, which refers to investment by companies in physical goods such as plant or machinery.)

To make personal investment choices, there are various techniques and tools available to investors. This book explains how these work and, in so doing, introduces you to the academic discipline of finance, a field to which many eminent economists have contributed. Key to this field of study is the lack of certainty about how returns from investment can be predicted. The share price of a particular company, for example, may be based on a calculation of future profits, which depend on a number of unknown factors. These might include the success of its future sales, how well it controls costs, the hiring of a new management team, or the trajectory of economic conditions. You will be introduced to the power of investment tools in turning unknown factors such as these into precise calculations, but also to the limitations of the tools in the face of uncertainty. That is not to say that such tools should be discarded, but their suitability must always be understood in the context in which they will be applied, just as, say, a hand lens would be a poor tool for scanning the horizon.

Table 1 A guide to common personal investment terms*

Term	What it means
Bonds	Investments that are loans to a government, company or other body. Typically, a bond has a set repayment date and, in the meantime, pays interest and can be bought and sold on the stock market.
Saving	The flow of money not used for current consumption and that contributes towards an individual's or household's savings.
Savings	The total value of all financial assets, including investments, that an individual or household has at a particular point in time.
Shares	Also called equities, securities or stocks. These are investments where each holder becomes part-owner of a company. The return may comprise regular dividends (a share of the company's profits) that are not guaranteed and/or a capital gain or loss when the shares are sold. Shares are often, but not always, traded on the stock market.

Investing	Saving is sometimes called 'investing', especially when the money is set aside for long-term goals. 'Investing' is often used to mean the purchase of financial or physical assets that involve some risk of capital loss. However, there is no set definition and the terms 'saving' and 'investing' are often used interchangeably.
Investment fund	A financial product that invests in a broad range of different bonds, shares and/or other assets.
Investments	This tends to mean assets that are traded on a stock market or products that invest in such assets. However, there is no set definition and across the financial services sector you will find the term used to mean different things.
Real value	The value or price of something after stripping out any change due to inflation. For example, if £100 is invested and grows to £110 but the general level of prices goes up 10 per cent, the real value of the investment is still only £100.

* These terms generally have different meanings when used by economists and business specialists. This book makes clear when a more specialist meaning is intended.

1 Themes in personal investment

Our intention, in writing this book, is to encourage you to think critically about personal investment. You will be encouraged to make informed decisions, to look at the implications in the small print when considering financial products, to understand how the operation of financial markets impacts on your planning, and to search behind the marketing messages and advice of providers and advisers. The book develops three main themes:

- *Risk and return.* To make a financial return from investments, individuals must take risks. Stocks and shares, for example, are more risky, but over long periods of time typically offer higher returns than bonds and cash. As you will explore in Chapter 1, even savings accounts are not risk free. This theme looks at the relationship between risk and return, and the extent to which investors can increase returns without necessarily incurring extra risk. It also highlights how our understanding of the risk–return relationship rests on some deeply embedded assumptions that we might want to question.

- *Uncertainty and change.* This theme explores the importance to personal investment of unforeseen forces and events. Some events occur suddenly, throwing investment plans into disarray. Other forces, such as population ageing, are more gradual, but generate great uncertainty for personal investment decisions.

- *Regulation and ethics.* Investors need to be assured that financial institutions are sound and that financial product providers and advisers are behaving in an ethical way. This may be achieved through formal regulation and the financial services sector's own ethical codes and practices. Both are forged within the context of government policies that aim to regulate the national and international economy in pursuit of stability and other goals. Ethics may also embrace a concern that the aims and actions of organisations issuing investments are compatible with social, religious, humanitarian and environmental objectives.

The following is a brief introduction to each theme, and why it is important to personal investment. Some key concepts will be introduced as part of this introduction.

1.1 Risk and return

Savers have a diverse choice when looking at ways to set aside resources for future consumption, and the options differ greatly in terms of risk. The least risky for personal investors is generally taken to be savings accounts, since they can easily be cashed in with no loss of the original capital invested (ignoring any erosion due to inflation). In other words, savings accounts have low **liquidity risk** and low **capital risk**.

Risk is related to return because the vast majority of investors must be persuaded to take on extra risk and the persuasion comes in the form of a higher potential return – a **risk premium** (only 'potential' otherwise there would be no risk). Of course, gamblers enjoy and seek out risk – they may be playing the financial markets for their own sake and require no extra reward, but most investors do not fall into this category.

The key choice that investors face over the degree of risk and return associated with their investments is illustrated in Figure 1. Risk is plotted along the horizontal axis of the chart and potential return on the vertical axis; the space created by these axes can be thought of as the **risk–return spectrum**. We have placed a number of investments in this space, choosing the position of each one according to the balance of risk and return that we think it offers. For example, we have put savings accounts in the bottom left-hand corner, corresponding to low risk but a potentially low return. Moving upwards and to the right, the investments become progressively more risky – generally because liquidity risk or capital risk or both increase – but the reward for the extra risk is a higher potential return; in other words the *risk premium* increases. Shares are very risky, which is why most people do not buy them individually but instead invest in a broad spread of different shares through an investment fund. On the whole, where we have placed each investment should be fairly uncontroversial. But the investments shown are broad types, and within each type there will be examples of some that are higher risk and some lower risk than the position on the chart suggests. For example, a fund investing in the shares of small, high-growth companies may be more risky than buying shares in a single well-established high-street name.

Don't worry if some of the investments in Figure 1 are unfamiliar to you at present. Chapters 1 to 4 will introduce you to them, explaining how they work and the nature of the risks involved.

Liquidity risk
The risk of being unable to cash in an investment rapidly or at an acceptable price.

Capital risk
The possibility that investors may lose some or all of their original capital and returns made to date.

Risk premium
The extra return that an investor expects as a reward for choosing a risky investment rather than a risk-free one.

Risk–return spectrum
The relationship between the risk of, and return from, investments: usually, lower-risk investments offer lower returns, while investments offering the chance of higher returns involve additional risk.

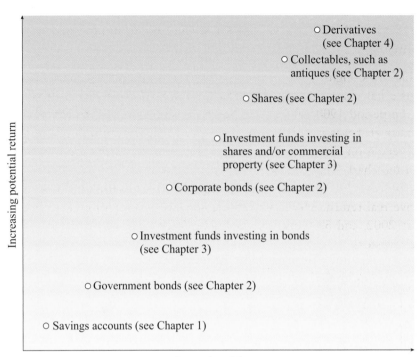

Figure 1 The risk–return spectrum

Activity 1

Many personal investors look on their home – or perhaps a buy-to-let property – as their most important investment and you may have noticed that neither of these is included in Figure 1. Where on the chart would you place them?

Whether or not a home should be viewed as an investment is debatable. Although the property may increase in value, there is the problem of selling it to realise the gain, since the owner will still need somewhere to live. It might be possible to sell and buy somewhere cheaper, but this is not certain. Setting that issue aside, investing in a single asset is always more risky than investing in many. In this case, the single property chosen could be affected by, for example, subsidence, a declining neighbourhood, plans to build a new road, and so on. By contrast, the fate of one property will have only a limited impact on a fund invested in a spread of many properties. However, the biggest impact on risk is the way in which homes and buy-to-let properties are usually bought: with a mortgage. You will explore in Chapter 1 how borrowing to invest (leverage) increases both the risk and potential return considerably. So there is no single position in Figure 1 where residential property comfortably fits.

The high-risk–high-return nature of shares is illustrated by Figure 2. This is a bar chart showing the annual real return on shares in the UK over the period 1900–2008. Each bar represents whether the return in a particular year was positive or negative. In 1975, for example, there was a real return on shares of 99.6 per cent, as represented by the highest bar in the chart. This contrasts with the real loss of 30.5 per cent in 2008, represented by the bar on the right-hand side showing this as a negative real return. The chart reports similarly big losses of 24.5 per cent in 2002, and 58.1 per cent in 1974. These were very bad years for share investors.

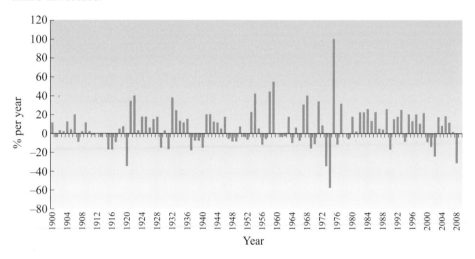

Figure 2 Annual real returns from shares quoted on the UK stock market 1900–2008

(Source: based on data from Barclays Capital, 2009)

One of the ways in which investors assess risk is by analysing information from the past like that in Figure 2. Although you will be looking at more sophisticated measures of risk later in the book, we can use the data in Figure 2 to calculate a simple indicator as follows. The chart shows that there were more years in which shares earned positive rather than negative returns: throughout the 1980s, for example, and most of the 1920s. We can see negative real returns for 39 years compared to 70 years in which investors made a positive real return. Investors made a negative return in 39 out of 109 years – or $(39/109) \times 100 = 36$ per cent of the years reported in Figure 2.

This type of calculation can be used to forecast the probability of making a real loss. An investor in 2009, for example, might say that there is a 36 per cent probability of making a real loss, based on information from the previous 1900–2008 period. As Paul Marsh, emeritus professor of finance at the London Business School, has argued: 'Bearing in mind that nothing can make shares "safe" over any time horizon – there is always going to be risk – the balance of probability and the record of history is on your side' (Wright and Cooper, 2009).

1.2 Uncertainty and change

What does it mean to say, as stated earlier, that risk can be calculated? This essentially means that we can assign probabilities to likely future developments, for example, on the basis of how often outcomes have occurred in the past. So if historically shares have earned higher returns than, say, bonds, we can assume that they also will in the future. A key problem with this type of calculation, however, is the uncertainty generated by major socio-economic change.

Would the 500 years of feudal history up to 1700 have provided much ability to forecast the development of technology in the 100 years of industrial revolution between 1750 and 1850? Or could anyone have predicted the aeroplanes crashing into the twin towers in New York? We now speak of 'the world after 9/11' to convey the idea that the world operates in such a different way after a major event that we can describe the world before and after that event.

These two examples illustrate how some major changes occur gradually, while others occur suddenly. For investors, a sudden tragic event such as 9/11 had an immediate unforeseen impact, for example, on the share values of airline and travel companies. Changes in technology during the industrial revolution – though more gradual – created uncertainty in a different way. Investors did not know the scope of the impact that the changes would have on industry and the economy. There were, for example, several railroad booms in the 1800s in which investors grossly overestimated the impact of new steam engines. Similarly, in 2000, investors overestimated the immediate impact of the internet, which led to a crash in share prices throughout the world.

Hindsight is a great thing. Events that now look as if they were bound to happen cannot always be predicted beforehand. The financial trader and academic Nicholas Taleb, in his book *The Black Swan*, gives the example of a turkey being fed each day. The turkey expects this to happen, since it has happened each previous day – but then it is Christmas time (Taleb, 2007, p. 40).

The global credit crunch that started in 2007 was not foreseen by most people. One key person was Adam Applegarth, chief executive of Northern Rock, the former building society turned bank. He presided over the first run on a British bank since 1866, but complained: 'I didn't see this coming. I have yet to find someone who did'; and Sir Callum McCarthy, then chairman of the Financial Services Authority (FSA), the regulator of the financial services in the UK, also insisted that the freezing of money markets was unprecedented (*The Economist*, 2007).

Northern Rock, like all other banks, was reviewed by the FSA to examine the risks in its business model, using probabilities of the type introduced earlier. But the FSA assessed Northern Rock as 'low probability' in terms of its risk framework (Financial Services Authority, 2008, p. 4). The problem was that Northern Rock's business model relied on the borrowing of funds from global financial markets, a source that had been readily available in the past. When these markets dried up, it suddenly lost its funding source – as suddenly as the turkey discovered Christmas.

Box 1 How they got it wrong

- 'Go back to Liverpool, Mr Epstein, groups with guitars are out.' Dick Rowe of Decca Records, rejecting the Beatles

- 'Get rid of the lunatic who says he's got a machine for seeing by wireless.' The editor of the *Daily Express* refusing to meet John Logie Baird – the man who invented television

- 'Everything that can be invented has been invented.' Charles H. Duell, commissioner, US Office of Patents, in 1899

- 'This "telephone" has too many shortcomings to be seriously considered as a means of communication. The device is of no value to us.' Western Union internal memo in 1876

- 'Drill for oil? You mean drill into the ground to try and find oil? You're crazy.' Drillers responding to Edwin L. Drake in 1859

- 'The wireless music box has no imaginable commercial value. Who would pay for a message sent to nobody in particular?' A businessman deciding not to invest in radio in the 1920s

> - 'Heavier-than-air flying machines are impossible.' Lord Kelvin, president of the Royal Society, in 1895
> - 'No flying machine will ever fly from New York to Paris.' Orville Wright
>
> (Symons, 2006, pp. 84–5)

The importance of uncertainty was emphasised by one of the great economists of the twentieth century, John Maynard Keynes, who you will read about in more depth in Chapter 5:

> By uncertain knowledge, let me explain, I do not mean merely to distinguish what is *known* for certain from what is only *probable*. The game of roulette is not subject, in this sense, to uncertainty … The sense in which I am using the term is that in which the prospect of a European war is uncertain, or the price of copper and the rate of interest twenty years hence, or the obsolescence of a new invention … About these matters there is no scientific basis on which to form any calculable probability whatever. We simply do not know!
>
> (Keynes, 1937, pp. 113–14)

Change and uncertainty go together for personal investors. If we believe that there are strong and violent undercurrents of social and economic change, then we may have less confidence in the predictive power of probability calculations. Each time there is a downturn in the stock market, for example, investors are unsure whether this will bring an end to previous returns, or whether the downturn is just a temporary correction. There is always a tension between recurring patterns of history and the enormous change that can be generated by improbable and unforeseen forces and events.

1.3 Regulation and ethics

Faced with this uncertain world, or just lacking the knowledge and tools of analysis, investors often turn to the advice of experts. Advice can help people to choose between the vast and complex range of financial products available.

The main business of the financial services sector is the selling of financial products: savings accounts, unit trusts, life funds and pensions are the main types of product available for private investing. Individuals requiring advice may rely either on providers, such as banks and life companies, and their agents for guidance on a relatively narrow range of products (tied advice), or turn to independent financial advisers, who can in principle recommend from the whole market. Advisers may charge a fee but historically have been paid by commission on products that they sell.

Although advisers are professionally committed to treating clients fairly, there is often a conflict of interest. While the self-interest of a commission-paid or tied adviser is to sell particular financial products, the interest of the client may be to purchase other products or even no products at all. There are numerous examples of products being sold without due care and attention to the needs of clients. In 2002, for example, Royal & Sun Alliance was fined £1.35 million for failing to pay compensation to over 13,000 of its customers who had been mis-sold pensions (Financial Services Authority, 2002). Between 2000 and 2005, nine providers were fined a total of £8 million for mis-selling mortgage-related endowment policies; and over £1 billion in redress was paid to 695,000 customers for whom these stock-market-linked products were unsuitable (Financial Services Authority, 2005). In 2009 John McFall, chairman of the Treasury Select Committee, called for an inquiry into the mis-selling of 'capital secure' savings products to 6000 UK investors (McFall, 2009). These products, in which some had invested all of their life savings, became suddenly worthless when the US investment bank Lehman collapsed in October 2008.

For the adviser–client relationship to work properly, the adviser must give advice that is in the interests of the client. This requires the adviser to have a moral approach, in which the interests of the client are paramount. Such an adviser follows ethics, a set of moral principles or codes that guide conduct. Ethics are a part of our everyday life. Whenever we choose to pay a bit more for fair-trade coffee, refrain from telling lies or give time to a local charity, we behave ethically: in a way that is not necessarily in our own self-interest, but is in the interests of another party or obeys an ingrained sense of what is 'right'.

Even some of the most vehement defenders of individual self-interest have recognised the importance of ethics. Adam Smith, often called the father of economics, famously argued that the reason why free markets work so well is because each individual acts according to their self-interest. But Smith also argued that individuals can trade with each other in a market only if they have a moral sentiment, or ethic, for the interests of others. When two individuals haggle over a price, they have to consider the interests of the other party in order to reach agreement.

But what if professional ethics do not prevail? Governments and other bodies often step in to impose rules and guidelines. We have seen, for example, that advisers face the prospect of fines if they are found guilty of mis-selling. This is an example of external regulation – the setting and implementation of rules and policies by government and other bodies – reinforcing or replacing professional self-regulation.

Regulation frequently transcends national boundaries, requiring international agreements and regulators. Countering this, a key socio-economic change that has characterised the world economy in the 30 years to 2009 has been a move towards liberalisation. Many of the rules that governed the behaviour of banks and stock markets were relaxed in the 1980s and 1990s, criticised as being out of date and inflexible, or just unworkable because of the changes wrought by financial innovation and globalisation. However, Robert Jenkins, chairman of the Investment Management Association, has complained: 'it has been the mantra in the UK that light bank regulation is good and heavy regulation is bad. The result: light touch became soft touch' (Jenkins, 2009). Throughout the book, and particularly in Chapter 7, the theme of regulation, its implementation and the tensions with the free development of markets will be explored.

At a higher level, economic policy can also be viewed as a form of regulation. As you will see in Chapter 5, important ways in which governments regulate the economic and financial system are through the setting of interest rates and taxation. Surprisingly, economic regulation is a relatively recent phenomenon. Before the Second World War, there was much less government involvement than we are used to today. The experience of many economies going into deep **depression** in the 1930's Great Depression convinced many governments that the economy had to be actively managed to keep it on track and prevent further crises. This structural change has had a major impact on personal investment. Investors have learned to anticipate how government intervention can impact on the prospects for economic growth and price inflation. Governments' economic management policies aim both to contain inflation and can be a source of inflation. You have already seen how inflation damages the returns to savers but conversely borrowers benefit (since their debts are reduced in real terms). So there are winners and losers, and this highlights the ethical dimension that is present in all regulation: who benefits and who bears the costs?

Depression
A prolonged period of low economic activity and high unemployment.

During the course of your journey through this book, you will learn how financial products, financial markets and financial regulation are interlinked and constantly changing together. Financial crises prompt the creation of new regulations. The regulatory framework stimulates new products, new markets and new strategies, often as ways to circumvent regulatory constraints. The three themes introduced here will help you to understand this dynamic tension between innovation and regulation, and its implications for personal investment.

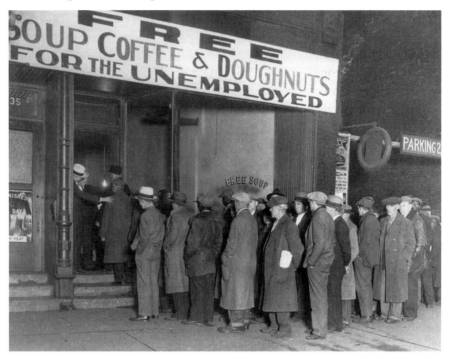

The Great Depression in the 1930s caused a structural change in government economic policies

2 Structure of the book

We have chosen these themes as key dimensions to the understanding of personal investment. Continuing the example of inflation, you will see how understanding inflation is fundamental to thinking about risk and return. Investors may accept higher risk in order to increase their chance of a return that will match or beat inflation. But looking into the future also means that there is uncertainty about what will happen: will investors face low inflation, as in the 1990s, or high inflation, as experienced in the 1970s? Ethics have a key role to play here, with financial advisers having a duty of care that the retirement incomes of customers are not eaten away by rising prices. And governments have to ensure through regulation that inflation is not allowed to get out of control.

The book is divided into four parts: 'Products and players', 'Strategies and markets', 'Bubbles and the economy', 'Regulation and the long term'. These parts gradually build from an understanding of the main tools of investment, through to the wider context and a critique of the role of personal investment. Throughout these four parts, the three themes develop, encouraging you to look at the big issues and wider context of personal investment, and providing a framework for considering the concepts, ideas and arguments that you meet.

In Part One, Products and players, we start in the lower left corner of the risk–return spectrum by looking at where most people in the UK put at least some of their money: accounts with banks and building societies. Chapter 1 examines how banks work in order to unravel the risks involved in placing your savings there and asks: are bank accounts really safe? Chapter 2 introduces the other three main assets considered in the book – bonds, shares and property – and demonstrates simple methods for calculating their potential return and inherent risks. The chapter highlights some of the assumptions behind these calculations in relation to uncertainty and change.

As we progress to Part Two, Strategies and markets, Chapter 3 demonstrates how investors can combine the main assets to create a portfolio. You will look at theories for selecting portfolios that suggest how investors can manage risk and improve the balance between the risks and returns that they face. In the process, you will consider whether investors should simply aim to follow the market or gain from actively choosing different companies' shares and timing their investments. Chapter 4 examines how financial markets work, with particular attention to one of the key socio-economic changes that have taken place in modern times: the growth of complex financial products such as derivatives. Not only has this change altered the economic context for all investing, it is also responsible for the growth of more complicated personal financial products that can leave investors unsure about what they have really invested in and the degree of risk involved.

Part Three, Bubbles and the economy, invites you to consider the context of financial planning in national economies and how these can be affected by financial crises and bubbles. In Chapter 5, you will be introduced to the driving forces of the economic landscape in which investors operate. It looks at key economic indicators that concern investors, such as inflation, economic growth and interest rates, and some of the main theories that have been developed by professional economists to explain their behaviour. Chapter 6 looks in more depth at how judgements are made about putting a value on assets. Of particular importance is the way in which investors behave during 'bubbles' (periods when asset prices rise dramatically without obvious reason). This chapter explores the implications of these financial anomalies for economic theories about investment behaviour and for practical decisions about which products to invest in.

In Part Four, Regulation and the long term, Chapter 7 focuses on the regulation of financial markets, looking at both the UK and the international context. Chapter 8 provides a conclusion, drawing together the main investment tools and theories developed throughout the book. The particular problem of long-term investment for retirement is used to illustrate how these personal investment tools can be applied and the limitations inherent in them. The book closes by raising some challenging questions about the interrelationship between personal investment and the goals of society as a whole.

References

Barclays Capital (2009) *Equity Gilt Study*, London, Barclays Capital.

Bucks, B., Kennickell, A., Mach, T. and Moore, K. (2009) 'Changes in US family finance from 2004–2007: evidence from the Survey of Consumer Finances', *Federal Reserve Bulletin*, vol. 95, pp. A1–A55.

Economist, The (2007) 'Lessons of the fall', 18 October.

Financial Services Authority (FSA) (2002) 'FSA fines R&SA 1.35 million for pensions review failings', press notice, London, FSA, 27 August.

Financial Services Authority (FSA) (2005) 'Mortgage endowments: progress report and next steps', London, FSA.

Financial Services Authority (FSA) (2008) 'The supervision of Northern Rock: a lessons learned review', London, FSA.

Jenkins, R. (2009) 'Speech to the Chartered Financial Analyst Society of the UK' [online], www.investmentuk.org/news/speeches/2009/CFAspeechbyRobertJenkinsApr2009.pdf (Accessed 3 July 2009).

Keynes, J.M. (1937) 'The general theory of employment', *Quarterly Journal of Economics*, vol. 51, no. 2, pp. 109–23.

McFall, J. (2009) 'John McFall urges FSA to investigate potential mis-selling' [online], www.johnmcfall.com/news2.aspx?i_PageID=105425 (Accessed 3 July 2009).

Symons, M. (2006) *How to Avoid a Wombat's Bum … And Other Fascinating Facts*, London, Doubleday.

Taleb, N. (2007) *The Black Swan*, London, Penguin Books.

Wright, M. and Cooper, K. (2009) 'Beat the stock market's lost decade', *The Sunday Times*, 8 February.

PART ONE: PRODUCTS AND PLAYERS

It is common sense that people armed with skills such as budgeting and planning ahead, as well as up-to-date information about new products, will be better able to cope with what life throws at them. It is also common sense that consumers will be more confident and trusting if they know a robust system of consumer protection is in place to ensure firms act in good faith. [...]

But there are limits. Will most consumers ever fully understand how a complex product works – indeed do most consumers even want to know? Can a consumer ever know as much about a product as the provider who sells it? Is it reasonable to expect consumers to be always up-to-date, given the levels of innovation in the market? Is it reasonable for consumers to assume that advisers know more about products than they do, and to rely on that advice? [...]

> Lord Adair Turner, Chairman of the UK Financial Services Authority, speech to 'Helping Consumers Through the Recession' conference, Cambridge, 15 July 2009

Thought-provoking questions for Chapters 1 and 2:

- What investment products can people use to maximise and manage financial provision through their life course? How can they identify appropriate investment strategies?
- How can higher returns on investment best be balanced against higher risks? Have recent financial crises changed our understanding of uncertainty and risk – and of the financial institutions that claim to spread and transfer them?

Chapter 1
From saving to investment

Alan Shipman

1 Introduction

Learning outcomes

After reading this chapter, you will:

- be able to describe the risk and return characteristics of savings accounts
- understand how banks operate and have changed
- be able to interpret a bank's financial accounts
- understand systemic risk and the need for bank regulation.

[handwritten note: money guaranteed up to 85k banks lend to others, but may not get it back]

For most people, managing money and making provision for the future begin with a visit to the local or online branch of a financial institution. In the UK, the ones to which most people entrust their money are banks or building societies. In other countries, credit unions and post offices also play an important role. These are called *retail* financial institutions – because, like other retailers, they deal directly with members of the public. Insurance companies are also financial institutions with large retail operations, selling policies that compensate for various unfortunate events, along with investment products and pensions. Most banking groups run large insurance operations, so banks are embedded in all aspects of personal investment.

New technology has allowed banks and building societies to conduct more of their interaction with customers through automated telling machines (ATMs) and via the internet. But most still centre their operations on a large branch network and this provides most of the jobs in financial services. Out of just under 1.1 million people working in UK financial services in 2008, around 500,000 were employed in banks and another 50,000 in building societies. In contrast, the City of London, one of the world's largest financial centres, employed fewer than 300,000 in banking, investment and insurance at its most recent peak in 2006–07 (Gordon et al., 2008, p. 14).

Our dealings with financial institutions often start early in life – perhaps via a deposit account taken out as a child, a student loan, or savings towards a first big purchase like a home or a car. In the UK, the USA and other higher-income economies, more than 90 per cent of people have a bank account, a far higher proportion than hold investments such as stocks and shares. Thus banks are an integral part of personal investment, and bank accounts are usually viewed as the safest, most basic way to hold savings. This is why they appear in the extreme bottom left of the risk–return spectrum that you met in the Introduction and which is reproduced in Figure 1.

This first chapter looks more closely at how banks help individuals and households to manage their resources to deal with an uncertain world, through loans and savings. It will explain how banks can offer savers accounts that are at the lowest end of the risk–return spectrum, while investing their money in much riskier ways. You will be looking at the problems that can arise from this transfer of risk from households and businesses to the banks. Most big banks use their long histories and the solidity of their buildings to reinforce their sense of permanence. But they perform a complicated and sometimes hazardous operation with the nation's money. This is demonstrated when something goes wrong with the banks' calculations, as has happened with some frequency since the rise of the modern economy – most recently in the crisis that began in 2007 – and is an example of the way uncertainty is an inescapable theme when considering investments.

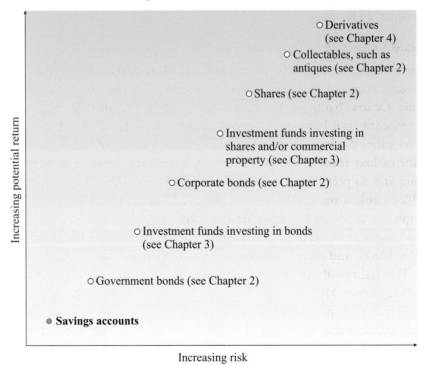

Figure 1 Savings accounts in the risk–return spectrum

Around the world a number of financial institutions, including some of the largest, came close to collapse during 2007–08. Northern Rock, a UK bank, was the first and most visible, because its depositors got involved in a 'bank run' – queuing up to withdraw their money – for fear that they'd lose it if they left it in any longer. The funding problem that Northern Rock ran into (explored further in Section 3.3) was also experienced by a number of other banks and building societies in the UK, and their counterparts elsewhere in Europe and the USA. But the others avoided a run, and were able to keep their doors open without long lines of worried customers queuing through them. The crisis was a reminder that, unlike people dealing with other large corporations, the customers of deposit-taking financial institutions, such as banks, have three lines of defence against losing their money, as described below.

Deposit insurance

Banks and building societies subscribe to a fund (in the UK, the Financial Services Compensation Scheme, FSCS) that repays savers if a subscribing institution fails. This 'deposit insurance' guarantees that deposits cannot be lost, at least up to a set limit. In the UK, the FSCS covered deposits up to £50,000 per person in each banking group after 7 October 2008.

Rescue measures for individual banks

Governments, usually working through a **central bank**, will often intervene to ensure the rescue of an institution that gets into financial trouble. Central banks, originally set up to extend and manage the government's own borrowing, now monitor banks, coordinating their actions when the banking system comes under strain and acting as their **lender of last resort**. The aim is to ensure that the banks continue trading and to prevent depositors from losing confidence. If possible, a troubled bank is rescued by others that are financially stronger. For example, in 2008 the UK government allowed the Spanish banking group Santander to take over the Alliance & Leicester and Bradford & Bingley banks, and relaxed its competition rules to enable Lloyds to take over The Halifax–Bank of Scotland (HBOS), while the US government sold Washington Mutual to JPMorgan Chase after taking it into public administration to prevent collapse. If private-sector rescuers cannot be found, governments can themselves take control of failing commercial institutions, as happened during 2008–09 in the UK with Northern Rock, Royal Bank of Scotland and Lloyds Banking Group (formed after Lloyds had taken over HBOS). The Belgian, Dutch and Luxembourg

Central bank
The bank that issues a nation's currency, sets its interest rates, manages its foreign currency and supervises other banks. Examples are the Bank of England (UK), the Federal Reserve System (USA) and the European Central Bank (eurozone).

Lender of last resort
A central bank function under which it lends to banks that are in difficulty and unable to borrow from elsewhere.

governments staged a similar rescue for Fortis, while the US government assisted Citibank and Bank of America.

Measures to stabilise the whole banking system

Banks are heavily interconnected – borrowing from and lending to one another, investing in one another, and insuring one another's investments. When one bank gets into financial trouble, it tends to endanger others, which find that money they've lent cannot be returned, and investments they've made are suddenly worth less. Widespread loss of confidence can create a **systemic risk** to all other banks; even the fear of trouble at one bank can be enough to trigger a run on other banks. So as well as rescuing particular financial institutions that run into trouble, governments and central banks use regulation to try to minimise systemic risk, a subject that you will look at more closely in Chapter 7.

Banks can therefore be considered to be safe, not because they never take risks with depositors' money, but because there are extensive regulatory safeguards against bank failure. Thus the theme of regulation is central to the role of banks and the savings and investments that they offer. Section 2 explains the importance of banks, which motivates governments to offer these safeguards. The risks that banks run, which make such protections necessary, are examined in Section 3. Finally, Section 4 examines why matching savers and borrowers cannot just be left to market forces, and how banks and other institutions have taken on the role of intermediaries that act as substitutes for the market.

Systemic risk
The danger that problems in one financial institution will spread through the whole system, due to the way in which institutions are financially interconnected. Because of its huge scale and unpredictability, it is not a risk that can be insured against without government help.

2 High-street banks: the first place to save?

Most people have to deal with banks – as a place to store and draw out money, or to borrow it if income isn't enough. Whenever we deal with a bank, we're connecting with a much wider financial system. Even if savers only ever put money into a current or savings account, the bank will channel this into investments in order to make it work harder and earn a return. When customers borrow from a bank, it uses similarly complicated strategies to keep down its costs and spread the risks. Although this means that banking is an inherently risky business, it is nonetheless essential to the whole economy.

2.1 Banks: important for households

The proportion of adults (and older children) with bank accounts has steadily risen over recent decades, with governments and employers encouraging this trend by paying benefits and wages direct into accounts. Compared with dealing in cash, storing and moving money in and through a bank has several advantages for households and small businesses:

- *Safety.* Less risk of money being lost, stolen or physically damaged.
- *Transparency.* Automatic record of receipts and payments through the account, useful for managing money and giving tax information.
- *Lower transaction cost and greater convenience.* Especially when transferring money long-distance, and for international and internet transactions where buyer and seller don't meet in the same place.
- *Interest.* Money not needed immediately can go into an account that earns interest. This offers some protection against inflation. But savings accounts offer a positive real interest rate only if the after-tax rate is above the rate of price inflation (see Box 1 overleaf).
- *Access to credit and other financial products.* Borrowing through a bank account is often easier and cheaper than arranging a separate loan from a financial institution, or borrowing from family and friends. Having a bank account is an important factor in assessing creditworthiness for other types of borrowing. Payments into insurance policies and pensions often have to be made from a bank account.

Box 1 Inflation

'Inflation' is a rise in the general level of prices, which means that over time a constant sum of money will buy less and less. The rate of inflation is published by the government and is measured as the percentage change in the price of a large basket of goods and services that are typical of the way households spend their money.

If inflation were 3 per cent over the next year, a household with typical expenditure would need £103 (3 per cent more) next year to buy the same things that it can buy today with £100. The impact of inflation is a key reason why households save and invest rather than just putting cash under the mattress. But savings and investments are not usually guaranteed to grow by enough to keep pace with or exceed inflation. For example, if a £100 deposit earned £3 interest over the next year after tax, the saver would get back £103. But if inflation were 4 per cent, that £103 would buy only the same as £99 today. The savings would have earned a negative real after-tax return of approximately −1 per cent.

Despite the advantages, an estimated 2.8 million UK adults (7 per cent of the adult population) were 'unbanked', having no account of their own, in 2003, prompting a government-backed initiative to extend basic account provision (British Bankers' Association, 2006). In the USA, surveys suggest that the comparable figure was 25–28 million, up to 14 per cent of the population, according to a Visa/BearingPoint study (Center for Financial Services Innovation, 2006). In the older (15) member states of the European Union (EU), 'two adults in ten lack access to transaction banking facilities' (EU Commission, 2008). At least as many are 'underbanked', with much of their income, expenditure and borrowing relying on cash transactions outside their account. Box 2 considers reasons why so many people remain unbanked.

Financial exclusion
The inability to access mainstream financial services, and employment and market opportunities linked to these. Factors contributing to exclusion may include low income, location, adverse history and inappropriate products.

Box 2 The unbanked: left out of account?

Financial exclusion has been defined as the inability, difficulty or reluctance of particular groups to access mainstream financial services. To this could be added that the services accessed are inappropriate ... In an increasingly cashless economy, the consequences of not holding a bank account increase financial exclusion. The fall in the proportion of low-income households without a bank account has coincided with the introduction of two new types of account – basic bank accounts and post office card accounts. Many of those with bank accounts are on the margins of banking and barely use their account. About half of basic bank account holders prefer to withdraw all their money each week and manage it as cash. They do this because it gives them more control over their finances than an account that does not suit their needs, or because they have a basic bank account that comes with only a cash card.

Causes of financial exclusion from banking or savings accounts are interlinked and can be conceptualised as follows:

- geographical exclusion, e.g. resulting from branch closures
- condition exclusion, e.g. the failure to qualify because of minimum deposit required, poor credit history or identity requirements
- price exclusion, e.g. the relative cost of financial products and services such as unauthorised overdrafts
- marketing exclusion – some less profitable groups of customers are not targeted by providers and so are unaware of the financial services available
- self-exclusion, reflecting cultural and psychological barriers – financial services as 'not for people like us'.

(Adapted from Mitton, 2008, p. 2)

Activity 1

Some financial institutions are relying on new technology to overcome the problem of financial exclusion. For example, with more people owning mobile phones than bank accounts, there are high hopes for mobile banking – managing an account online through the phone and eventually using it as a payment card. UK-based consultancy Juniper Research (2009) forecast that, globally, the volume of mobile financial transactions would rise from 2.7 billion in 2007 to 37 billion by 2011. Can you think of technological changes that may have led you to make more use of a bank or to put more money into your account?

The arrival of cash machines and internet banking encouraged bank use by making deposited money more accessible. But not all changes are so visible. Behind the scenes, new techniques have helped banks to assess which services to offer different customers. Financial innovation has enabled them to design new products, such as flexible mortgages (that allow customers to vary their monthly repayments) and equity-linked products (where the interest paid is based on movements in the stock market). While customers stay in the low-risk, low-return area of the risk–return spectrum shown in Figure 1, banks must incur more risk to deliver some of these products, moving up the spectrum. They claim that they are able to do this because of improved risk-management techniques.

2.2 Banks: important for business

Working capital
Raw materials, unsold stocks, and other expenditures on production from which money is recovered at the end of the production process when goods or services are sold.

It's not just households but also the companies that employ their members and the small businesses that they run that depend heavily on banks. Because businesses have to buy materials and pay wages before they get any revenue from selling their goods or services, new and expanding businesses especially need loans to cover **working capital**. This term covers raw materials and parts that haven't yet been made into output, stocks of output that haven't yet been sold, and revenue from sales that hasn't yet been collected from customers. When companies incur costs before they obtain revenues, 'profits can only become fully available as cash income to entrepreneurs if their working capital is financed by borrowing' (Godley and Cripps, 1983, p. 66). Banks are therefore key suppliers of **liquidity** to the business world – helping companies to turn future sales, and potential gains from a rising value of stocks, into ready cash.

Liquidity
In accountancy, the ability of a business to pay its debts as they fall due.

Fixed capital
Machinery, buildings, communication and transport networks, and other physical installations that sustain many runs of a production process.

Unless they can pay for new buildings and equipment through retained profit or share issues, companies must also look to banks to finance their **fixed capital** investments. A few large corporations are able to borrow for such investments by raising money from investors by selling them bonds (which you will be looking at in Chapter 2). But for most smaller businesses, a bank is the only affordable source of such large loans. Banks are therefore also key suppliers of **leverage**. This is a frequently used term in both the accounting and investment worlds. The availability of loans makes it possible for businesses to exploit profit-making opportunities that would not be available if they had to assemble their own capital beforehand. It also multiplies the potential profit from the venture. This is similar to a household being able to buy a home early in life by taking out a mortgage secured against it, and profiting from any rise in its value. Leverage made available by banks has been credited with fuelling a long production boom in the early

Leverage
Technically, the ratio of a company's debt to its total capital (which also includes, for example, money raised through issuing shares). More generally, it means using borrowed funds to increase the return from an investment (whether made by a business or an investor).

twenty-first century by creating a virtuous circle, in which debts secured against existing assets led to investment in new assets, allowing economies to grow much faster than if businesses and households had had to save before they spent. 'Leverage' has now become a general word for making productive use of assets without having to own them first.

Activity 2

A company spots a good business opportunity. By investing £100,000, after a year it expects to get back £110,000, making a profit of £10,000. This represent a return of £10,000 / £100,000 = 10 per cent.

If instead the company invests £50,000 of its own money and borrows the remaining £50,000, what return will it make?

Comment on the position if the opportunity turns out badly and pays back only £90,000.

For simplicity, ignore any costs of borrowing.

If a company invests £50,000 of its own money and £50,000 of borrowed money and gets back £110,000, first the £50,000 has to be repaid, leaving £60,000 for the company. This represents a profit for the company of £10,000 / £50,000 = 20 per cent. So borrowing – leverage – has significantly increased the return that the company gets. If the opportunity pays back only £90,000, this would be a loss of £10,000 / £100,000 = 10 per cent, assuming that the company had invested only its own money. But the loss would be £10,000 / £50,000 = 20 per cent if it had invested £50,000 of its own money and £50,000 of borrowed funds. So leverage has also magnified the loss.

[handwritten margin note: 50k me gets 110k   50k bank   profd 10/50 = 20%]

2.3 Banks: important for the economy

By financing loans through deposits taken from households, banks play a key role in channelling savings to investment. As you will explore in Chapter 5, using household savings to fund business investment is important for maintaining the growth of an economy and preventing falling economic activity that could lead to the types of depression that we looked at in the Introduction. But banks do more than channel savings. They offer long-term loans to companies (and households), while still giving savers immediate or short-term access to their deposits, a feat called **maturity transformation**. In this way, businesses can

Maturity transformation
Turning short-term, highly liquid liabilities (such as households' bank deposits) into longer-term, less liquid assets (such as loans to companies to fund investment in their business).

invest in long-term projects that generate profits and economic growth. Some of these profits flow back to banks through the interest that they charge on loans and, as a result, banks should be able to offer savers extra interest on their accounts.

By channelling savings to investment, banks prevent a growing economy from being held back by a lack of either profits to reinvest or investment finance. And they can also promote growth, by multiplying profits through leverage and by turning short-term deposits into longer-term loans. Although banks deny that they create money, a widely used model of the banking system suggests that they do. If banks' loans to businesses or households exceed the amount that they are collectively saving, this puts extra money into circulation, which can accelerate economic growth. The money multiplier model described in Box 3 and Figure 2 shows how this works.

Box 3 The money multiplier

This expansion can be illustrated with a simplified example in which ABC Bank lends £1000 to a business to buy a new machine (step 1 in Figure 2). After the purchase, the business has £1000 worth of new machinery, and the machine-seller has £1000 in cash (step 2). The machine-seller deposits the £1000 in its own bank, the XYZ Bank (step 3). I've assumed that banks in this system need to keep 10 per cent of their funds in cash, to meet depositors' withdrawal demands – this 10 per cent is called the banks' reserves (step 4); the other 90 per cent can more profitably be lent out to generate interest income. The extra £1000 deposit thus enables XYZ Bank to offer £900 of new loans (step 5). Once borrowers have used these loans to buy goods for investment (step 6), the people and firms that they buy from deposit £900 in their own banks (step 7). Those banks in turn keep back £90 (step 8) and lend out the other £810 (step 9). This process continues, as shown in Figure 2, until the original £1000 advance by ABC Bank has been multiplied several times. In fact, if you were to trace the process through – always assuming that each new loan gets spent so that it ends up in another bank within the system – you'd find that the original £1000 loan by ABC Bank eventually generates £10,000 in new deposits and loans across the banking system (which is the original loan divided by the proportion kept in reserves expressed as a decimal, in other words £1000 / 0.10). The multiplier has a value of 10.

As we'll see later (Section 3.4), banks would actually be unusually cautious if they kept as much as 10 per cent of their customers' deposits as cash. Most of them lend out more than 90 per cent of their deposits. And the lower the proportion that they retain as reserves, the higher the money multiplier. For example, if banks were to keep only 5 per cent of their deposits as cash, the total amount of new loans would be £1000 / 0.05 = £20,000.

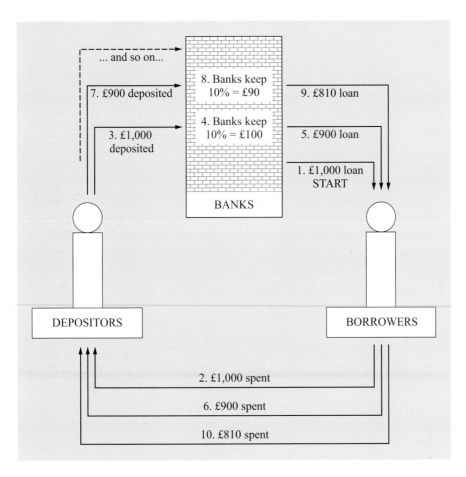

Figure 2 The money multiplier model

3 Risk and return in banking

Maturity transformation is the reason why banking is an inherently risky business. Provided that short-term savers have confidence in the banking system – so that they do not all want their money back at the same time – this risk is managed. But there have been important structural changes in the way that banks organise themselves and operate, which have created additional risk and uncertainty. This is often harder to identify and manage and is thus a key reason why banking is subject to a high degree of regulation.

3.1 Three into one: universal banks

When first set up, banks tended to specialise in particular types of lending, matched to a particular way of raising funds. There were essentially three distinct types of bank:

- *Savings banks* took deposits from ordinary households, offering them interest. They lent mostly to the government, local authorities or other very safe borrowers (Horne, 1947, Chapter 4). They could get these loans repaid quickly if savers wanted their money back, and savings banks also kept large amounts of cash for this purpose. Some who had saved with a bank for a time were allowed to take loans from it, but many were not allowed to borrow, even by becoming overdrawn for a short period.

- *Commercial banks* took deposits from wealthier households, who could generally keep their money locked away for longer. So these banks were able to make loans to businesses. But the loans were mainly confined to working capital, so that loans could be repaid frequently and the bank's cash stock could still remain high. Large stocks of cash had to be kept to meet clients' unexpected demands, and this meant that commercial banks had to forego a lot of interest and investment income – a cost that they tried to spread across many savers and borrowers, by growing to a large size (Kashyap et al., 2002).

- *Investment banks* lent to businesses and governments for fixed investment (in, for example, factories, offices and machinery). These banks often needed to leave their capital tied up in projects for several years in order to make a higher return, so did not traditionally finance themselves through customer deposits. Instead, they raised capital from individuals or companies that were willing to invest it for a long period, via shares or bonds. Some countries legislated to keep commercial and investment banking separate.

A century ago, most banks chose either the commercial or the investment model. Some countries later passed laws to enforce this separation. For example, the US Glass–Steagall Act 1933 required commercial banks to make no more than 10 per cent of their income from stock-market investment. They were required to concentrate on retail customers, rather than stock-market investments. There were several motives for this, including:

- *Risks to households*. Commercial banks had previously lost depositors' money in the USA through being allowed to speculate on share prices that fell suddenly in the 'Great Crash' of 1929.

- *Systemic risks*. By cutting their lending after the loss of depositors' money, banks were accused of causing the subsequent Great Depression in the USA.

- *Moral hazard*. Governments had set up deposit insurance schemes to reassure savers that they would still get their money back if a bank collapsed. But such insurance might tempt banks to take excessive risks with depositors' money, unless commercial banks were explicitly banned from getting involved in stock-market activity.

- *Conflicts of interest*. Ethical business standards might deteriorate if banks could hold (or advise others to hold) shares in companies that they also lent to. Owning shares (whose value can fall to zero if a company goes bankrupt) might deter a bank from letting a failing corporate borrower go out of business, even if this were the best option for other creditors and for the economy. Banks' tendency to keep lending to companies, so as to protect the value of their shareholdings, is widely believed to have slowed down corporate restructuring and efficiency improvement after 1990, notably in post-communist Eastern Europe and Japan. This conflict is reduced if commercial banks focus on lending to companies, while trading their shares is left to investment banks.

Moral hazard
The risk that insuring or otherwise protecting someone against a bad outcome will make them less careful about the consequences of their actions and so encourage more risky behaviour.

Over time, unless regulation has prevented it, the three forms of bank have tended to merge together. And there has been a process of deregulation, thus allowing the erosion of rules separating commercial and investment banking. The UK 'Big Bang' financial deregulation of the 1980s enabled commercial banks to expand investment banking operations, and the USA repealed the Glass–Steagall Act in 1999. So most big banks in Europe, the USA and Asia now run savings, commercial and investment banking operations within one group. The same large bank can now offer instant-access accounts, twenty-five-year mortgages, investment funds, and insurance to go with its longer-term loans. These changes have increased the uncertainty surrounding the way that banking activities have an impact on the wider economy.

To carry on the three distinct types of banking activity under one roof, financial institutions have to engage in some sophisticated 'financial engineering'. Anyone engaging with the financial services industry needs to assess how risky a particular bank is as a home for savers' money. Insight into this can be gained from the financial accounts that banks and similar institutions must publish every year.

Activity 3

Think of the financial products that you have. How many are with the same provider? What are the advantages of using your bank or building society as a 'one-stop shop'? What are the disadvantages?

Transaction cost
A cost incurred when buying or selling an asset, or taking out or closing an investment.

You might have got a better deal by taking several products (for example, a savings account, a loan and life insurance for the loan) from the same provider. Often it's cheaper for the provider to sell several products to one customer than to find a separate buyer for each, and they pass on some of these cost savings to the multiple buyer. Sometimes the knowledge that they've gained about you from selling one product gives them the confidence to sell you another for less (the knowledge reduces the risk, so they can charge less of a risk premium). Sometimes they will offer a second product cheaply when you buy the first, because the branch or sales representative has been given an incentive to sell more products: for most businesses, selling more to existing customers is a much easier and cheaper way to raise sales than finding additional customers. And because this provider already has your details, it's usually easier to open new accounts there than with another provider you've not dealt with before – there is a **transaction cost** saving through buying several products from one provider. You might, however, have shopped around so that the first product was the best available – but when you added the second, were you able to check that other providers weren't offering the same for less? And if this provider went out of business, might you regret having 'all your eggs in one basket'?

3.2 Understanding a bank's accounts

Two financial statements are at the core of a company's accounts: the income statement and the balance sheet. The annual income statement shows how banks (and non-financial companies) have made (or lost) money in the past financial year. The balance sheet shows their net asset position (what they own and what they owe). Both are drawn up according to accounting regulations and conventions, which are set nationally but are gradually being harmonised internationally.

The income statement: profit and loss

For any company, the income statement shows the income that the enterprise has generated in the financial year and the expenses that it incurred in doing so. Profits are calculated by examining the difference between income and expense, so the statement is also often referred to as the profit and loss account. Banks and building societies make money in rather different ways from most non-financial companies, so their income statements are set out along the lines of Table 1.

Table 1 Layout of a typical bank income statement

Income	Expenditure
Net interest – interest received on loans minus interest paid on deposits	**Operating cost** – wages, raw materials, other items that went into creating and delivering the services
Net fees and commissions from sale of financial products and advice	**Administrative cost** – amount spent running these operations
Net trading and investment income from holding assets, and selling those that rose in value	**Depreciation and amortisation** – cost of buying and maintaining tangible and intangible assets
Net insurance premiums from policies sold to customers	**Net insurance payouts** on policy claims
Other income from outside normal operations, e.g. property sales	**Interest and tax** on outstanding loans, income and capital gains
Total Income – **Provisions** against bad debt – **Provisions** on loss-making investments	**Total Expense**
Net Income	

Handwritten margin notes:
income statement = profit & loss account – how much made or lost in the previous financial year
balance sheet – net asset = what they own – what they owe
profit = income – expense

The left-hand column of Table 1 shows the various sources of income for the bank. Income from interest, fees, commissions, investment and trading are quoted 'net'. In this case, the 'netting' involves subtracting money paid out from money received under each of these headings. For example, if the bank earns £100 from commissions, but pays out £75 in commissions to others, its net commission income is £25. Specific to a bank's income statement are provisions for bad debt and loss-making investments that the bank has made, or for losses it fears will arise in future. These are subtracted from the bank's Total Income to derive its Net Income.

The right-hand column of Table 1 shows the bank's various expenses, such as staffing and administrative costs, which all add up to Total Expense. The bank's Operating Profits are then calculated by subtracting Total Expense from Net Income:

> Operating Profits = Net Income – Total Expense

These operating profits can become losses if expenses exceed income. The bank pays taxes on its operating profit, after adjusting this for income or costs from any associated companies and profits or losses on acquiring or selling these. Its post-tax profit is available for distribution to shareholders.

On the income side of the bank statement, the proportions of income obtained by the major UK banking groups in 2007 are show in Table 2. The year 2007 has been chosen because it was a generally good year for the banks, with most groups making a profit on all their main operations. The following year, most experienced losses on their trading and investment activities, and some had to realise capital gains by selling assets in order to stay in profit before tax. Bank chiefs were quick to suggest that this was exceptional, and that the all-round profitability of 2007 was more typical of the performance to be expected of their institutions, though it would take several more years to determine whether this would be the case.

Table 2 Breakdown of total income, main UK banking groups, financial years ending 2007

%	Barclays	HBOS	HSBC	Lloyds	RBS
Net interest	40.9	34.3	43.1	33.6	40.7
Net fees and commissions	32.8	5.9	25.1	14.4	19.8
Net trading and investment income	21.2	22.5	19.7	17.2	4.3
Net insurance premiums	4.3	26.4	10.4	29.7	20.6
Other	0.8	10.9	1.7	5.1	14.6
Total	**100.0**	**100.0**	**100.0**	**100.0**	**100.0**

Sources: Consolidated income statements in Barclays plc, 2008, p. 176; HBOS plc, 2008, p. 153; HSBC, 2008, p. 337; Lloyds TSB, 2008, p. 10; RBS, 2008, p. 120

The integration by banks of formerly separate savings, commercial and investment operations, and the addition of large insurance units, has diversified their income away from what can be gained from borrowing and lending. The proportion of total income obtained from net interest is now less than 50 per cent for the largest groups. Net interest is the return that banks get from lending to borrowers less the interest that they have to pay out to savers – the margin between the rates on loans and savings is income for the bank. By contrast, there has been a rise in income from fees and commissions, trading and investment and insurance. Fees and commissions are mostly earned from advising businesses and households on how to invest their money, and from carrying out investments on their behalf. Trading and investment income arises when the bank buys and sells, or holds, investments on its own account.

Activity 4

Look back over the material in this chapter so far and draw on any of your previous study or general knowledge to consider the following questions:

- Why do you think banks now make more of their money from fees and commissions, and less from interest charges, than they did in the past?
- Why do you think banks now make more of their money from trading and investment than they did in the past?

Cyclical
Rising and falling with the state of the economy. Thus income and profits of a cyclical business will tend to be high at times of fast economic growth, and low or negative when the economy is stagnant or shrinking.

There are several possible reasons for the shift in the sources of banks' income. First, banks have targeted the growth of commissions and fees because these are less **cyclical**. That is, they tend to be steadier from year to year than net interest income, which rises and falls with the state of the economy and the volume of lending. Second, competition among banks has tended to push down the gap between depositors' and borrowers' interest rates (which determines net interest income) more than it pushes down fees and commissions. Third, as national income has risen, many customers have less need to borrow and incur interest, whereas more customers have money to invest, for which they will pay fees and commissions. Finally, people are having to make more personal financial provision for future events such as big purchases, unemployment, illness and retirement, for which financial institutions can sell them products that generate fees and commissions.

Thinking about income from trading and investments, one reason for the increase here could be that banks now have more opportunity to make money this way. There are more financial instruments to trade in, more markets to trade on, and cleverer ways to make money from trading than there were in the past – as will be examined in more detail in Chapters 2–4. Another reason is that banks are under more pressure to engage in these types of business. Financial institutions compete to attract savers with higher interest rates, and to attract good-quality borrowers with lower interest rates. To absorb the resultant reduction of net interest income, and still make profits, they have to look for ways to make more money by trading and investing with the funds that depositors give them.

Before they can start calculating the year's profit, banks (and building societies) have to take one more step, to get from their total income as calculated in Table 1 to net income. Because some of a bank's borrowers may fail to repay their loans on time, and some of its investments may not perform as well as expected, it has to set aside provisions to cover for possible losses from lending, trading and investing. These provisions are shown as a subtraction from Income (not as an Expense) because the money won't necessarily be paid out – the loans might be recovered and the investments move back into profit. But in some years when the lending and investment climate becomes difficult, as in the years 2007–09, banks must increase these provisions, in case they later have to write off loans and investments whose capital cannot be recovered.

The balance sheet: matching assets and liabilities

The income statement shows whether a bank, or any other company, operated at a profit in the past year. But it doesn't tell you whether the company can stay in business, or continue to make profits in future years. To be sure of this, we need to know that the bank or company is solvent: that its

- assets – what it owns (or can collect from others who owe it money)

exceed its

- liabilities – what it owes to others, and has to pay back to them.

An insolvent company can't repay all the money that it owes to other people, even if it sells off everything it owns. When its liabilities exceed its assets, a company still has some means of survival. It could generate profits to make up the difference (some countries, such as the USA, have bankruptcy laws that allow a company to keep trading in search of extra profit). Or, if it's a public company – one that has raised capital by selling shares to the public – it can ask shareholders for more capital. But a company with liabilities exceeding assets is in danger of being wound up by those that it owes money to – who can step in to sell off what remains of it to recover as much of their money as possible.

Solvency
The ability to repay all debts and remain financially viable, usually indicated by assets exceeding liabilities on the balance sheet.

The extent of a company's **solvency** is shown by its balance sheet, an annual inventory of its assets and liabilities. This is similar to the balance sheet that households may draw up, as you may have seen in previous study. Banks make money in a rather different way from other service or manufacturing companies, so their balance sheets look different, even though they are drawn up on the same basis as those for other companies. A typical bank balance sheet is set out in Table 3.

Table 3 Typical bank balance sheet

Assets	Liabilities
Cash, including reserves at central bank	
Items to be collected from other banks	Items to be collected by other banks
Trading assets	Trading liabilities
Financial investments	Financial liabilities
Derivative contracts	Derivative contracts
Loans to other banks	Deposits from other banks
Loans to customers	Customer deposits
Available-for-sale investments	Issued debt
Collateral on assets lent	Collateral on assets borrowed
Goodwill	Provisions
Intangible assets	
Physical assets, including property	
Total assets	**Total liabilities + shareholders' equity**

The difference between assets and liabilities for a company – whether a non-financial company or a bank – is known as shareholders' equity. If assets exceed liabilities, this is a positive sum to which the shareholders are entitled (though they will tend to leave it with the company for use in its business). If liabilities exceed assets, shareholders' equity is negative, and they may be asked to pay in more capital to restore solvency (though they do not have to agree to this request). To avoid shareholders being responsible for all the losses that a company might incur, company law gives shareholders limited liability. This means that the most that they can lose, if a public limited company (plc) goes bankrupt, is the full value of the shares at the time they bought them.

Usually a company balance sheet divides the assets and liabilities into short-term and long-term – short-term usually means assets that can be turned into cash and debts that will have to be paid within a year. You'll notice that in Table 3 this division was not made, as it is hard to do in the case of banks. However, the bank's assets and liabilities are still listed on the balance sheet in order of liquidity. Cash is the most liquid asset. But it is also one that generates little or no income, so banks hold only as much as they need to meet immediate withdrawals. Traditionally, most of a commercial bank's assets consisted of loans to customers and other banks, which count as assets because they represent a future payment and can be sold to other investors. But many of these loans are for relatively long durations, so can't be quickly called in, and they aren't always easy to resell. So, more recently, banks and building societies have expanded their holdings of other financial assets that can be turned back into cash more easily. These include: trading assets that are bought and sold frequently to take advantage of price changes; financial investments (principally shares and bonds); and derivative contracts, involving the exchange of financial assets, which you will explore in Chapter 4.

Several categories of item that form a bank's assets also appear among its liabilities. Thus a bank will owe money to other banks and on some of its trading assets, financial assets and derivative contracts. In normal times, there will often be a close match between assets and liabilities in these categories. Indeed, the purpose of some items, especially derivatives, is often to **hedge** the bank's balance sheet so that its assets and liabilities rise and fall together.

Hedge
To invest in a way that protects income or wealth against unpredictable price movements.

In other areas of the balance sheet, there are large and long-lasting gaps between assets and liabilities in the same category. Perhaps most significantly, loans to customers (an asset) have tended in recent years to be much larger than customer deposits (the corresponding liability). For banks as a whole, the difference between them – known as the 'customer funding gap' – grew in the UK from close to zero in 2001 to £700 billion in 2007 (Bank of England, 2008) as shown in Figure 3. Banks allowed this gap to develop partly because customer deposits, which are often short-term liabilities (because of instant access), are not well matched with customer loans, which are more often medium- or long-term assets. Banks sought to fill the gap with trading assets, financial investments and derivative contracts, and issues of tradable debt. These are longer-term assets, better matched to longer-term liabilities. However, downturns in the economies and housing markets of Europe and North America after 2007 challenged this new balance-sheet structure, causing asset values to fall and liabilities to increase. Shareholders' equity became squeezed, forcing banks to seek government assistance in raising extra capital if their shareholders were unwilling to pay in more.

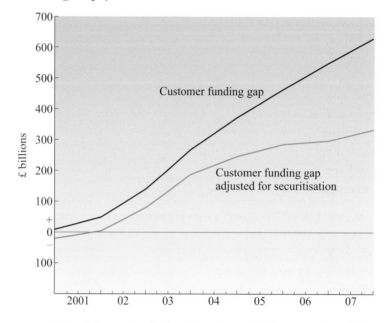

Note: Where not available stocks of securitisations are estimated from issuance data.

Figure 3 Major UK banks' customer funding gap

(Source: Jenkinson, 2008, p. 224)

3.3 Banks and the credit crunch

Because of their maturity transformation (sometimes summarised as 'borrowing short and lending long') and the very small proportion of assets that they keep in cash, banks are inherently vulnerable to a run. If depositors decide, even mistakenly, that a particular bank is having liquidity or solvency problems, their panic reaction – queuing up to withdraw cash – can create the feared liquidity problem. When Northern Rock, in 2007, experienced the first UK bank run since 1866, it claimed to be the victim of just such a self-fulfilling expectation. Some officials even blamed the Bank of England for unnerving Northern Rock's depositors by casting doubt on its financing – even though the Bank soon became its rescuer, subscribing an immediate £25 billion to help it to meet depositors' demands.

Banks that temporarily run short of cash can normally expect help from other banks. At the end of every trading day, some banks are in debt to others because more has moved out of their customers' accounts than into them. As most of the money that flows out of one bank goes straight into another, these momentary gaps are regularly plugged by inter-bank lending. If a run on one bank starts purely because of self-fulfilling panic, most of the money flows into other banks, which can then in principle help out the troubled bank, offering to support it until customers regain confidence and stop taking their deposits away. Though this may mean lending the troubled bank money at low interest, other banks have a reason to do this because a loss of public confidence could spread, prompting further runs and a general downturn in lending, investment and growth.

A bank that runs short of cash won't receive help from others if they suspect that it has a genuine solvency problem. That was the fate of Northern Rock in 2007, which eventually was forced to seek state support and ended up being nationalised. As a small bank that wanted to expand its lending much faster than it could capture more deposits, Northern Rock had turned to other sources of funding. In particular, it had exploited a way to expand the 'debt securities' side of its balance sheet, by packaging up and reselling its existing loans to raise money for new loans. **Securitisation** – selling these securitised loans to other investors – in Europe and the USA, raised capital more cheaply than using higher interest rates to attract additional savers. Larger banks, seeing that they were losing market share to Northern Rock, began a similar move towards this **originate-and-distribute** lending model.

A form of securitisation that became widespread after 2000, focused on home mortgages, seemed at first to provide similar advantages. As Figure 3 shows, UK banks' customer funding gap looked substantially smaller when funds raised by securitisation were included. But the subsequent rise in mortgage defaults, fall in house prices and drying-up of the market for mortgage-backed securities ran many banks into trouble. Although many securitised loans had been of high quality, they had been bundled with low-quality 'sub-prime' debt, and the value of securitisations fell sharply when the UK and the USA encountered slower economic growth and falling house prices after 2007. This vividly highlights the theme of uncertainty: banks had measured the risks involved in their securitisation strategies, but their calculations did

Securitisation
Turning an asset that produces a regular flow of income (such as a bundle of bank loans, or properties generating rents) into a tradable investment such as a bond that can be sold to other banks and non-bank investors.

Originate-and-distribute
A strategy by which a bank securitises and sells its customer loans, instead of retaining them for a long-term relationship with the borrower.

not take into account the possibility of the unexpected events that undermined the value of their mortgage-backed securities.

Investors realised that the originate-and-distribute strategy gave rise to moral hazard and **adverse selection**. Banks following this strategy were more likely to take on unreliable borrowers, because they expected to sell on the loans quickly rather than stay connected with them. To the extent that banks tried to offset extra risk by charging a higher interest rate, they scared off more prudent borrowers, concentrating the proportion of riskier ones. Northern Rock foundered because other banks stopped buying its securitised debt, cutting off its main source of funding. But other much larger banks hit comparable financial problems shortly afterwards, because securitised debt that they had counted among their assets – and classified as having high liquidity – suddenly became worth much less and harder to sell for cash. Through the course of 2008, many other UK banks and building societies (and US and European banks that had also been trading securitised debt with them) had to admit that they were running short of capital.

In most other sectors of the economy, companies that miscalculate risks or adopt an inappropriate business model are allowed to go out of business, and their departure is often seen as making life easier for rival companies. But systemic risk means that central banks and governments are wary of allowing any financial institution to collapse. If one bank were to cease trading or experience a run, others could be similarly affected as the public lost confidence in the banking system as a whole. Any withdrawal of deposits to be held instead as cash would shrink the amount of money circulating in the economy, reverse the money multiplier and cause a downward spiral in economic activity (the kind of economic downturn whose causes and consequences for personal finance are examined further in Chapter 5). So while the UK government took over Northern Rock, assigning over £100 billion to guarantee its debts, the Bank of England also doubled (to £200 billion) its scheme for assisting other banks. The US government and most European Union member states were forced to make similarly large capital injections into major banking groups. One government, that of Iceland, found that its banks had grown too large for the state to support them, so UK and Dutch savers with struggling Icelandic bank subsidiaries had to look to their own governments to refund their deposits.

Adverse selection
The disappearance of profitable or trustworthy buyers or sellers from a market, due to the prices or rules set, leaving only less profitable or less trustworthy participants.

Prompt action persuaded the public that it was safe to keep their money in banks. But it could not prevent a sharp fall in banks' other assets, as they lost the other sources of cheap finance that had allowed them to widen the customer funding gap. Because their capital and cash flow had been seriously eroded, banks drastically reduced their lending during 2008. The importance of banks to households and the economy, outlined in Section 2, was painfully confirmed. A 'credit crunch' led to a severe downturn in production and employment, sending the UK, the USA and many other economies into **recession**. Fearing another Great Depression, European and US governments abandoned their previous commitments to conservative economic policies, driving interest rates down towards zero, cutting taxes and boosting government spending in a bid to stimulate economic activity.

Although it involved relatively new financial instruments, and had an unusually widespread, even global, impact, the crisis that started in 2007 was the return of a problem that has afflicted banks repeatedly: the inherent risk of maturity transformation. The banks' move into the

Recession
Economic downturn, technically defined as two or more successive quarters of declining national output (or 'negative growth').

mortgage business, formerly left to building societies, strained their balance sheets, as they tied up more capital in long-term loans while still allowing most depositors to withdraw their funds overnight.

3.4 Gauging a bank's health

The income statement and balance sheet enable customers, shareholders and analysts working in the financial services sector to put a bank's profitability into proportion. They can look at the profits in relation to the amount of capital that shareholders and depositors have put at their disposal. Key measures that help in interpreting the financial data are:

- *Return on assets.* Net income as a percentage of total assets.
- *Return on equity.* Net income as a percentage of shareholders' equity.

Customers and shareholders can also use the balance sheet to look beyond the past year's financial performance to a bank's underlying financial condition. It shows to what extent assets exceed liabilities and therefore indicates whether in future the bank may be able to invest in expansion or return capital to shareholders – or, conversely, whether it may need to appeal to find more capital, from shareholders or elsewhere. As you have already seen, because of the way in which they try to offer higher returns to savers by investing their money while also allowing instant access to that money, banks run two significant risks:

- *Liquidity risk.* Because banks hold only a small fraction of their assets as cash – far less than their deposit liabilities – they may not be able to return all the cash that depositors want to withdraw.
- *Solvency risk.* If its assets fall in value, or its liabilities rise, a bank may not have sufficient assets to repay all its liabilities. Whereas illiquidity would mean a delay before depositors' money can be returned, insolvency would mean that there are insufficient funds for this even when all assets have been turned back into cash.

The scale of these risks is indicated by a set of key ratios, derived from the balance sheet. The most important are described here.

Liquid assets ratio

The liquid assets ratio is the ratio of cash and immediately cashable assets to total assets. This is also the ratio of cash and other quickly cashable assets to the other side of the balance sheet, i.e. liabilities + shareholders' equity. So it shows the proportion of what is owed – to creditors and shareholders – that could be paid back today, or in the next few days, from assets that are sufficiently liquid to be turned into cash immediately.

Over time, banks have steadily reduced their liquid assets ratios. In the UK, banks' average ratio was 60 per cent in the 1850s, but it dropped to 30 per cent in the 1860s. In addition, Figure 4 shows how three of the ratios used by the Bank of England dropped even further in recent times to less than 5 per cent (Jenkinson, 2008, p. 226). As financial markets were deregulated and developed, banks moved steadily more of their funds out of liquid assets and into other types of investment that offered higher returns. They were also increasingly confident that these investments could be easily sold if more cash were needed.

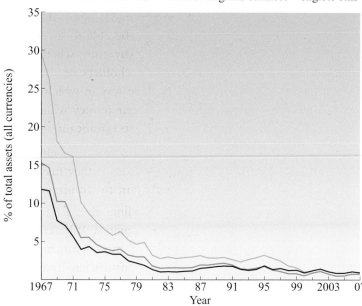

Definition of liquid assets
—— Broad ratio: cash + Bank of England balances + money at call + eligible bills + UK gilts
—— Reserve-ratio eligible assets
—— Narrow ratio: cash + Bank of England balances + eligible bills

Figure 4 Sterling liquid assets relative to total asset holdings of UK banking sector

(Source: Jenkinson, 2008, p. 226)

Capital ratio

This is the proportion of a bank's assets that can reliably hold their value as shown on the balance sheet – as distinct from investments that could fall in value, or loans that could be diminished by a wave of

capital ratio : assets that will hold their value

defaults. This so-called core capital is needed to ensure that assets stay above liabilities, even if the riskier assets fall in value. Whereas liquid assets ratios have shown a long downward trend, ratios of capital to assets have risen in recent years. Under an international regulatory agreement, called Basel II (see Chapter 7, Section 6), banks undertook to achieve a minimum capital ratio of 8 per cent by 2008. This ratio is applied on a risk-weighted basis. This means that if the balance sheets of two banks show the same total assets, but one bank has taken fewer risks in its lending and investment, then it will have a smaller capital requirement than the other. However, banks that take fewer risks can also expect lower returns on their assets – the familiar risk–return trade-off that you have already met and which is a recurrent theme throughout this book.

4 Banks and financial markets

Most goods and services, in most countries, are traded through the market system. A 'market' exists where buyers and sellers come together to exchange goods and services. For a market to work well, and set prices efficiently, there must be large numbers of buyers and sellers all competing with one another to get the best deal. Today, most of what people consume, and much of the activity that they engage in, is subject to market pressures. Even publicly provided services, such as the UK's National Health Service and railway system, operate with a form of market. Wages and employment are affected by the state of the 'labour market', and interest rates for savers and borrowers, along with the amount that they can borrow, are determined by the 'capital market'. Banks are major participants in the capital markets, as both buyers and sellers of investment products. However, because of the way in which they decide who gets to borrow, and on what terms, there is also a way in which banks can be viewed as *substitutes* for a completely free capital market.

Activity 5

Think about yourself in the market for jobs as a seller of your labour. Is there a price (wage) below which you would not be willing to take a job? For extra income, would you be willing to work overtime or at weekends? Now think of yourself in the market as a buyer – in the supermarket, say. If your favourite food is on special offer, are you persuaded to buy more of it? Have you ever set out to buy something but changed your mind because it cost more than you were happy to pay?

In a normally functioning market, the supply of any product will rise as its price rises, because this increase in the amount received encourages more people to offer it and in larger amounts. This is why you may be willing to work extra hours (supply more labour) if the rate (price) offered is high enough. But demand for the product will fall as its price rises, because people can't afford so much of it and are more likely to find a cheaper alternative.

4.1 Markets and prices

Supply rises but demand falls as price adjusts upwards. This means that there is only one equilibrium point at which demand exactly matches supply. (Economists, who like to show that they have studied ancient languages, took the word 'equilibrium' from the Latin for 'balance', because it's the point at which supply and demand are exactly in balance.) Equilibrium is reached through the working of the **price mechanism**. If buyers aren't offering a high enough price, they won't be supplied with as much as they want, and will have to offer more. But if sellers ask for too high a price, they won't find enough buyers, and will have to charge less to avoid being left with unsold stocks.

Price mechanism
The adjustment of prices, upwards when there's a shortage and downwards when there's a surplus, so that market supply and demand move into balance.

The price mechanism keeps supply and demand in balance, and any mismatch between supply and demand can usually be traced to an inflexibility that has prevented prices from adjusting. For example, the UK used to try to keep housing affordable by putting a limit on rents, the 'price' that landlords charge for living in their property. But this low limit deterred owners from renting out homes, so there was still a shortage of affordable housing. Governments tried to solve this problem by removing the controls, allowing rents to move up to their market level. There are some goods and services of which, to ensure affordability, prices are still set below the market level – or where there's no price at all. However, the result is almost always more demand than supply, and a long queue (think of the last time you visited a doctor in the UK, or went to a free concert). Sometimes, prices are set in the market but there's another constraint that makes it hard to increase supply, and then you also find queues – as at a bus stop. The bus company can't run more frequent services because there's limited space on the roads, however much it offers to pay for space.

4.2 The market for saving and borrowing

The market process described here might apply to many markets – including those for most goods and services, houses and even jobs. Economists used to argue that it applied to capital as well. Savers would put money into the market for loanable funds, offering a larger amount if they were promised more interest for it. Borrowers would draw money out of this market, though reducing their demands as the interest rate went higher. The equilibrium interest rate would be reached at the point where savers were offering exactly the amount of funds that borrowers wanted to take as loans. In this way, the price mechanism would also determine the equilibrium amount of saving and borrowing. However, there are sound reasons why this is not a good description of the market for capital. In particular:

- *The amount of interest that borrowers are willing to pay indicates only how much they want the money, not how reliably they will actually make the repayments.* A borrower's willingness to pay a high rate of interest might be signalling that they have a really good business idea that's sure to generate lots of income. But it could also mean that they will struggle to repay the loan, however good their business idea; or even that they're an unreliable borrower who never intended to repay. Offering loans at high interest rates can cause adverse selection – good borrowers are deterred, and only reckless or dishonest borrowers take up the offer. Charging high interest on a loan can cause moral hazard: even the initially sensible borrowers may, in order to meet their interest payments, start to take more reckless actions that increase the **default risk**.

- *The amount of interest that savers are offered might not greatly affect the amount they save.* Many people's savings are determined by the amount of future expenditure that they are planning or just by the amount that's left over when they've spent their income – so offering higher interest may not persuade them to save more.

- *Interest rate changes have a wider economic impact.* It isn't safe to assume that an adjustment of prices in the capital market has no effect on other markets. A change in interest rates can have effects across the whole economy (an idea developed further in Chapter 5), which may cause unexpected responses to the change.

Default risk
The likelihood that a borrower will fail to repay a loan, or make other due payments, usually because of *insolvency*.

4.3 Banks as a substitute for the market

These doubts about how the market for saving and borrowing works are confirmed by the way that banks operate in practice. They don't appear to operate a market in which competing savers and borrowers set an interest rate at which the supply of funds equals the demand. Instead, they carefully assess prospective borrowers, determining the size of a loan and its interest rate according to an assessment of the borrower's ability and willingness to repay, a process known as credit scoring. The better the bank's assessment of the borrower, the lower the interest rate they tend to charge. So, often, the people who could afford to pay most (because they are the best money managers and have the best business ideas) are actually charged the least interest.

Once credit assessments have been made, the bank offers an interest rate on savings that is below the market rate. The amount of deposits that it attracts is therefore less than the amount that prospective borrowers would like to borrow at this rate. With more demand for loans than it can supply, the bank rations the amount of capital available by setting interest rates for borrowers that are above the market rate, and/or by capping the amount that people can borrow at their specified rate. The bank rations its funds according to applicants' credit scores. A low-risk borrower might be charged a rate not much higher than the savings rate, while a higher-risk borrower might be charged a lot more. Through this rationing, based on borrowers' anticipated success at repaying the loan with interest, the bank avoids the adverse selection that might arise if it simply sold off its funds to the borrowers who offered the highest interest rate.

Rather than acting like a capital market, banks have traditionally operated as **intermediaries** that replace the market mechanism, connecting savers and borrowers through administrative processes (such as credit scoring). A further sign of banks operating in place of the market is the spread between borrowing rates and savings rates, which is still wide enough to produce around half the net income even of larger, more diversified banking groups. This gap would not exist in the market where the price mechanism was left to set the equilibrium interest rate, which would be the same for savers and borrowers. With banks acting as intermediaries between savers and borrowers, the spread between the rates is one cost of intermediation. The spread, plus other fees and charges for bank services, represents a source of income for banks, but a transaction cost for their customers. In this way, you can see how the relationship between risk and return may be determined by the way in which institutions, such as banks, operate rather than the way in which markets work.

Intermediary
A financial institution that connects buyers and sellers, or borrowers and lenders.

Activity 6

Log on to at least two websites of banks or building societies and compare the current interest rates on their savings accounts (the annual equivalent rate, AER) and loans (the annual percentage rate, APR). How do these rates compare, and why?

You would expect the APR to be above the AER, because banks make some of their profit by charging more interest on loans than they pay out on savings. If there are AERs above the APR, the chances are that the borrowing rate was fixed some time ago, and interest rates have risen since; or savings are long-term while the borrowing is short-term.

4.4 Why banks intermediate

A market brings together sellers and buyers who may not have met before, and who choose to transact solely on the basis of the other party's willingness to pay an agreed price or hand over an agreed product or service. In contrast, a bank seeks to connect savers and borrowers after collecting more detailed information about them, and channels money between them in a way that does not rely only on price. Traditionally, banks form an ongoing relationship with their depositors and borrowers, for at least the duration of their loan, so that they can monitor the use of the funds and ensure that they are achieving the return that will repay the loan. They try to overcome the information problems that tend to be encountered by people who lend to a company at 'arm's length' through the market.

Lenders' amassing of information about borrowers before they transfer the capital, and monitoring of their behaviour afterwards, is intended to overcome the adverse selection and moral hazard problems outlined earlier. Getting to know the clients – 'relationship banking' – is a way of dealing with the hazard of **asymmetric information**. Banks assign funds according to borrowers' *ability to pay*, rather than a *willingness to pay* that may imperfectly signal that ability. This intermediated, non-price way of rationing credit can overcome information and incentive problems that might arise from market allocation. This can help banks to gauge the likely risk and return of their lending activities more accurately.

Asymmetric information
One party in a transaction knowing more than the other. Sometimes the one who knows more can get a better deal; but if the other side knows this, they adjust prices to offset their risk, so that sharing the information can actually produce a better deal.

4.5 Alternatives to banks

When first set up, commercial banks with shareholders competed with a range of other institutions in the retail financial market. These were membership organisations, owned mutually by those who signed up to them, and included:

- *Building societies*, which took deposits from members and gave them loans with which to build houses (or later to buy existing houses).

- *Credit unions*, which took deposits from members, offered them unsecured loans when their ability to repay was deemed adequate, and channelled any profits into community improvement, including members' financial education.

- *Friendly societies*, which took deposits from members that were used to finance insurance, pensions and funeral expenses, some also offering forms of credit.
- *Post offices*, which offered accounts linked to safe savings products underwritten by governments.
- *Cooperative banks*, which operated comparable loan and savings-account facilities to commercial banks but were owned by their depositors and borrowers, not by external shareholders.
- *Trade unions*, which when first formed often made borrowing, saving and insurance facilities available to members; many still link with banks and insurers to offer financial services.

All these types of institution still exist, often on a large scale; for example, credit unions remain widespread in the USA and Ireland, and cooperative or post-office based banks are strong in several European countries. But in almost all countries they have lost market share, for savings and loans, to commercial banks. This can be traced partly to structural economic changes relating to different institutions' fundraising and risk-spreading abilities, and partly to social change as societies become more industrialised and urbanised. To compete with banks, mutuals have also retreated from their distinctive use of 'membership' to gather information and establish trust. Whereas they used to rely on members' mutual monitoring to enforce good standards of financial behaviour, often requiring members to save before they borrowed and giving them financial education, mutuals have now adopted more impersonal methods, including the credit-scoring techniques used by banks. This has been in part because efficiency required growth in size and geographical coverage, and mutual membership inevitably loses value once there are millions of members spread across a whole region or nation. Here, then, is another example of the way in which change has fundamentally altered the investment landscape, contributing to greater risk and uncertainty.

4.6 The marketisation of mutuals and banks

Commercial banks have moved steadily into the activities pursued by these 'mutual' institutions, and captured market share from them. In the UK, banks took up long-term mortgage lending that was previously the preserve of building societies, raising their share of residential mortgages from less than 1 per cent in 1970 to 30 per cent by 1989 (Coleman, 1996, p. 191). The share then rose to well over 50 per cent as banks outgrew building societies – helped by their ability to raise more capital from external shareholders – and as many mutuals responded to competitive pressure by converting into banks. 'Demutualisation' was driven by a perception that other financial institutions could no longer compete with commercial banks unless they offered the same range of services, and that they could not do this without external shareholding. Halifax (which had been the world's largest mutually owned financial institution, with over 8 million members) and Abbey (acquired by Spanish bank Santander in 2004) were among the best-known demutualisers.

Activity 7

Were you, or one of your parents, a member of a building society that demutualised? If so, did you/they get a vote on demutualisation? How did you/they vote, and why?

If you're under 30 you may never have had the chance to experience demutualisation, as most UK building societies that chose to convert had done so by the late 1990s. Most societies whose managers wanted them to become banks had put this to a vote of members (depositors and borrowers), as these were the 'shareholders' who collectively owned the society. Most members voted for demutualisation, for two reasons. They accepted managers' predictions that turning into a bank would mean cheaper capital, greater operating efficiency, and lower risk due to more diversified activity. And they stood to make an immediate financial gain. Members were usually assigned shareholdings in the newly created bank, which they could sell for an immediate profit to institutional investors. Many were also given a bonus, paid out of the society's reserves, as these were now replaced by shareholders' equity as the cushion between assets and liabilities.

5 Conclusion

In this chapter you have seen that high-street banks remain the most accessible place for households to deposit their savings and raise loans. Although they also do much corporate business, the value to commercial banks of borrowing and lending by households has increased over time. The value of banks to households and businesses arises from their unique ability to turn instant-access deposits into long-term loans. This plays a vital role in generating a return on people's savings, making loans available to people who want to buy houses or other large items, for financing business investment and making the economy grow. But it also makes banks' operations risky.

In the past, banks and other (mutual) financial institutions sought to reduce the risks by separating short-term deposits from long-term loans, and by developing strong relationships with savers and borrowers so that they could channel funds between the two groups. More recently, 'savings bank' and 'investment bank' functions have been brought together in single institutions. However, to achieve this, banks that once served as an alternative to financial markets have had to become significant users of financial markets. New techniques of risk management, such as debt securitisation, have been brought under new forms of regulation. Despite these safeguards, serious global financial problems led to a worldwide recession that started in 2007 and raised significant questions over the safety of the ways in which banks were operating.

Governments' reactions to the global financial crisis reaffirmed that the banking function is essential to the economy. Systemic risks and the recession triggered by the crisis reinforced the perceived need to regulate the financial system to stop such events happening again. Maintaining savers' confidence in the banking system is essential for banks' continuing roles in converting savings into investment and ensuring the availability of credit. This explains the reluctance of governments to let banks fail and the establishment of compensation schemes to ensure that the majority of savers do not lose in the event of failure. Thus banking may be inherently risky, but – owing to regulation and lenders of last resort – bank savings accounts probably do justify their position in the lowest corner of the risk–return spectrum, representing low risk but low return. In the next chapter, you will explore the options available to personal investors as they move across the spectrum in search of higher returns.

References

Bank of England (2008) *Financial Stability Report*, no. 24, 28 October.

Barclays plc (2008) *Annual Report 2007*, London, Barclays plc.

British Bankers' Association (BBA) (2006) *Banks' Commitment to Financial Inclusion Continues*, 16 November [online], www.bba.org.uk/bba/jsp/polopoly.jsp?d=145&a=7874 (Accessed 3 July 2009).

Center for Financial Services Innovation (CFSI) (2006) 'America's 84 million underserved underbanked', *U.S. Banker*, supplement, vol. 116, no. 8, pp. 29–32.

Coleman, W. (1996) *Financial Services: Globalization and Domestic Policy Change*, London, Macmillan.

EU Commission (2008) *Financial Inclusion – Ensuring Adequate Access to Basic Financial Services*, Memo/08/344, Brussels, 28 May [online], http://europa.eu/rapid/pressReleasesAction.do?reference=MEMO/08/344&format=HTML&aged=0&language=EN&guiLanguage=en (Accessed 3 July 2009).

Godley, W. and Cripps, F. (1983) *Macroeconomics*, London, Fontana.

Gordon, I., Travers, T. and Whitehead, C. (2008) *London's Place in the UK Economy 2008–9*, London School of Economics/City of London Corporation.

HBOS plc (2008) *Annual Report and Accounts 2007*, Edinburgh, HBOS.

Horne, H. (1947) *A History of Savings Banks*, Oxford, Oxford University Press.

HSBC (2008) *Annual Report and Accounts 2007*, London, HSBC.

Jenkinson, N. (2008) 'Strengthening regimes for controlling liquidity risk: some lessons from the recent turmoil', *Bank of England Quarterly Bulletin*, vol. 48, no. 2, pp. 223–8.

Juniper Research (2009) *Banking on the Mobile* [online], www.juniperresearch.com/shop/viewwhitepaper.php?id=167&whitepaper=79 (Accessed 20 April 2009).

Kashyap, A., Rajan, R. and Stein, J. (2002) 'Banks as liquidity providers: an explanation for the coexistence of lending and deposit-taking', *Journal of Finance*, vol. 57, no. 1, pp. 33–71.

Lloyds TSB (2008) *Report and Accounts 2007*, London, Lloyds TSB plc.

Mitton, L. (2008) *Financial Inclusion in the UK*, York, Joseph Rowntree Foundation.

Royal Bank of Scotland (RBS) (2008) *Annual Report and Accounts 2007*, Edinburgh, RBS.

Further reading

Bank of England (2008) *Financial Stability Report*, no. 24, London, Bank of England [online], www.bankofengland.co.uk/publications/fsr/2008/fsrfull0810.pdf (Accessed 17 December 2009).

Tett, G. (2009) *Fool's Gold*, London, Little, Brown.

Chapter 2
Investment choices

Jonquil Lowe

1 Introduction

Learning outcomes

After reading this chapter, you will:

- understand some of the factors that may influence investment choice
- be able to measure the intrinsic value of an investment
- understand how investors can measure risk
- be able to apply these measures to compare different investments.

Having identified a need to save or invest, private investors have a wide range of assets and products to choose from. There are many different types of savings and investment product, with a variety of different features. Some offer income, some capital gain, others both; some have guarantees, some do not; charges may be explicit or subsumed into the interest rate offered; and tax treatment may vary. But whatever the make-up of the product, the attributes come down to three basic features that can be characterised by the questions:

- *How much* will the return be?
- *When* will the return be paid?
- *What is the risk* that the amount or timing of the return might not turn out as expected?

The first two questions relate to the return from the product; the last concerns risk. Essentially, investment choice is about assessing where in the risk–return spectrum (see Figure 1 overleaf) each option lies. Section 2 of this chapter looks at methods investors may use to answer these questions, particularly in the context of straightforward investments such as bonds. Section 3 explores risk in more depth and introduces another fundamental building block of financial investment: shares. Section 4 considers how investors may employ measures of risk and return to evaluate and choose between different investments, but invites you to think about the limitations of these techniques, especially in the face of uncertainty. Finally, Section 5 shows how the methods you have learned can be applied to any other investment opportunity, such as investing in collectables, property or even your own human capital.

Where relevant in this chapter, questions will be raised about the ethical aspects of investment and borrowing decisions, both for the individual and for society as a whole. But we start by considering how changes in the wider socio-economic context within which investment choices are made can influence those decisions.

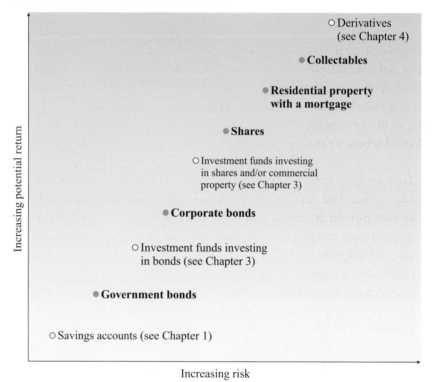

Figure 1 Bonds and shares are the basic building blocks of investment

2 Investment choices

In this section, we will explore how investment choices may be influenced by the prevailing economic, social and political framework but also depend crucially on the underlying method by which investors are assumed to make decisions.

2.1 Choice in context

Looking back over the last two centuries, different investments have been popular at different times. Important factors driving these changing trends are changes in the structure of the economy and even prevailing social attitudes. For example, commenting on British investors in the nineteenth century, Keynes (whom you briefly met in the Introduction to this book) noted:

> To save and invest became at once the duty and the delight of a large class. The savings were seldom drawn on, and, accumulating at **compound interest**, made possible the material triumphs we now all take for granted. The morals, the politics, the literature, and the religion of the age joined in a grand conspiracy for the promotion of saving … The atmosphere thus created well harmonised the demands of expanding business and the needs of an expanding population with the growth of a comfortable non-business class. But amidst the general enjoyment of ease and progress, the extent to which the system depended on the stability of money to which the investing classes had committed their fortunes was generally overlooked; and an unquestioning confidence was apparently felt that this matter would look after itself. Investments spread and multiplied, until, for the middle classes of the world, the **gilt-edged bonds** came to typify all that was most permanent and most secure.
>
> (Keynes, 1963/1931, pp. 84–5)

Compound interest
Interest earned not just on the amount originally invested but also on the interest previously earned and reinvested.

Gilt-edged bonds
(also called gilts) Bonds issued by the UK government.

As Keynes goes on to explain, 1826 to 1914 was a period of remarkably stable prices. Inflation was very low and at times even negative, as will be explored in Chapter 5. Therefore investors had no qualms about investing in bonds whose return comprised a stream of fixed payments on set future dates. As shown in Chapter 1, Section 2.1, inflation erodes the buying power of money. Not surprisingly, then,

Logarithmic scale
A scale used for plotting graphs where the values on the scale reflect the ratios of the underlying quantity, such as a percentage increase.

investors' complacency was shattered by the rise in inflation that accompanied the First World War – see Figure 2. The chart shows a price index for the UK over the period 1800 to 2008. It is plotted on a **logarithmic scale** so that the vertical distance between any two values on the chart gives a measure of the proportionate difference between them (or, put differently, it looks at the *ratios* of the underlying quantity, such as a percentage increase). For example, the distance on the scale between 10 and 100 is the same as the distance between 100 and 1000 because both represent a tenfold increase. Plotting the data this way makes it easy to see how stable prices were throughout the 1800s and the strikingly different trend since 1914. The long period of price stability led investors to expect continuing low rates of inflation in future and to make their investment choices accordingly. This is an example of how basing predictions of the future on what has happened in the past can lead investors badly astray because it fails to take into account the uncertainty of future outcomes.

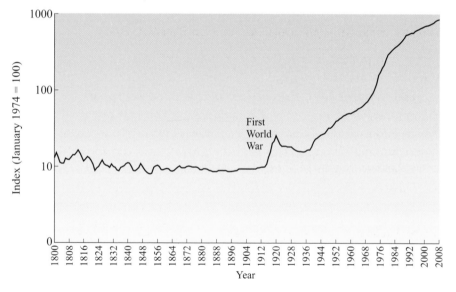

Figure 2 Retail Prices Index 1800 to 2008

(Source: Office for National Statistics, 2009)

In the inflationary environment that became the norm as the twentieth century progressed, UK private investors shifted away from bonds and instead turned their attention to shares, which, as we will see later in this chapter, offer a reasonable chance of beating inflation over the long term. Figure 3 illustrates how important private share ownership had become by the mid twentieth century, with private investors owning two-thirds of all the shares quoted on the UK stock market.

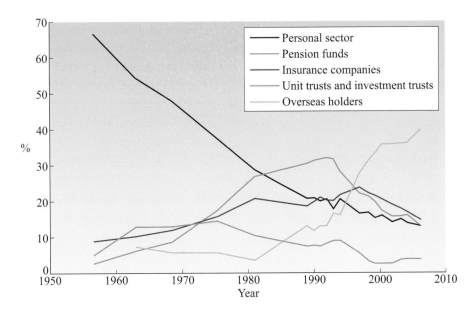

Figure 3 Ownership of UK quoted shares 1957 to 2006

(Sources: Proshare, 1997; Office for National Statistics, 2007)

Activity 1

In the second half of the twentieth century, shares remained popular but private shareholders became less important to the market as a whole, despite Government privatisation programmes during the Thatcher government of 1979 to 1990. By 2006, the proportion of UK-quoted shares held by private investors had fallen to less than 13 per cent. Can you suggest reasons for this decline?

Figure 3 tells an interesting story: as the proportion of shares held directly by private investors declined, we can see that the proportion held by pension funds and, to a lesser extent, insurance companies rose. These are both important ways in which private investors hold shares indirectly. This shift reflects a major socio-economic change arising from a shift in the social and political approach towards welfare, with a move away from reliance on the state. In the case of pension funds, the pattern in the chart mirrors the growth of non-state pension schemes, especially occupational schemes provided through the workplace. In 1936, just one worker in eight belonged to an occupational pension scheme, increasing to one in three by 1956. It peaked at nearly half the workforce in the 1960s before falling back to around two in five today (Pension Law Review Committee, 1993, pp. 67–8; Office for National Statistics, 2008).

The other dominant pattern in Figure 3 is the rising proportion of UK shares held by overseas investors. The Office for National Statistics (2007), which produces these data on share ownership, suggests that the rise reflects the increasing globalisation of the economy, with UK firms becoming part of international groups, and overseas companies launching UK subsidiaries quoted on the UK stock market.

2.2 Individual choice

Simply observing the outcomes of investors' decisions cannot take us very far in *explaining* their choices. A commonly held assumption is that economic agents, such as investors, behave rationally.

Rationality

In economics, the pursuit by individuals or organisations of goals in the most efficient way possible, usually by maximising financial or material gain subject to constraints of income or wealth. For example, businesses are assumed to maximise profits, and rational investors are assumed to maximise subjective well-being (linked to wealth), given the resources that they have available to invest.

Rational investors systematically weigh up options

In economics, **rationality** is defined in a very particular way: it means that an economic agent pursues goals in the most efficient way possible, usually by maximising something given any constraints that apply. For example, businesses are assumed to maximise their profits. Rational investors are assumed to have the goal of maximising their wealth given the resources that they have available to invest. Faced with a number of options, a rational investor is assumed to weigh up the expected return from each option according to a systematic set of preferences. The choices made will be internally consistent, so that, for example, if A is preferred over B and B preferred over C, then A will be preferred over C. An important element in these preferences will be the investor's attitude towards risk.

Investors may be 'risk-averse' or 'risk-preferring' and, again, economists define this in a precise way, which can be explained here in terms of a simple bet. Suppose that an investor is offered the following choice:

- Option 1: a guaranteed sum of £100.
- Option 2: an amount determined by the toss of a coin, with £110 paid if the coin comes up heads and £90 if the outcome is tails. The chance of a head is ½ and so is the chance of a tail. Therefore the investor has an equal chance of getting either amount and the average return that the investor could expect if he or she took the gamble many times would be the average of the two amounts: (£110 + £90) / 2 = £100.

Since the average return from Option 2 is the same as the guaranteed sum from Option 1, economists call this a 'fair bet'. Investors are termed **risk-averse** if they reject a fair bet (in other words, they reject Option 2 and choose Option 1) and **risk-preferring** if they accept it.

If investors are both risk-averse and rational, it can be assumed that, for a given level of return, investors will always choose the option offering the lowest risk. Similarly, for any given level of risk, investors will choose the option with the higher return. Some evidence about attitudes to risk was provided by a research study for the Department for Work and Pensions in March 2009. The authors reported:

> As a whole there was a general consensus that most participants were unwilling to take much risk with their money. This was the case even over the long term (five years or more) and few participants mentioned the potential for risk and return to balance out over time. The most common reasons cited for being averse to taking risks related to life stage: the responsibility of raising a family, taking on large financial commitments such as a mortgage and, among older participants, the need to protect any savings they had built up over time.

(Collard and Breuer, 2009, p. 19)

Risk-averse
Tending to choose an investment with a lower level of risk than another comparable investment.

Risk-preferring
Tending to choose an investment that offers a higher level of risk than another comparable investment; the opposite of risk-averse, also known as risk-seeking.

In the rest of this chapter, I will assume that investors are risk-averse, but you should bear in mind that in reality this assumption is unlikely to hold for all people and all situations.

2.3 Society's choice

Just as individuals make choices about deferring consumption (by saving) or bringing consumption forward (by borrowing), so too do governments. If a government decides to spend more than it receives in tax revenues and other receipts, it must fill the gap by borrowing. Issuing government bonds is the main way of doing this.

As well as affecting the supply of bonds available to investors, such decisions also affect the allocation of resources between different generations, which can make government borrowing a controversial issue. In effect, future generations, whose taxes will fund the eventual repayments, are being made to pay for investment or consumption by people today. This may be justified by arguing that future generations benefit from today's spending on, for example, infrastructure such as roads and hospitals or rescuing the banking system, as described in Chapter 1.

Views about the ethics of government borrowing have changed over time. In the eighteenth and nineteenth centuries, when economies were relatively much simpler, particularly with regard to their financial mechanisms and institutions, the prevailing view was that prudent governments should aim to balance their budgets just as a prudent household would. This policy proved disastrous during the Great Depression of the 1930s. From the 1940s, following the then revolutionary ideas of Keynes, running a government deficit gained acceptance as a legitimate way of stimulating economic growth to reduce unemployment, especially, but not only, in periods in which business investment is too low, as occurs during economic crises (see Chapter 5). Deficits can then be closed, and debts repaid, once the economy returns to health. This approach again came to the fore during the global financial crisis that started in 2007.

Gross domestic product (GDP)
The value of all the goods and services produced by a country over a year.

Figure 4 shows the total government debt outstanding for selected countries as a percentage of their **gross domestic product (GDP)** in 2008 (the bars on the chart) and the level forecast for 2010 (indicated by '+'). The level of debt outstanding at a point in time reflects past decisions to borrow (plus any missed interest payments which were subsequently added to the debt). A fall in debt outstanding occurs when a government pays back more past debt than it borrows in new debt. Conversely, the level outstanding rises if a government borrows more than it pays back. You can see that the borrowing experience of different countries varies markedly. In 2008, Australia had the lowest level of debt at 14.2 per cent of its GDP. Japan's debt stood at 172.1 per cent of GDP, reflecting past attempts to spend its way out of a persistent depression that started in the early 1990s. Against these extremes, the UK debt level of 54.1 per cent looked relatively modest in 2008 but was forecast to rise steeply to 90.5 per cent of GDP by 2010 as a result of measures to tackle the impact of the global financial crisis (OECD, 2009).

Now you have looked at the context in which governments issue bonds, the next section considers how bonds work as an investment.

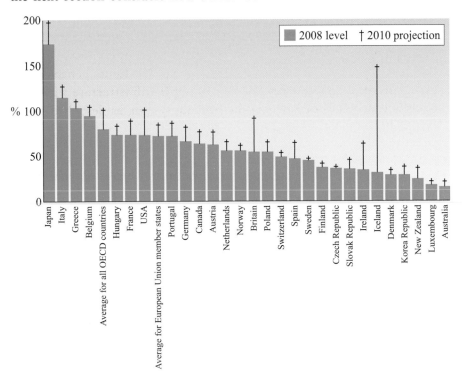

Figure 4 Government debt outstanding as a percentage of GDP for selected countries

(Source: OECD, 2009, Figure 3.6)

2.4 Introducing bonds

All bonds, whether issued by the government, a company or some other body, work in basically the same way. A bond, which is a contractual loan, typically has a fixed lifetime. For example, UK government bonds (gilts) are divided into short-, medium- and long-dated, with lifetimes of up to seven years, seven to fifteen years, and more than fifteen years, respectively (Debt Management Office, 2004). The date on which a bond reaches the end of its life is called the redemption date. At that time, the bond issuer will repay the loan. In the meantime, the issuer pays interest to the holder of the bond on set dates – usually at six-monthly intervals. An important feature of bonds is that they can be traded on a stock market. This means that an investor does not have to hold a bond until redemption, but can sell at any time before then at whatever price prevails on the stock market at that time. Note that a few bonds are undated, meaning that they have no redemption date at all and can continue indefinitely.

For convenience, bonds are often referred to in units of £100 though investors can buy smaller or larger sums and part-units. These units are called '£100 nominal'. The price that the investor pays on the stock market may be higher or lower than the unit price – for example, a lower market price might be £90 for each £100 nominal of the bonds held. By this stage, you have probably noticed that bonds have their own language with lots of jargon – Figures 5 and 6 will help you to get your head around this.

There are two types of government bond: conventional and inflation-linked. Conventional bonds pay a fixed sum of interest each period until redemption and then a redemption value of £100 for each £100 nominal. The name of the bond reveals the amount of interest and indicates the redemption date – see Figure 5. With inflation-linked bonds – such as index-linked gilts in the UK and Treasury Inflation-protected Securities (TIPs) in the USA – the interest payments and redemption value are increased in line with inflation throughout the life of the bond.

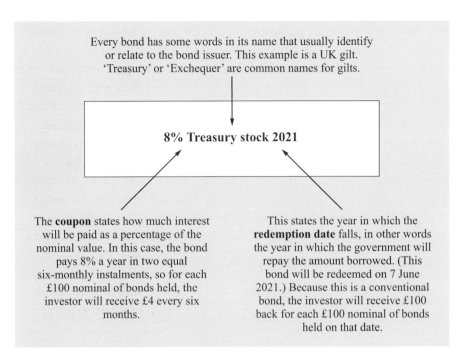

Figure 5 Bonds: it's all in the name

Figure 6 Getting your head around the jargon!

The interest payments ('coupon') and redemption value for a conventional bond are fixed. Therefore, based on the current market price, investors can work out exactly what return they will get if they buy a bond and hold it until redemption.

Interest yield
The income that a bond will produce expressed as a percentage of the current market price.

In market reports and newspapers, you will see that the return is called the 'yield' and two yields are usually quoted. The **interest yield** (sometimes called the running yield) expresses the coupon as a percentage of current market price. Although the coupon is fixed, the market price is not, so the interest yield on offer to new investors varies with the market price. For example, if the market price of the 8 per cent Treasury Stock 2021 in Figure 5 is £140 for each £100 nominal, the interest yield would be 8 / 140 × 100 = 5.7 per cent a year. If the market price were £90 per £100 nominal, the interest yield would be 8 / 90 × 100 = 8.9 per cent a year. The interest yield is particularly useful for investors who are seeking income and want to compare government bonds with other income-producing investments.

Most investors will be more interested in the total return that they can get, which includes the redemption value as well as interest. This is called the **redemption yield**. If the current market price of a bond is higher than its redemption value, the investor will make a capital loss when the bond is redeemed, which drags the redemption yield down below the interest yield. If the current market price is lower than the redemption value, the investor will make a capital gain that will boost the overall return.

Redemption yield
The total return that a bond will produce expressed as a percentage of the current market price, assuming that the bond is held until redemption. It takes into account both the interest and the redemption value.

Because the coupon and redemption value of a bond are fixed and do not change, the interest yield and redemption yield vary only with changes in the bond's stock-market price. If the market price falls, the yields go up. If the market price rises, the yields go down. In other words, there is an inverse relationship between the market price of a bond and its return.

In the UK, interest on bonds, including gilts, is subject to income tax but gains on nearly all government and corporate bonds are tax-free.

3 Understanding risk

At the start of this chapter, risk was described as the likelihood that the actual return from an investment will not turn out as expected. We assigned two dimensions to risk: amount and timing. Risk is the chance that the actual return will:

- *be more or less than expected.* This is known as **capital risk** and/or, if part or all of the return is in the form of income, **income risk**. You will find a fuller definition in Table 1 on page 84.

- *not be available when expected.* This is an aspect of **liquidity risk**; again, you will find a fuller definition in Table 1.

Note the assumption here that risk is symmetrical: the probability of a gain is equal to the probability of a loss. Although investors typically want to avoid the downside risks of a lower return, they do want exposure to the chance – risk – of a higher return. We will follow the normal convention of describing different types of risk in terms of the bad outcomes that may result, but you should bear in mind that the risk–return trade-off means that the reward for running the risk of bad outcomes is the chance of superior returns. Later in the chapter, we will consider whether to question this assumption that risk is symmetrical.

3.1 Types of risk

In Figure 7, an investment contract has been broken down into the following elements: (1) the provider who offers the investment, possibly having outsourced some aspects of it to (1A) a third party; (2) the investment itself; (3) the investor who takes up the offer; and (4) the wider economic, social and political context within which the contract takes place. The investment may display some or all of the three high-level risks identified above: capital risk, income risk, liquidity risk. But these high-level risks are fed by a wide variety of underlying risks that stem from the various elements of the investment contract. Figure 7 considers some of the most important risks, but as you read this book you may identify others that you can add to the diagram.

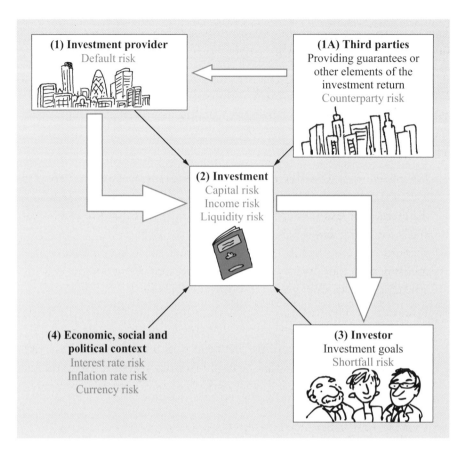

Figure 7 Sources and types of investment risk

Starting at the top left of Figure 7 with the provider, a key risk is that the investment contract is broken: in other words, default risk (first introduced in Chapter 1 and also called credit risk). For example, a company may issue a bond that is due to pay a fixed stream of payments over a set number of years. The investor has to weigh up the possibility that the company might fail to make these payments. See the short extract in Box 1 on page 85 for an example of default risk and the consequences that it may have for investors.

Where the investment provider has passed on some of the obligations of an investment contract to a third party, default risk shifts with the obligation and is then called **counterparty risk**. If the third party becomes insolvent or reneges on its part of the deal, the loss may feed through to the investor. Chapter 3 looks at some investments that involve counterparty risk.

The main risk that can be highlighted in connection with the investor is **shortfall risk**. This can be viewed as a special type of capital or income

Counterparty risk
The risk that the counterparty to a transaction or contract will default on their obligations.

Shortfall risk
The risk that a predefined savings or investment target will not be met.

risk. It arises only where the investor has a predefined target, such as building up a lump sum large enough to pay off a mortgage, or generating enough income to meet school fees. Shortfall risk is the chance that the target will be missed.

Turning to the wider economic, social and political context, there is a multitude of events that could affect the return from an investment. Three key risks are:

- *Interest-rate risk.* The risk that, having based an investment choice on a view about how future interest rates will change, the outcome is different. For example, an investor expecting interest rates to be stable or rising might put their money into a variable rate savings account and lose out if interest rates actually fall. Similarly, an investor who has opted for a fixed return may be unable to take advantage of an unexpected rise in interest rates.

- *Inflation risk.* The risk that the return from an investment will be worth less than expected in real terms because of unanticipated increases in the level of prices between now and payment. This risk is greater with longer- rather than shorter-term investments and, as we saw earlier (Section 2.1), is a particular problem with investments paying a fixed income.

- *Currency risk.* Where an investment is denominated in a foreign currency, unexpected changes in the exchange rate may cause the sterling (or other home currency) value of the holding to be less than expected. Similarly, this can be a risk when a person borrows in one currency to purchase an investment or other asset in another currency (for example, borrowing in euros to buy a home in the UK).

With each of these risks, it is *unexpected* changes that are important. In assessing possible outcomes, rational investors will build in an assumption about future changes in interest rates, inflation and exchange rates. Investors will make their choices in light of these assumptions, so the risk is that the future will turn out differently from the assumptions. The importance of how these expectations are formed is returned to in Chapter 6.

The next section looks at shares, which are important investments that involve many of the risks introduced in this section.

Table 1 Summary of common investment risks

Risk	Definition
The high-level risks	
Capital risk	The possibility that investors may lose some or all of their original capital and returns made to date.
Income risk	The risk, where payments are variable, that they may fall below the amount the investor had expected or fail to be paid.
Liquidity risk	The risk of being unable to cash in an investment rapidly enough or at an acceptable price either to pay bills or debts as they fall due or to take advantage of better investment opportunities.
Examples of risks underlying the high-level risks	
Counterparty risk	The risk that a third party responsible for some aspect of the investment fails to meet its contractual obligations (for example, because it becomes insolvent).
Currency risk	Where an investment is denominated in a foreign currency, the risk that unexpected changes in the exchange rate will alter the sterling (or other home currency) value.
Default risk	The risk that income or other payments due under the investment contract will not be made (usually because the investment provider becomes insolvent).
Inflation risk	The risk that the return from an investment will be worth less than expected in real terms because of an unexpected rise in prices.
Interest-rate risk	The risk that, having based investment choice on a view about how future interest rates will change, the outcome is different.
Shortfall risk	The risk that a predefined savings or investment target will not be met.

Box 1 Investors in 'safe bonds' at risk of wipeout

Private investors who put thousands of pounds into bonds that were deemed to be low risk are set to lose all their money in the wake of the collapse of Bradford & Bingley (B&B), which is now controlled by the government. The investors hold B&B permanent interest-bearing shares (PIBs). Their worst fears were confirmed last week when the bank said that investors would not be receiving their six-monthly interest payment due in July. PIBs are undated fixed-income bonds issued by building societies to raise money, which have proved popular with older investors because they pay a decent income and are perceived to be low-risk and secure.

About 1600 private investors invested in B&B PIBs when it was a building society. These PIBs were converted into 'subordinated notes' when the society converted to a bank. One investor who bought £18,000 worth of B&B PIBs in 1998 faces the prospect of losing the lot as a result of the former society's collapse. Notionally, he thinks his investment is worth about £3100 but, not surprisingly, he is unable to sell because the market for his PIBs is illiquid and no one wants to buy them. 'We went into PIBs because they were meant to be a sensible and safe alternative to leaving our money in the bank.'

(Adapted from Farrow, 2009)

3.2 Introducing shares

Unlike bonds, which are contractual loans, shares make the holder a part-owner of a company, usually in proportion to the number of shares owned. Many people own shares in their own small business. Provided that they own over half, they not only receive the lion's share of the profits but can also control the running of the business. Usually these shares are unquoted. A major risk with unquoted shares is liquidity risk because when owner–managers of small businesses want to cash in their investment, there is no guarantee that anyone will want to buy their shares. By contrast, quoted shares have the advantage of being readily bought and sold on a stock market.

The return on shares comes in the form of regular dividends and a capital gain or loss when the shares are sold. Dividends are the share of the company's profits that the company directors decide to pay out to shareholders, and can vary (income risk). In the UK, profits have already been taxed in the hands of the company. Therefore the amount received by the shareholder is treated as a net sum and comes with a tax credit that exactly satisfies the liability of most taxpayers, but capital gains are taxable (though UK investors have a substantial capital gains tax-free allowance).

The total return will depend to some extent on the technical type of share held (see Table 2), but far more on the type of company concerned. For example, high-growth companies in new technology areas might not pay any dividends for years, so investors will be looking for return through an increasing share price to generate a gain on sale. Capital risk is high, which means that losses can be large but so too can gains. As the boom in internet companies in the late 1990s (the dot-com bubble) turned to bust for the likes of boo.com and Webvan, others such as Amazon and Google have stayed the course to become household names (you will return to this dot-com bubble in Chapter 6). Shares such as these, expected to have high growth potential but with a high risk of failure, are often called 'aggressive stocks'. By contrast, shares in utilities, such as water and electricity companies, have a reputation for delivering a solid stream of dividends and relatively less variation in price – they are examples of 'defensive stocks' that are likely to carry on performing steadily even if the economy hits a downturn. 'Blue-chip' shares (named after the highest-value chip in poker) are shares in large, well-established companies that typically pay dividends and are expected to deliver growth in line with the general economy.

Table 2 Different types of share

Ordinary shares	Investors may receive a share of the company's profits in the form of dividends, which are not guaranteed to be paid at all and may vary in amount. Usually each share carries one vote that the holder can cast to try to influence the running of the business. If the company fails, its assets are sold to pay off its debts and other obligations. Ordinary shareholders are last in line and may get nothing back at all.

Preference shares	Investors receive a fixed-rate dividend provided that the company's profits are sufficient to cover it. These dividends must be paid before any ordinary share dividends, and if the company is wound up, preference shareholders are entitled to a share of the liquidated assets, if any are left, before the ordinary shareholders. Preference shares may have one or more of the following additional features: • *Redeemable*. The shares have a fixed date on which the company will buy the shares back, typically at £100 for each nominal £100 of share held. Because they offer a fixed return, preference shares can seem more like bonds than shares, and this is especially true when they are redeemable. • *Cumulative*. Any missed dividend payments must be paid before any ordinary dividends can be paid. • *Participating*. The dividend may be increased if the company performs better than a pre-specified target. • *Convertible*.* The shares can be converted to ordinary shares on set future dates at pre-set prices.
Convertible unsecured loan stock (CULS)*	Investors buy corporate bonds but these can be converted to ordinary shares on set future dates at pre-set prices. As a conversion date gets closer, CULS tends to behave more like the underlying shares than like bonds.
Warrants*	Investors buy a right to purchase the company's shares on one or more set future dates at pre-set prices. The warrants themselves can be traded on the stock market. Warrants are typically issued by companies to the purchasers of newly issued shares to make the share offering more attractive.

* These securities all offer the right (but no obligation) to buy or convert to a company's shares on one or more set future dates (the exercise date) at pre-set prices fixed in advance (the exercise price). If, on the exercise date, the market price of the underlying shares is lower than the exercise price, the holder can simply let the right lapse. If the market price of the shares is higher, the holder can exercise the right and either sell the shares immediately for a profit or continue to hold the shares.

3.3 Reducing and managing risk

For an investment to be completely risk-free, its return must comprise one or more fixed payment(s) on one or more set future date(s) with no possibility of a different outcome. In the real world, there is no such thing as a completely risk-free investment. Even if a fixed return is guaranteed on a set date, there is still some chance that the provider might default. However, this default risk is usually considered negligible when looking at investments issued by the governments of large, well-developed economies, such as the USA and the UK, since, as a last resort, the government could raise money from taxpayers or print extra money in order to pay off its debts (which can have dangerous consequences, as discussed in Chapter 5). But, as you have seen earlier in this chapter, government bonds generally are not free from inflation risk, so a risk-free investment needs to be fairly short-term. In practice, in both the USA and the UK, short-term transactions in government-issued bonds over terms ranging from a few days to a few months are taken to be a close proxy for a risk-free investment. Although few private investors hold these risk-free investments, they are important for banks and play a key role in the way interest rates are set in the economy as a whole, which you will be considering in Chapter 5. The risk-free rate is also important in providing a baseline against which to compare other investments. Investors should normally expect a higher return from any investment that involves risk – this is the risk premium that you met in the Introduction to this book.

The closest that personal investors get to risk-free investing is by choosing inflation-linked investments, such as the index-linked government bonds mentioned earlier or, in the UK, index-linked savings certificates, a savings product issued by National Savings & Investments (a government agency). Coping with inflation risk is a common problem for investors, especially those investing for income. By paying a return that rises with inflation, index-linked investments remove the impact of unexpected inflation. The drawback is that the real return on offer is often low compared with the real return that investors expect to get from non-indexed savings and investments, given their view about future inflation. This is an example of the risk–return trade-off, with the cost of removing inflation risk being a reduction in expected return.

Many investors seeking protection from inflation turn to a different strategy by choosing investments whose return is linked to economic growth, such as shares. Unlike bonds, the return from shares is not fixed, so share investors are exposed to both capital and income risk. The risk premium for taking on these risks provides the opportunity to beat inflation. Table 3 overleaf compares, for three main asset classes, the average real return for each decade over a period of 100 years. It shows that historically, equities have beaten inflation more often and by a larger margin.

Investors with little or no appetite for capital risk might prefer to stick to savings accounts, where the return of their original capital is assured – at least up to the limit of any deposit guarantee scheme (see Chapter 1, Section 1). But the cost of this strategy may be an increase in shortfall risk, because the return on such accounts may be too low to enable a large goal, such as saving for retirement or paying off a mortgage, to be achieved at an affordable cost. Again, Table 3 highlights the generally superior long-term performance achieved in the past by equities.

Table 3 reveals that the worst three decades for equities have been 1908–18 (First World War), 1968–78 (sterling crisis, oil price crisis and stagflation) and 1998–2008 (dot-com bubble bursts and global financial crisis). The real returns during those decades were all negative. In other words, after taking inflation into account, investors in shares lost money over each of these decades. Since the real return is broadly the nominal return less inflation, to find the nominal return, we need to add inflation back. For example, for 1908–18, the nominal return was −3.5 + 8.0 = +4.5 a year. Similarly, the nominal return during 1968–78 was +8.3 a year, and during 1998–2008 it was +1.1 a year. Comparing the return on shares with savings accounts, in 1908–18, although the real value of an investment in shares fell by 3.5 a year, the real value of a savings account fell even further, by 4.8 a year. In both 1968–78 and 1998–2008, savings accounts gave a better return than an investment in shares.

Keynesian
Usually describes a policy of pumping money into the economy, in particular by boosting government spending; derives from John Maynard Keynes, who showed that economics could operate with permanently high levels of unemployment.

[handwritten note: Nominal return = real return + inflation]

[handwritten note: ? what is nominal]

Table 3 Real investment returns in the UK (% a year)

Decade	Equities (shares)	Government bonds (gilts)	Index-linked gilts	Savings account	Inflation	Major events during the decade
1908–18	−3.5	−7.4	n/a	−4.8	8.0	First World War
1918–28	10.3	7.0	n/a	6.9	−2.7	Regeneration following the war
1928–38	3.6	6.7	n/a	2.4	−0.7	Great Depression
1938–48	3.9	0.8	n/a	−2.6	3.5	Second World War and adoption of **Keynesian** economic policies
1948–58	7.1	−4.5	n/a	−1.8	4.5	Aftermath of war
1958–68	11.0	−1.4	n/a	1.9	3.2	'Stop–go' economic cycles
1968–78	−3.5	−3.3	n/a	−2.7	11.8	Sterling crisis. Oil price quadruples. Slow economic growth, rising unemployment, high inflation ('stagflation').
1978–88	12.4	5.8	n/a	3.8	7.9	Inflation brought under control. Privatisation and financial deregulation.
1988–98	11.1	8.7	6.0	4.7	4.1	Financial deregulation continues. Internet boom.
1998–2008	−1.5	2.4	1.9	2.4	2.6	Dot-com bubble bursts. Housing boom ends. Global financial crisis.

(Sources: Barclays Capital, 2009, pp. 55, 70; Thompson, 1989, pp. 15–47)

Activity 2

Using the data in Table 3, over the last century, which have been the worst three decades for investing in equities? What was the real return on equities during those decades? What was the nominal return? Compare your answers with the return on savings accounts during those decades.

Real retn = Eq
Nominal retn = Eq + Inf

Real ret sav = Sav
Nom ret sav = Sav + Inf

4 Evaluating risk and return

An investor checks the stock market and finds that Tesco plc is trading at 348p, 5 per cent Treasury 2018 at 114p and HSBC corporate bonds at 97p. Are they worth investing in at those prices? Are there other shares or bonds that would be better? How can investors make sense of the many options for investing their money? In order to make rational decisions, investors need a method for putting a value on the stream of payments that an investment is expected to produce – the dividends from holding Tesco shares or the interest payments from the gilt or the HSBC bond. Moreover, the method needs to take into account the risk that the actual outcome may differ; for example, Tesco dividends might rise or fall, or the bonds might have to be sold before redemption.

There are two approaches that investors can use, which are really flip sides of the same coin. The investor can ask: what would be a reasonable price to pay today for the return on offer? In other words, the investor is looking for the **intrinsic value** of the stream of payments, which can be compared with the market price to see if the investment appears to be underpriced or overpriced. Alternatively, the investor can ask: given the stream of future payments and the current market price, what rate of return would this investment give? Here, the investor would compare the rate of return with that available from competing investment options. In this section, we introduce a technique for answering both these questions.

The simplest case is an investment on which the return is virtually certain to turn out as expected, so we will start by looking at government bonds held until redemption. We will then consider scenarios and investments where the return is less predictable.

4.1 The return on government bonds

A standard technique for working out either the intrinsic value of an investment or, given its market price, the rate of return that it offers is to use a process called **discounting** in order to find the **present value** of the stream of future payments. You are probably comfortable with the idea that if you invest a sum of money at a constant compound rate of interest, you will get back a larger sum in future because your investment earns interest not just on your original capital but also on any interest that is reinvested. Discounting simply puts this process into reverse to find out what sum you would need to invest today (the

Intrinsic value
The fundamental, underlying or actual value of an investment as opposed to its market price, which may be out of line with its underlying value.

Discounting
The process of reducing a future payment to find out how much it is worth today.

Present value
The value today of one or more payments due to be received in the future when the future payments have been discounted to reflect that money in future is generally worth less than money today.

present value) to produce that future sum, given a specified rate of interest.

For example, £100 invested in a savings account at a return of 3 per cent a year would grow to £100 × 1.03 = £103 by the end of the first year, £100 × 1.03 × 1.03 = £106.09 by the end of the second year, and so on. Putting this into reverse, we can say that the present value of £103 paid in one year's time, assuming a constant rate of interest of 3 per cent, is £103 / 1.03 = £100. Similarly, we can say that the present value of £106.90 paid in two years' time, assuming a constant interest rate of 3 per cent, is £106.09 / (1.03 × 1.03) = £100.

Alternatively, the discounting technique can be used to find out the constant compound rate of interest, called the **discount rate** (or internal rate of return), that would turn the sum available for investment today into the future amount. Using the previous example, if we know that £100 is invested and after two years it is worth £106.09, we could work out that the interest rate (the discount rate) must be 3 per cent a year.

Discount rate
The rate of return that will set a stream of future payments from an investment equal to its present value.

The discounting process is straightforward in an example like the one above where there is just one future payment. Where there is a stream of future payments – for example, 5 per cent Treasury 2018 paying out interest every six months and £100 at redemption – the detail of the calculations is more complicated, but the principle remains the same. Figure 8 summarises the process and is explained here.

Figure 8(a) represents a five-year government bond with a current market price of £75, shown as a negative payment in Year 0. The bond produces a stream of payments: £5 coupon each year (making the simplifying assumption that this is paid out once a year as a single lump sum), and in the final year the investor also gets the redemption value of £100. If we just added up all those payments, we would get a total of £125, but that is not a helpful measure of value because we know that money paid in future is worth less to us than money today, so adding £105 payable in five years' time to £5 payable next year, £5 the next, and so on, is like adding apples and pears.

In Figure 8(b), this problem has been resolved by discounting the payments to find the present value of each one. A discount rate of 11.9 per cent has been chosen – you will see why in a moment. To discount the payment of £5 paid in the first year, you need to divide it by 1 plus the discount rate: £5 / 1.119 = £4.47. To discount the £5 paid in the second year, the calculation is £5 / (1.119 × 1.119) = £3.99.

(a) Stream of payments before discounting

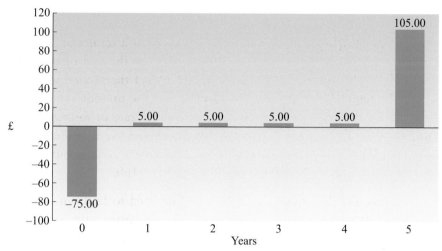

(b) Stream of payments after discounting at a constant discount rate of 11.9%

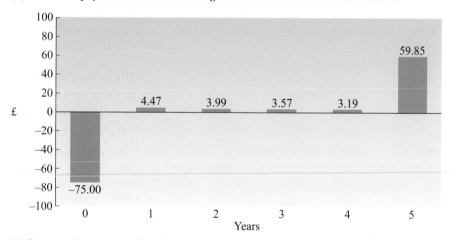

In Example (b), 11.9 per cent is the redemption yield, in other words the rate that sets the sum of the discounted payments equal to the market price of £75.

(c) Stream of payments after discounting at a constant discount rate of 3%

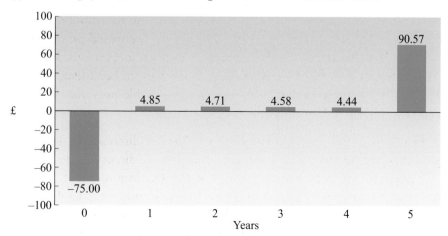

Figure 8 Example of discounting to evaluate a government bond

And the same approach is used for each of the subsequent years. Now if you add up the payments, £4.47 + £3.99 + £3.57 + £3.19 + £59.85, the total comes to £75 (give or take a few pence due to rounding). So discounting using a discount rate of 11.9 per cent has made the sum of the discounted payments equal to the current market price. Another way of interpreting this is to say that, if an investor buys this bond at £75 and holds it until redemption, the return will be 11.9 per cent a year.

Suppose that we had used a different discount rate. Maybe investors are weighing up whether to invest in this bond or in a savings account offering 3 per cent a year. If we use a discount rate of 3 per cent (Figure 8(c)), the present value is much higher at £109. This makes the current market price of £75 look very cheap – the bond must be a bargain!

Using a lower discount rate has increased the present value. Conversely, using a higher discount rate would reduce the present value. There is an inverse relationship between the discount rate and the present value. Do you remember that the same was true when we looked at the price of a bond and its yield in Section 2.4? In fact, when we choose a discount rate that sets the stream of payments to redemption exactly equal to the current market price of the bond, the discount rate is the redemption yield.

There are some problems with evaluating a bond in this way. The main one is capital risk. We have assumed that there is none because the bond is held to redemption. In practice, the period for which the investor wants to hold the investment may be shorter. In that case, they will be selling the bond on the stock market before redemption and the price that they will get cannot be known in advance. The resulting capital gain or loss will need to be estimated before the stream of payments can be discounted. Worse still, the investor might not know in advance what their holding period will be, in which case there is uncertainty even about how many interest payments they will receive before sale.

Therefore, while discounting is a very widely used technique, which gives a useful general basis for comparison, it does not necessarily give a realistic indication of the actual return that a particular investor may get.

4.2 The return on corporate bonds

Corporate bonds are loans to a company that work in essentially the same way as government bonds. The main difference is default risk. While investors may be confident that a government will repay its loans, a company might not. To compensate for default risk, the return on corporate bonds is normally higher than the return on government bonds with a similar maturity – this premium is called the 'corporate bond spread'. Figure 9 shows by how many basis points the return on different types of UK investment-grade corporate bond exceeds the return on government bonds. A basis point is one-hundredth of a percentage point, so a spread of 100 basis points means a premium of 1 per cent over the return on a comparable government bond. During 2008, spreads widened dramatically, especially for banks and other companies in the financial sector. For most of the preceding decade, the spread was generally between 50 and 150 basis points (Bank of England, 2008, p. 11). By 2009, the spread for financial sector bonds had widened to nearly 800 basis points. This wide spread reflected the global financial crisis and fears of an ensuing recession, indicating investors' perception of an increasing risk of companies defaulting and high uncertainty about the future of the economy and investment markets.

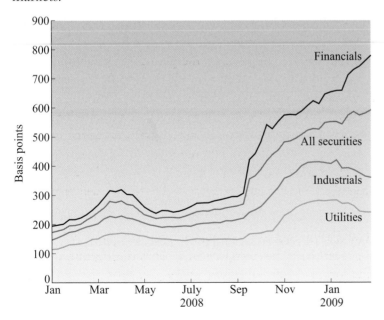

Figure 9 Corporate bond spreads for UK investment-grade bonds

(Source: Bank of England, 2009, p. 10)

Few investors, personal or professional, have the time or means to investigate the creditworthiness of a company. One way to deal with this information gap is to refer to a credit rating agency, an organisation whose business is assessing risk and disseminating this type of information. Figure 10 shows the rating scale used by one of the main international agencies. Personal investors will normally be looking only to invest in 'investment-grade' bonds, as defined in the figure. At the top end of the scale, a company assigned an 'AAA' rating is thought very unlikely to default on its bond payments, but this is not a guarantee or seal of approval – there is still some risk. The extent to which investors can and should be able to rely on the information from credit reference agencies is discussed in Chapter 4.

General summary of the opinions reflected by Standard and Poor's ratings		
	'AAA'	Extremely strong capacity to meet financial commitments. Highest rating
	'AA'	Very strong capacity to meet financial commitments
Investment Grade	'A'	Strong capacity to meet financial commitments, but somewhat susceptible to adverse economic conditions and changes in circumstances
	'BBB'	Adequate capacity to meet financial commitments, but more subject to adverse economic conditions
	'BBB–'	Considered lowest investment grade by market participants
Speculative Grade	'BB+'	Considered highest speculative grade by market participants
	'BB'	Less vulnerable in the near-term but faces major ongoing uncertainties to adverse business, financial and economic conditions
	'B'	More vulnerable to adverse business, financial and economic conditions but currently has the capacity to meet financial commitments
	'CCC'	Currently vulnerable and dependent on favorable business, financial and economic conditions to meet financial commitments
	'CC'	Currently highly vulnerable
	'C'	A bankruptcy petition has been filed or similar action taken, but payments of financial commitments are continued
	'D'	Payment default on financial commitments

Ratings from 'AA' to 'CCC' may be modified by the addition of a plus (+) or minus (–) sign to show relative standing within the major rating categories.

Figure 10 A credit rating scale

(Source: Standard & Poor's, 2009)

4.3 The return on shares

As with bonds, an investment in shares may be expected to produce a stream of payments, but there are some very important differences:

- shares do not have a redemption date
- the amount the investor gets back on sale depends on the market price at that time
- dividend payments are not contractual or guaranteed
- the amount of each dividend may vary.

This means that there are many possible outcomes, depending on how well the company performs, the proportion of its profits paid out in dividends to shareholders, and how the share price performs over the holding period. Estimating the intrinsic value of shares is the essence of **fundamental analysis**. In a classic work on the subject, *Graham and Dodd's Security Analysis*, the authors (Cottle et al., 1988) define the intrinsic value of a company as: 'its economic value as a going concern, taking account of its characteristics, the nature of its business(es), and the investment environment'. Fundamental analysis is an important technique, widely used by people working in the financial services industry. While some personal investors carry out their own analysis, more often they rely on reports and forecasts from stockbrokers, but some understanding of the techniques, ratios and measures used by analysts is necessary to interpret these reports.

A key task for analysts is to estimate a company's future earnings and to give some idea of how confident they are that their forecasts will prove correct. There are various ways in which the analyst can work from the earnings forecasts to estimating the return from investing in the company's shares. One is to assume the proportion of earnings that will be paid out as dividends (called the **dividend payout ratio**). This produces a stream of future dividend payments that can be discounted using the same method that we employed for bonds in Section 4.1.

The stream of payments must include an estimate of the price at which the shares will eventually be sold. But assuming that it matches the intrinsic value, that future sale price will itself reflect the present value of the future dividends to be paid to the new shareowner. Therefore, instead of trying to estimate the sale price directly, the present value of the shares can be assumed to equal a discounted stream of dividends that goes on being paid indefinitely. This is called the **dividend valuation model**. In its most basic form, the model assumes that

Fundamental analysis
A method of trying to find the intrinsic value of an investment by examining the factors that may affect it. Typically these factors include the financial and operating situation of the provider, the sector that it operates in, investment markets and the wider economy.

Dividend payout ratio
The percentage of a company's earnings (profits) for a given period paid out to shareholders as dividends.

Dividend valuation model
A method of trying to find the intrinsic value of an investment in shares by discounting an assumed flow of dividends that continues indefinitely.

dividends continue at their current level. Other forms of the model allow for dividends that increase over time either at a steady growth rate or at a reduced rate once an initial period of rapid growth has passed. These models cannot be used to value companies that have yet to start paying dividends – typically relatively new, high-growth firms.

Another commonly used bridge from the analyst's earnings forecast to a share valuation is the price–earnings (P/E) ratio. This is the share price divided by the company's yearly earnings per share. The resulting number can loosely be thought of as the number of years that it would take to recoup the price paid, but its main function is as a measure of relative value. For example, suppose that the analyst has forecast that earnings for a drug company will be 20 pence per share next year and the P/E ratio for the pharmaceuticals and biotechnology sector is 9.6. The analyst could estimate the intrinsic value of the company's shares as 9.6 × 20p = 192p per share. The valuation can then be compared with the actual market price to assess whether the shares look cheap or overpriced. Once again, this technique cannot be used to value companies that have no earnings, since this makes it impossible to calculate a P/E ratio.

Investors more often start by looking at a company's P/E ratio, then compare it with the ratios for similar companies or the relevant sector as a whole. A high P/E ratio may indicate investors' expectations that a company's earnings are set to rise significantly, but equally it could suggest that the shares are overpriced. Figure 11 briefly considers some of the other ratios that investors use to estimate the worth of a company.

Any one investor is comparing the value that he or she puts on a share with the price in the market, which from the individual's point of view is a given amount determined externally and over which the investor normally has no influence. However, it is worth bearing in mind that the market price is set by the collective actions of all investors, so that the price can be seen as an average of all investors' views about the value of the share – you will return to this point in Chapter 6.

$$P/E = \frac{\text{share price}}{\text{yearly earnings per share}}$$

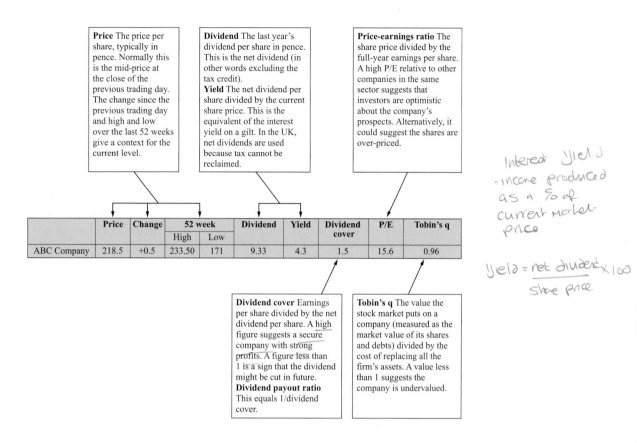

Handwritten margin notes:

Interest Yield
- income produced as a % of current market price

Yield = net dividend × 100 / share price

Figure 11 Share price information and ratios

Activity 3

- If Company X made earnings per share of 34p last year and the market price of its shares is £5.00, what is the P/E ratio?

Handwritten: 500/34 = 14.7

- If the average P/E ratio for similar companies is 8.4, would Company X look like a good or a poor investment to make?

The P/E ratio is the price divided by the earnings per share, but make sure to use the same units in the top and the bottom of the fraction. Working in pence, the P/E ratio for Company X = 500 / 34 = 14.7. If the average for truly similar companies is 8.4, Company X seems heavily overpriced and looks like a poor investment, but maybe Company X is expected to grow exceptionally well in future. However, high growth expectations may be met by bad news (for example, no new drugs coming out of the biotechnology sector). This is the reason that very high P/E ratios are sometimes the sign of trouble ahead – something that you will consider in Chapter 6.

4.4 Shares: taking account of risk

Whatever valuation technique is used, any forecast of share price or return will not necessarily turn out to be accurate and will be just one of a wide range of possible outcomes. Investors and analysts will either implicitly or explicitly assign probabilities to at least some of the possibilities. In the example in Table 4, an analyst has forecast six possible outcomes with probabilities ranging from 5 per cent for outcome F (not very likely to happen in this analyst's view) up to 40 per cent for outcome A (the most likely outcome). We now look at a technique that the analyst can use to turn these forecasts into the basis for an investment decision by a rational investor.

Weighted average
An average that allows for the relative importance of each component.

The first step is to work out the **weighted average** of all the possible outcomes, using the probabilities of each as the weights. The answer is the best estimate of the expected return and is called the **expected value**.

Table 4 An example of finding the expected value

Expected value
(also called the mean)
The average of possible returns from an investment, where each possibility has been weighted by the probability that it will occur.

Forecast outcome	Analyst's estimate of how probable the outcome is	Implied rate of return from investing in the shares[*] % a year
A	40% (i.e. 0.4)	19.7
B	15% (i.e. 0.15)	16.2
C	10% (i.e. 0.1)	−5.2
D	10% (i.e. 0.1)	30.7
E	20% (i.e. 0.2)	25.3
F	5% (i.e. 0.05)	−10.4

[*] Given the analyst's earnings forecasts, dividend payout ratio and current share price.

The analyst has forecast six possible outcomes, which imply six possible rates of return from investing in the company's shares, ranging from −10.4% up to 30.7%. You might be tempted to work out the average return by adding the six values in the last column and dividing by 6. But that would be correct only if the analyst thought that each outcome was equally likely. We know from the middle column that the analyst doesn't believe that to be so. The most likely outcome, with a 40% probability, is that the return will be 19.7%. The least likely outcome, with just a 5% chance, is −10.4%. So, to find a more meaningful average, pre-multiply each outcome by its probability and add together the answers.

Expected value = (0.4 × 19.7%) + (0.15 × 16.2%) + (0.1 × −5.2%) + (0.1 × 30.7%) + (0.2 × 25.3%) + (0.05 × −10.4%) = 17.4% a year.

In this example, the expected value is therefore 17.4 per cent. This seems a very attractive return, but the expected value is only part of the picture. Investors also need to know whether there is any risk involved, and how much. One way of conveying a visual indication of the risk would be to plot the possible outcomes on a chart like the one in Figure 12. Each possible return from the example in Table 4 has been plotted along the horizontal axis with a bar whose height against the vertical axis corresponds to the probability of that return being the actual outcome. For example, the tallest bar (fourth from the left) corresponds to outcome A with a 40 per cent chance that the return will be 19.7 per cent a year. The shortest bar (first on the left) shows outcome F with a 5 per cent chance that the outcome will be a loss of 10.4 per cent a year. If the possible returns were bunched closely around the expected value of 17.4 per cent, the risk of the actual return being very different from the expected value would be small. However, if, as in this example, the returns are spread over a large range, the risk of the actual outcome being very different from the expected value is quite large.

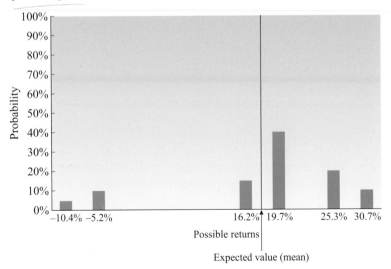

Figure 12 An example of the spread of possible returns

It would be useful if, instead of using qualitative descriptions such as 'quite large', we could quantify the risk so that we could compare the riskiness of one investment opportunity with another. We can do this if, using a chart similar to the one in Figure 12, we make some special assumptions, which are: the expected value lies exactly in the middle of the spread of possible returns; the returns spread out symmetrically either side of the expected value; the returns tend to bunch around the expected value, with extreme values (either lower or higher) being increasingly unlikely the further we move away. In such a world, the spread of possible returns plotted on the chart would form a bell shape, as in Figure 13. This is called a **normal curve** (sometimes also referred to as a 'bell curve').

Normal curve
A graph that shows the probability of an outcome taking on different values and which has some specific characteristics: the possible outcomes are distributed symmetrically around the expected value (mean); a known proportion of the outcomes lies within a specified distance of the expected value.

Many naturally occurring statistics conform to a normal curve. For example, if you drew a chart with height along the horizontal axis and the number of UK men of each height measured by the vertical axis, the data would form a bell-shaped curve, with the majority of men bunched in the centre around the average height of 5 feet 8.37 inches (NHS Information Centre, 2008) and progressively fewer as you moved out towards the far tails of the curve. Neil Fingleton (2009), the UK's tallest man at 7 feet 7.56 inches, would be way out on the right-hand tail.

Mean
The weighted average of a set of values. Provided all values are equally probable, it is obtained by adding them up and dividing the total by the number of values.

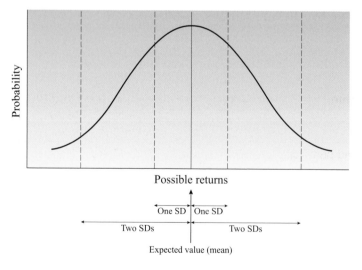

Figure 13 A normal curve

Standard deviation
A measure of the extent to which outcomes spread out to either side of the mean. Commonly used in investment as a measure of risk.

The beauty of a normal curve is that it can be completely described with just two statistics: the expected value (the **mean**), which is a line going through its centre; and the **standard deviation** (SD), which measures the way that the returns spread away to either side. Although the size of the standard deviation varies depending on how far the values spread out across the chart, with a normal curve the following relationships always hold:

- 68 per cent of all the values lie within one standard deviation either side of the expected value
- 95 per cent of all the values lie within two standard deviations either side of the expected value
- 99 per cent of all the values lie within 2.5 standard deviations either side of the expected value.

It follows that if the values are tightly packed around the expected value, the standard deviation must be small and the risk of an outcome very different from the expected value will also be small. If the values are widely spread out, the standard deviation must be larger and the risk of an outcome that is very different from the expected value is therefore larger. In this way, the standard deviation gives us a numerical measure of risk. Using data for the example in Table 4, it turns out that the standard deviation is 11.1. Another investment with a standard deviation lower than 11.1 would be less risky; one with a larger standard deviation would be more risky.

Activity 4

An analyst forecasts the following possible returns from investing in Company Y, which sells umbrellas.

Outcome	Probability	Return from investing in Company Y's shares (% a year)
A: Wet winter and summer	50%	10.4%
B: One season wet and the other dry	30%	5.0%
C: Dry winter and summer	20%	−2.5%

Using the same approach as that shown in Table 4, work out the expected value of an investment in Company Y's shares.

Assuming that standard deviation is a useful measure of relative risk, which is more risky: an investment with an expected return of 6 per cent and standard deviation 10.2, or one with an expected return of 20 per cent and standard deviation 3.5?

Expected value is worked out by multiplying each possible return by the probability that it will occur, and summing the total. The sum is easiest if you turn the probabilities into decimals before you start. In this case, the expected value is $(0.5 \times 10.4\%) + (0.3 \times 5.0\%) + (0.2 \times -2.5\%) = 5.2\% + 1.5\% - 0.5\% = 6.2\%$. A higher standard deviation indicates a higher degree of risk, so the higher-risk investment is the one offering an expected return of 6 per cent with standard deviation 10.2. However, this question poses an unusual scenario. Usually investments offering higher returns are higher-risk. An investment offering a high return but seemingly low risk should be treated with suspicion.

Fat tails – not so unlikely

Standard deviation is very commonly used in the investment world as a measure of risk. For example, standard deviation figures are published in most tables of investment funds, so that the riskiness of one fund can be compared with that of another. But the measure is controversial. Particularly given the roller-coaster ride of stock markets in modern times, is it reasonable to assume that the range of likely returns from a share-based investment really does bunch around the expected value, as the normal curve suggests, or that extreme values are really highly improbable? Some experts suggest that unusual outcomes are much more common than we generally suppose. This would mean that the distribution of possible returns around the expected value would describe a much flatter curve, with **fat tails** that indicate a higher

Fat tail
A distribution of data (such as possible investment returns) where even values that are a long way from the expected value have a relatively high probability of occurring.

probability of extreme results than a normal curve would suggest (see Figure 14). This issue will be considered further in Chapter 6, Section 7.

Also open to question is the assumption that the possible returns are arranged symmetrically around the expected value. Looking back at the example shown in Figure 12, if we drew a curve joining the top of each bar, it would have a longer tail on the left than on the right – this is called a **skew**. If actual outcomes are skewed, risk is not symmetrical. Bad outcomes might be more likely than good, or vice versa, so standard deviation would not provide an accurate measure of risk.

Skew

A situation where the data (such as possible investment returns) are not distributed symmetrically around the expected value.

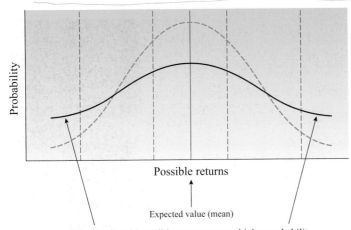

The fat tails of the solid curve suggest a higher probability of extreme rates of return than the dashed normal curve would suggest

Figure 14 A fat-tailed curve

5 Non-financial investments

The techniques applied in this chapter to financial investments such as bonds and shares can equally be applied to any other investment that offers the prospect of a future monetary return: for example, collectables such as wine, antiques and art, property and even ourselves, if we think about investing in **human capital**. The main problem is the difficulty of estimating the nature, amount and probability of future payments from non-financial investments, particularly where there is no formal market in which the investments can be readily traded.

Human capital
Capacity, based on qualifications, skills and experience, to produce income through working.

In the UK, owning a home is often viewed as an investment as well as a place to live. Most homeowners think of the capital gain that they hope to make on selling their home as being the expected investment return. But there is also an income stream in the sense that rent would otherwise have been paid out and is saved as a result of buying rather than renting – economists call this **imputed rent**. If the homeowner has a mortgage, then the monthly mortgage payments should be deducted from the imputed rent to determine the income stream from the investment. The capital gain or loss on sale, net of any final mortgage repayment, is the final element in the calculation.

Imputed rent
The financial benefit that a homeowner is deemed to receive as a result of not paying rent.

Let's consider a very simplified example of someone who buys a home for £100,000 and sells it two years later for £110,000, making a gain of £10,000. During the two years, they saved on rent equal to £6000 a year. So the stream of payments is £6000 in Year 1 and £6000 + £110,000 = £116,000 in Year 2. What rate of return has the homeowner received? By trial and error (or using a computer), it is possible to work out an answer of 10.745 per cent. If we are right, using a discount rate of 10.745 per cent should set the flow of imputed rent and the proceeds from selling the house exactly equal to the price that the owner paid. Let's check that below.

> Year 1: the imputed rent is £6000. The discounted value is £6000 / (1.10745) = £5418.

Year 2: the imputed rent and sale proceeds are £116,000. The discounted value is £116,000 / (1.10745 x 1.10745) = £94,582.

Present value: this is the sum of the discounted values, which comes to £5418 + £94,582 = £100,000. And that is indeed the purchase price of the home.

Of course, most people buy their homes with a mortgage. Let's now adjust the example, so that the homeowner takes out a mortgage of £90,000, putting up only £10,000 of his or her own money. He or she still gets the benefit of the £6000 a year imputed rent, but now has to pay back £7000 a year in mortgage payments. When he or she sells the home, the sale proceeds are still £110,000 but he or she has to pay back the remaining mortgage balance, which we'll assume is £87,000. Using a computer to work out the answer, the rate of return is now an amazing 43.408 per cent. This is how the flow of payments and calculations works out.

Year 1: imputed rent of £6000 less mortgage payment of £7000 makes a net amount of −£1,000. The discounted value is −£1000 / 1.43408 = −£697.

Year 2: the imputed rent less the mortgage payment is −£1000. The sale proceeds less repayment of the outstanding balance come to £110,000 − £87,000 = £23,000. So altogether the payment for this period is £23,000 − £1000 = £22,000. The discounted value is £22,000 / (1.43408 x 1.43408) = £10,697.

Present value: the sum of the discounted values is −£697 + £10,697 = £10,000. And that is the amount of the homeowner's own money that he or she invested.

Buying a home with a mortgage is another example of leverage, which you met in Section 2.2 of Chapter 1. You can see how borrowing to buy a home can hugely magnify the profit if property prices rise. This is a key reason why many personal investors view their own home as their most important investment and may even be planning to rely on it for their pension. But as you saw in Chapter 1, leverage also magnifies losses if prices fall. Therefore borrowing to buy your own home should be viewed as a high-risk way of investing.

Activity 5

'Human capital' may be defined as the capacity to produce income through working. Think of a way in which someone could improve (invest in) their human capital. What costs and rewards would make up the stream of payments from this investment?

A common way to invest in human capital is to study for a qualification that can be used as a basis for getting a better-paid job. The stream of payments might include on the negative side (the investment) tuition fees, cost of books and earnings foregone net of any student grants or loans received. After gaining the qualification, the investment will hopefully generate extra earnings compared with what earnings would have been without the qualification, from which should be netted out any loan repayments.

6 Conclusion

In this chapter, you have looked at the way in which economic and social change can influence investment fashions. You have also considered how rational investors may approach investment decisions, assessing the nature of risks involved, attempting to establish the intrinsic value of the investment and measuring the degree of risk. You have considered some criticisms of the techniques used, and perhaps you have some doubts about the extent to which investors are able to follow the rational approach described. For example, do investors have access to adequate information, are they in a position to estimate probabilities, and do they really make these carefully calculated decisions? As you work through the book, you'll explore these and other questions about investor behaviour. But, first, Chapter 3 builds on the basic investments considered in this chapter to examine a variety of more sophisticated products, techniques and strategies that may be used to adapt and alter the risk–return relationship.

References

Bank of England (2008) *Financial Stability Report*, October, no. 24.

Bank of England (2009) *Quarterly Bulletin*, vol. 49, no. 1.

Barclays Capital (2009) *Equity Gilt Study 2009*, London, Barclays Capital.

Collard, S. and Breuer, Z. (2009) 'Attitudes towards investment choice and risk within the personal accounts scheme: report of a qualitative study', Research Report no. 565, London, Department for Work and Pensions.

Cottle, S., Murray, R.F. and Block, F.E. (1988) *Graham and Dodd's Security Analysis*, New York, McGraw-Hill.

Debt Management Office (DMO) (2004) *A Private Investor's Guide to Gilts*, London, DMO.

Farrow, P. (2009) 'Investors in "safe bonds" at risk of wipeout', *Sunday Telegraph*, 31 May, Money, p. 4.

Fingleton, N. (2009) [online], www.neilfingletonlive.com (Accessed 8 June 2009).

Keynes, J.M. (1963/1931) *Essays in Persuasion*, New York, W.W. Norton & Co.

NHS Information Centre (2008) *Health Survey for England 2007*: *Latest Trends* [online], www.ic.nhs.uk/webfiles/publications/HSE07/Health%20Survey%20for%20England%202007%20Latest%20Trends.pdf (Accessed 8 June 2009).

Office for National Statistics (2007) *Share Ownership* [online], www.statistics.gov.uk/StatBase/Product.asp?vlnk=930&Pos=1&ColRank=1&Rank=272 (Accessed 19 February 2009).

Office for National Statistics (2008) *Private Pension Scheme Membership* [online], www.statistics.gov.uk/CCI/nugget.asp?ID=1277&Pos=&ColRank=1&Rank=224 (Accessed 20 February 2009).

Office for National Statistics (2009) *Composite Price Index* [online], www.statistics.gov.uk/statbase/TSDtables1.asp (Accessed 9 April 2009).

Organisation for Economic Co-operation and Development (OECD) (2009) *Economic Outlook: Interim Report* [online], www.oecd.org/dataoecd/18/1/42443150.pdf (Accessed 2 June 2009).

Pension Law Review Committee (1993) *Pension Law Reform*, Cm 2342-1, London, HMSO.

Proshare (1997) *Individual Share Ownership: Facts and Figures*, London, Proshare.

Standard & Poor's (2009) *Guide to Credit Rating Essentials* [online], www.AboutCreditRatings.com (Accessed 24 February 2009).

Thompson, P. (1989) 'The British stock market since 1918', *BZW Equity-Gilt Study*, London, Barclays de Zoete Wedd Research.

Further reading

Becker, G.S. (1992) *The Economic Way of Looking at Life*, Nobel Prize lecture [online], http://nobelprize.org/nobel_prizes/economics/laureates/1992/becker-lecture.pdf (Accessed 2 October 2009).

Debt Management Office (DMO) (2004) *A Private Investor's Guide to Gilts*, London, DMO.

PART TWO: STRATEGIES AND MARKETS

I have been an advocate of index funds from even before index funds even existed. If there is one thing that I am certain about in investing, it is that the lower the fees you pay to the purveyors of investment products, the more money will be in your pocket rather than in the pocket of the seller of the investment product. The best and lowest cost investment product is what is called an index fund. An index fund simply buys and holds all of the stocks in a market, or all of the bonds in a market. […]

All of the statistical work that I have done throughout my life suggests that year after year, index funds outperform, give a higher net rate of return to the investor than the average high expense actively managed fund, which is what most mutual funds are.

Each year the index fund beats about two-thirds of the actively managed funds because the five that win in one year aren't the same five that win the next year, so that when you compound this over 10, 20, 30 years, you find that you can really count on the fingers of your hands the number of actively managed funds that have beaten the index. So indexing is not guaranteed mediocrity as some critics will call it, but actually one of the surest ways that the individual investor can get above average returns.

Malkiel, B.G. (2007) Chemical Bank Chairman's Professor of Economics, Princeton University, 'How do index funds compare to the performance and movement of other investments?', transcript of an interview carried out on 10 September [online], www.wttw.com/main.taf?p=46,2,3,9 (Accessed 15 October 2009)

Thought-provoking questions for Chapters 3 and 4:

- Is beating the market index average performance only a matter of skill, and what strategies can investment clubs and individual investors adopt?
- Why are financial markets so important, and what are their advantages and limitations for personal investment?

Chapter 3
Risk–return strategies

Janette Rutterford

1 Introduction

Learning outcomes

After reading this chapter, you will:

- understand how theory and practice can be used to improve the balance between risk and return
- be aware of the implications of diversification and the Capital Asset Pricing Model for risk–return management
- distinguish between different types of fund and investment strategy
- understand how performance is measured.

In the Introduction to this book, you looked at the risk–return spectrum of financial products, ranging from assets such as short-term government bonds, which are virtually risk-free, to shares, which can make or lose a lot of money for the investor. And you found that the riskier the investment, the higher the expected return over time. So, for example, 3 per cent a year might be acceptable on a government one-year gilt, 5 per cent a year on a building-society three-year bond, and 8 per cent a year for an investment in Marks & Spencer shares. Investors who are risk-averse, as defined in Chapter 2, take on more risk only if they can expect higher returns.

The purpose of this chapter is to look in more depth at how investors can improve their trade-off between risk and return. Either they can increase expected return for a particular level of risk, or they can reduce the risk underlying a particular expected return.

Section 2 considers two straightforward ways in which this trade-off between risk and return can be improved. First, investments can be structured in a way that is tax-efficient, for example by choosing investment products that are tax-free. Second, investors try to keep a lid on transaction costs: fees, commissions and management charges that are charged by financial institutions and product providers.

In managing risk and return, investors are often advised to spread their risks across a range of investments. If a particular company's share price loses its value, say due to a particular circumstance that has a negative impact on that company's business, the risk incurred may be cushioned if savings are also invested in a range of other companies. This chapter will consider the theory that underpins this type of investment strategy. This is referred to by financial analysts as 'portfolio theory', and is introduced here in two stages. Section 3 introduces the theory by examining the spreading of risk across a small number of shares. In Section 4, the spreading of risk across a range of investments is explored – in relation to the stock market as a whole, and in relation to other assets such as cash and government bonds. Of particular importance to investors is the Capital Asset Pricing Model, which will be introduced to you here.

Section 5 will show how portfolio theory is used by investors, either by investing in funds or by tracking stock-market indices. Section 6 will look at some of the issues involved with investment in practice.

2 Taxation and transaction costs

Tax is a key practical consideration for UK investors. Having introduced some of the main tax issues, the second part of this section will turn to the practical matter of transaction costs.

2.1 Tax-efficient investment

There are two main types of tax for UK investors: income tax and capital gains tax. Interest from savings and bonds, and dividends from shares, are taxed as income; the profit from selling something for more than it originally cost is typically taxed as a capital gain. Income and gains from some savings and investments are tax-free and, even when they are taxable, the investor may have tax-free allowances to use so that in practice no tax is due.

Tax-free investments take many forms

Tax-efficient investment means choosing tax-free products, using allowances and taking advantage of the difference in tax rates between different types of income and between income and gains – for example, choosing an investment that pays gains rather than income when gains are taxed at a lower rate. In practice, calculating income tax is relatively complicated, since this involves combining income from savings and investments with other income, such as from employment. Capital gains tax is simpler and was charged in 2009–10 at a single rate.

Certain specific investments offer reduced tax liabilities. For example, saving via a friendly society (see Chapter 1) is largely tax-free, though some tax is paid on income from dividends. Some National Savings & Investments (NS&I) products are free of income tax – these include savings certificates, children's bonus bonds and premium bonds. Gilts (government bonds) and most corporate bonds are a half-way house – the income from the coupons is taxable but any capital gain, from say buying at £98 and selling to get £100, is tax-free.

Tax wrapper

An administrative structure that shields an investment from either some or all tax.

As well as investing directly, an investor can place their investments in what is called a **tax wrapper**, for example in the UK, using an Individual Savings Account (ISA). A tax wrapper shields the underlying savings or investments from tax, but the amounts that can be invested tax-free are usually limited. For an ISA, the maximum in 2010–11 was £10,200 of which £5,100 could be in cash. Figure 1 illustrates how this works by imagining the tax wrapper as the cling film around a cake.

Imagine a couple of cakes, one chocolate (cash) and one strawberry (shares). Usually, the tax man comes along, picks up a slice and takes a bite from it. But each year, to encourage saving, you're given a tax-free wrapper, like cling film, which you can put around some cake as you choose.

Once inside the cling film the nature of the cake hasn't changed; the chocolate's still chocolate (cash is still cash) and the strawberry still strawberry (shares are still shares) but because it's wrapped up in cling film the tax man can no longer take a bite.

Figure 1 The irresistible tax wrapper

(Source: moneysavingexpert.com, 2009)

But the tax-free label is not always as attractive as it seems, even in the case of ISAs. First, with a tax-free allowance of over £10,000 a year, few investors pay capital gains tax anyway. Second, the income from shares is still taxed at 10 per cent in the ISA which for many is the same tax rate as would be paid on non-ISA income. Lastly, any costs of buying the wrapper will reduce or eliminate the tax advantages.

In the UK, under current legislation, by far the two biggest tax-efficient investments that individuals can make are their own home – there is no capital gains tax on the primary residence – and a pension where contributions attract income-tax relief. Pension funds grow largely tax-free, but with a 10 per cent tax on dividend income still applying.

Box 1 Property as a pension?

After the dot-com boom and bust of the early 2000s, and with property prices rising rapidly, investors looking to save for their old age turned their attention to property. In a 2006/07 government survey, 60 per cent of adults below pension age when interviewed agreed with the statement 'Investing in property is the best way to save for retirement' (ONS, 2009, p. 80). Some traded up the property ladder in the hope of making larger tax-free capital gains which could eventually be used to live on, once they had downsized in retirement. Others borrowed and bought additional properties to form a specific pension nest egg.

There were a number of apparent advantages to investing in property rather than stock-market investments for one's old age. First, the investor could choose which bricks and mortar to buy rather than investing in a stock market which was relatively hard to understand.

Second, by borrowing (see Chapter 5, Section 5), the investor could increase the return (and risk). For example, putting £5000 down and borrowing £95,000 to buy a flat for £100,000 increased the potential expected return. If the flat's value went up to £120,000, the mortgage would still be £95,000 leaving a £20,000 gain on an investment of £5000, a phenomenal 400 per cent return.

For those borrowing to buy properties which they then rented out, there was generally no income tax to pay on the rental received since mortgage interest payments, management charges and maintenance costs could be used to offset rental income.

> By the peak of the property cycle in 2007, it is estimated that there were 920,000 'buy-to-let' mortgages which were taken out by people buying property not as a home but as an investment.
>
> (Source: Clark, 2008)

2.2 Transaction costs of investment

Buying investments involves transaction costs. These can include:

- the bid–ask spread
- brokerage commission
- transaction taxes
- management charges.

If we look first at a simple transaction of 100 Royal Dutch Shell shares, the bid–ask spread is the difference between the price at which the investor can buy the Shell shares (the ask) and the price at which the investor can sell them (the bid). Suppose that the bid–ask spread for 100 Royal Dutch Shell shares is £17.10 – £17.20. This means that the investor can sell 100 shares at £17.10 or buy 100 shares at £17.20, to allow a profit for the so-called **marketmaker**. The bid is the price at which the marketmaker bids for shares; the ask is the price at which the marketmaker asks investors to buy shares.

Marketmaker
An individual or firm that buys and sells assets in large amounts, ensuring a liquid market in them.

For the investor, the bid–ask spread represents a transaction cost. The price at which they can buy shares is always more than the price at which they can sell them, so there is an inbuilt capital loss from day one – in this case 10p per share. Also, the smaller the number of shares traded, the larger the bid–ask spread, to reflect relatively fixed handling costs. **Institutional investors**, trading in large amounts, say 100,000 shares, will experience a much narrower bid–ask spread than will the small investor.

Institutional investor
A financial institution that invests large sums of money on behalf of others.

It is normal to buy or sell shares through a stockbroker or brokerage firm, either by telephone or on the internet. Here again, charges vary according to the size of the trade, with a minimum brokerage commission of, say, £12 for each transaction. This is a relatively small percentage of a £10,000 trade, but makes trading in £100 amounts uneconomic. Online brokers tend to be cheaper than traditional brokers as they provide no investment advice, usually restricting themselves to basic information on the companies in which they trade.

There may be government taxes on transactions. Stamp duty, for example, is payable at 0.5 per cent of the value of any share purchase, with nothing payable on sale. Finally, there are the management charges payable to institutional fund managers in return for choosing the investments on behalf of clients. These charges have to be disclosed in the documentation but are taken by the manager from the funds invested with them and so are rather hidden from view, particularly with long-term investments. Although a 1.5 per cent annual management charge does not sound that large, it can mount up and reduce returns substantially over the long term, as, for example, with pensions (Box 2).

Box 2 The impact of management charges on pensions

The 2006 White Paper on Personal Accounts, published by the Department for Work and Pensions, examined the case of a male median earner (£23,000 a year in 2006/07 terms) who was aged 25 in 2012. By contributing 8 per cent of his earnings each year for 43 years to a pension scheme, with a real rate of return of 3.5 per cent, he would have a pension fund worth £87,000 at the age of 68. However, by introducing a 0.5 per cent annual management charge, the fund would be worth £78,000, with £9,000 having been deducted in management charges. With a 1.5 per cent management charge, typical of active pension fund management charges, the fund would be worth only £63,000, with £24,000 having been deducted in management charges. With charges of 0.5 per cent instead of 1.5 per cent a year, the fund would be worth approximately 25 per cent more on retirement. Stakeholder pensions are an attempt by government to force pension providers to offer pension products whose charges have been capped.

(Source: Department of Work and Pensions, 2006a)

3 Building a portfolio

Chapter 2 looked at the risk and return for each share on its own. But many investors hold a **portfolio** of shares. Instead of all the risk being focused on one share, it can be spread across a portfolio of shares. This section will explore how the trade-off between risk and return can be improved by adding shares to a portfolio.

Portfolio
A set of financial assets held by an individual (or a bank or other financial institution).

3.1 Diversification

Company shares that trade on the stock market are often closely associated with each other. Say, for example, one company sells sun hats and another ice cream in the UK. On a cold day both companies might suffer from low sales and low profitability. Their share prices will fall. Putting both these shares in a portfolio may not be a good idea, since they are both exposed to a similar risk from bad weather.

But what if an investor also bought some shares in a company selling hot chocolate? High sales and profits on a cold day can lead to an increase in the share price, and their portfolio is in better shape for including the hot chocolate company. The risk of loss from cold weather has been reduced through **diversification**: holding a combination of shares that are unlikely to all move in the same direction at the same time.

Diversification
Reducing risk by combining a variety of investments that are unlikely to all move in the same direction at the same time.

Investors use statistics to help establish which combinations of shares are most suitable for diversification. The type of statistics used can be illustrated by considering the example of three companies: Gelato, Solcap and Hotchoc. Gelato makes ice cream, Solcap makes sun hats, and Hotchoc is a manufacturer of hot chocolate.

Consider first the share prices for Gelato and Solcap over a period of sixty months, as displayed in Figure 2. The two shares are closely associated with each other, with prices tending to move together over time. In statistics, this type of close association is described as strong **correlation** between variables. When variables, in this case share prices, are not very well associated with each other, this is described as weak correlation.

Correlation
The extent to which movements of variables are associated with each other.

In addition to the strength of correlation, we also look at the direction of an association, which can be positive or negative. The association between Gelato and Solcap share prices is positive. After seven months, Solcap is priced at £160 per share and Gelato at £150 per share; but in month nineteen they have higher prices of £227 (Solcap) and £313 (Gelato). When Gelato's share price is low, the share price of Solcap is low; when Gelato's share price is high, Solcap's is high.

This type of association is referred to as positive correlation. It seems likely that in month seven the weather was worse than expected, so both shares were low in price, but in month nineteen a sequence of good weather led to better results than expected for ice cream and sun hats.

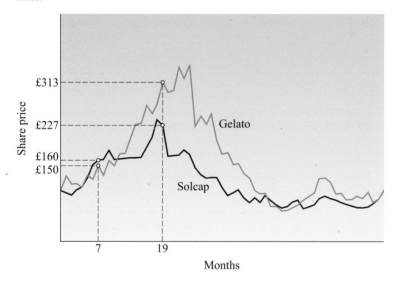

Figure 2 Positive correlation between share prices

Now consider an example of negative correlation in Figure 3, which compares the share price of Gelato with that of Hotchoc. These shares tend to move in opposite directions to each other, with higher share values of Gelato tending to be associated with lower values of Hotchoc. When Hotchoc is £66 per share, the share price of Gelato is £150; but when Hotchoc goes down to £46, we see that Gelato is up to £313.

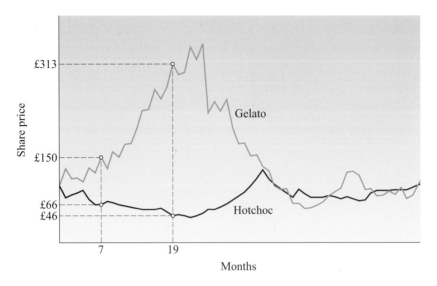

Figure 3 Negative correlation between share prices

When there is negative correlation between the price changes, this provides an opportunity for diversification. (Positive correlation also offers the possibility for diversification, but not to the same extent as negative correlation.) In our example, the investor might combine Hotchoc shares with shares in Gelato, in order to spread the risk associated with future weather conditions.

3.2 Portfolio theory

In Chapter 2 you were introduced to how investors measure the risk and return associated with each investment. We will now use these measures, along with the idea of correlation, to see how a portfolio can be constructed. This is called **portfolio theory**.

Portfolio theory
An approach that determines the risk and return of a portfolio given the risk, return and correlation of its assets.

For the example of Gelato and Hotchoc, it has been suggested that these shares could be combined for the purpose of diversification. To be more precise, portfolio theory considers the correlation between returns from shares. Chapter 2 explained that returns are made up of capital gains (or losses) from changes in share prices, and from dividends that are regularly paid to shareholders. To keep things simple, we can ignore the role of dividends for the illustration that follows. This means that in Figure 3, returns are represented just by the changes in share prices. Between months seven and nineteen, the return (capital gain) on Gelato is £313 − £150 = £163. Over the same period, the return on Hotchoc is represented by the fall in share price from £66 to

£46: a negative return (capital loss) of £20. This example illustrates the negative correlation between returns for Gelato and Hotchoc.

To illustrate how portfolio theory works, suppose that there are, in all, four different possibilities for types of weather:

- cold but sunny period
- hot but rainy period
- cold and rainy period
- hot and sunny period.

Now suppose that over the last sixty months we observed that each type of weather period occurred 25 per cent of the time. It is therefore estimated that each will have a 25 per cent chance of occurring in the next sixty months. These 25 per cent probabilities are shown in Table 1, alongside the average monthly returns observed in the past sixty months for Gelato and Hotchoc. Consider the hot and sunny period. The return for Gelato is expected to be 17.21 per cent (great ice cream sales), but a *loss* of 9.07 per cent is expected for Hotchoc (not much call for hot chocolate).

Table 1 Risk and return for Gelato and Hotchoc

Types of weather	Average monthly return		
	Probability	Gelato	Hotchoc
Cold/sunny	25%	−11.38%	−6.44%
Hot/rainy	25%	12.01%	7.16%
Cold/rainy	25%	−13.84%	9.78%
Hot/sunny	25%	17.21%	−9.07%
Expected return (monthly)		1.00%	0.36%
Expected return (yearly)		12.7%	4.4%
Risk (standard deviation)		13.8%	8.2%

In Chapter 2, you were introduced to two key measures: expected return and risk, both of which are included in Table 1.

Activity 1

Table 1 reports a monthly expected return of 1 per cent for Gelato. Explain how this measure is calculated.

Monthly expected return is calculated by multiplying each monthly outcome by its probability (see Chapter 2, Section 4.4). For Gelato, 1 per cent = $(0.25 \times -11.38\%) + (0.25 \times 12.01\%) + (0.25 \times -13.84\%) + (0.25 \times 17.21\%)$.

Then, the annual (yearly) equivalent return is just the compound value of the monthly return. You came across compounding in Chapter 2, Section 4.1. For Gelato, each £1 invested earns a monthly return of 1 per cent. In the first month this would grow to £1 × 1.01, in the second month to £1 × 1.01 × 1.01, and so on for 12 months. Using this method, the annual equivalent return for Gelato is 12.7 per cent. The annual expected return is the usual way to express returns on shares.

Risk is measured using the standard deviation (or dispersion) of returns. The more highly dispersed or spread out the returns, the higher the risk involved in holding the share. These risk measures are also reported in Table 1: 13.8 per cent for Gelato and 8.2 per cent for Hotchoc.

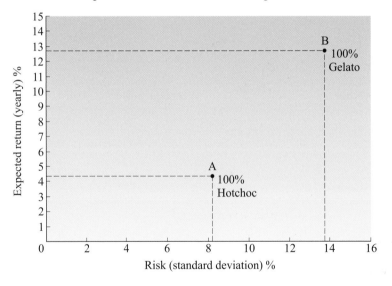

Figure 4 Risk and return for Gelato and Hotchoc

These measures can be displayed in the risk–return diagram, which has been shown to you in the previous three chapters. In Figure 4, the vertical axis represents the expected return, and the horizontal axis represents risk. Point A shows what happens if the investor chooses to invest 100 per cent of the investment outlay in Hotchoc. The risk measured at 8.2 per cent can be read off the horizontal axis of the diagram, and the expected return of 4.4 per cent can be read off the vertical axis. However, at point B, where only Gelato shares are held, both risk and expected return are higher (13.8 per cent and 12.7 per cent). This example of Gelato and Hotchoc provides a very good illustration of the risk–return trade-off, where to get higher returns the investor has to take on higher risk.

However, by combining the two shares in a portfolio it is possible for the investor to reach a better outcome. Consider point C in Figure 5: a portfolio of 62 per cent Gelato shares and 38 per cent Hotchoc shares. This portfolio bears the same risk as at A, where the investor holds 100 per cent in Hotchoc shares. But the expected return is now 9.5 per cent, significantly higher than the 4.4 per cent expected at A. So by combining the two shares in a portfolio it is possible to increase expected return without increasing risk. This shows how powerful diversification can be in tackling risk and return.

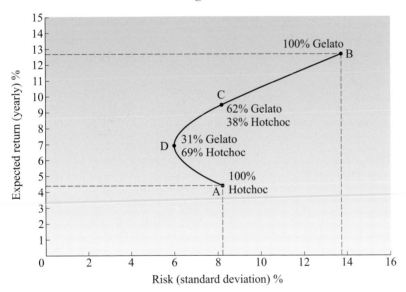

Figure 5 Combining two shares in a portfolio

For an investor seeking the least amount of risk, point D might be chosen, where the risk is 6.0 per cent. All possible combinations of Gelato and Hotchoc shares are shown by the curve in Figure 5 that links together all the possible portfolios.

Of course, in the real world, the investor can choose between thousands of shares, in any number of combinations. To illustrate how diversification works for three shares, consider Figure 6. An additional share is introduced for a company making ice lollies: Icepop. At point E, 100 per cent of the portfolio is allocated to Icepop shares. Various combinations of Icepop and Hotchoc are available in the curve drawn between A and E, as are combinations of Hotchoc and Gelato already shown in the curve joining A and B.

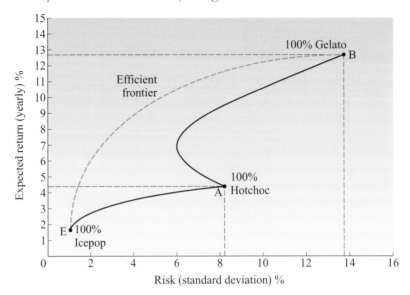

Figure 6 Combining three shares in a portfolio

The key to this new scenario is that the investor can now choose to combine all three shares in a portfolio. A third (dashed) curve can be drawn, which draws together all combinations that are possible from the three shares. This is called the **efficient frontier**. It represents points at which the investor can get the highest expected return for a given risk, and the lowest level of risk for a given expected return. Economists refer to these as 'optimal' combinations of risk and return.

By reaching the efficient frontier the investor is unable to improve their risk–return trade-off. The portfolios on the efficient frontier are said to be **Markowitz efficient**, named after Harry Markowitz (1959), who was the first person to work out the implications for the mathematics of combining shares into portfolios. By following a strategy to reach the efficient frontier, investors are said to employ **Markowitz diversification**. In summary, this use of statistical tools to achieve efficient diversification is just a particular way to apply in practice the well-known adage 'don't put all your eggs in one basket'.

Efficient frontier
A curve representing the most efficient combinations of risk and expected return.

Markowitz efficient
Describes a portfolio that has the highest expected return for a given level of risk.

Markowitz diversification
Combining portfolio assets in an effort to lower risk without sacrificing expected return.

Don't put all your eggs in one basket

3.3 Choosing the size of a portfolio

In practice many more than three shares could be chosen: let's call the number *n*. What should *n* be? The investor should diversify to improve the balance between risk and return, but to what extent?

Suppose that we adopt a simple investment strategy to find out. We invest equal amounts in randomly chosen portfolios that consist of two, three, four, five and more shares. This type of diversification is less efficient than choosing portfolios on the efficient frontier. Indeed, it is an example of **naïve diversification**: simply choosing to expand the number of shares in the portfolio without examining their risk–return characteristics. The portfolio will not necessarily be Markowitz efficient, but there are still benefits to naïve diversification.

Naïve diversification
When shares are combined without reference to their risk–return characteristics in an effort to lower portfolio risk.

The benefits of naïve diversification can be seen in Figure 7, which plots the typical risk for holding portfolios of one, two, …, ten, up to hundreds of shares, in equal proportions. For example, portfolios consisting of, say, ten shares have less risk than portfolios consisting of one share. Portfolios consisting of thirty shares have less risk than portfolios consisting of ten shares. But, beyond that, the benefits to diversification taper off. Why is that? This is because there are common factors affecting all shares that cannot be diversified away: interest rates, economic conditions, tax rates, inflation, and so on. Indeed, the benefits of diversification come from diversifying away what is known as

Specific risk
Risk specific to a
company, which can be
reduced through
diversification.

Systematic risk
Market risk that cannot
be reduced through
diversification.

Investment trust
A company that invests
in a diversified
portfolio of shares
and/or other
investments. Investors
buy shares in the
investment trust.

Unit trust
A trust that holds
shares on behalf of
investors. Investors
hold units in the unit
trust.

specific risk, that is, risk specific to individual companies. A limit is
then reached beyond which risk cannot be reduced further. This
*un*diversifiable risk is called **systematic risk**, that is, risk that is endemic
to the stock market and cannot be diversified away, no matter how
many shares are included in a portfolio.

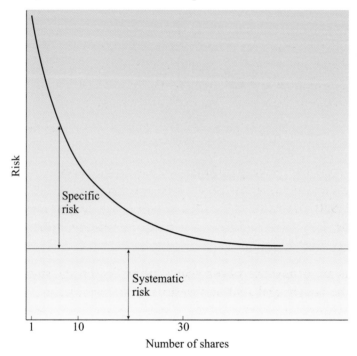

Figure 7 The effect on risk of the number of shares in the portfolio

(Adapted from Evans and Archer, 1968)

Figure 7 has two major implications for investors. First, small investors
need only diversify by holding 10 to 15 shares to have substantially
reduced risk from holding just one share. Second, institutional investors
do not need to hold vast numbers of shares to be diversified. The extra
reduction in risk gained by holding 100 rather than 30 different shares
is very small and may well be more than outweighed by the additional
transaction and monitoring costs involved in holding the extra 70
shares.

3.4 Diversification in practice

Investment trusts and **unit trusts** were designed to allow small
investors the benefits of diversification, when the amounts that they had
to invest did not allow them to buy, say, ten different shares in

reasonable quantities. The earliest British investment trust, the Foreign & Colonial Government Trust, was founded in 1868 with the declared investment strategy of buying 18 foreign government bonds, from Brazil to Turkey, Egypt to New South Wales, in amounts ranging from 3 per cent to 20 per cent of the value of the overall portfolio. The prospectus read:

> The object of this Trust is to give the investor of moderate means the same advantages as the large Capitalists, in diminishing the risk of investing in Foreign and Colonial Government Stocks, by spreading the investment over a number of different Stocks.

(Foreign & Colonial Government Trust, 1868)

It was such a success that it soon had many imitators, primarily investing in fixed-interest securities. Unit trusts, first launched in the UK in the early 1930s, based on a US idea, concentrated on shares rather than bonds, and overtook investment trusts in popularity during the 1960s.

Investment trusts are companies whose shares are traded on the stock market and can be bought and sold by investors. Investment trusts invest in shares whose total market value is called the **net asset value** of the trust. Interestingly, the market value of an investment trust company's shares does not have to be the same as the net asset value of the underlying portfolio. The investment trust share price can be at a discount or premium to the net asset value per share. Consider, for example, an investment trust with a market value of £100 million divided into 10 million shares priced at £10 each. It may, in fact, hold a portfolio worth £120 million, which represents £12 per share. In this case the shares would be trading at a discount of £2 to the net asset value of £12. The size of the discount or premium is what balances demand with supply. Although popular investment trusts may trade at a premium, typically investment trusts trade at a discount. This discount can vary, adding an additional risk to investment. Investment trusts, being companies, can also borrow, which also adds to investment risk.

Unit trusts are structures that hold shares in trust for the beneficiaries, the unit trust holders. **Open-ended investment companies** (OEICs – pronounced 'oiks') are similar but use a corporate rather than trust structure. The value of the underlying investment portfolio of a unit fund is also called the net asset value; but in this case the market price at which the units are bought or sold is the same as the net asset value

Net asset value (NAV)
The market value of the portfolio underlying a unit trust or investment trust. The net asset value per share is the net asset value divided by the number of shares (for an investment trust) or units (for a unit trust or OEIC).

Open-ended investment company (OEIC)
Similar to a unit trust but better understood internationally.

(with a spread between the bid and the ask price). There is no discount or premium. The balance of supply and demand determines the number of units, so that popular unit trusts grow in size, and unpopular ones shrink. This is why unit trusts are sometimes called 'open-ended'. In contrast, investment trusts are called 'closed-end' because they cannot create additional shares as can unit trusts – unless they make a new share issue in the stock market. So demand for investment trusts is reflected in the premium or discount to net asset value, whereas demand for unit trusts is reflected in the number of units. Unit trust managers have to keep a certain amount of the portfolio in very liquid assets to allow for possible redemptions. Unit trusts do not borrow money.

Life insurance company investment funds are run along the lines of unit trusts and are funds in which investors invest through the wrapper of a life insurance company policy.

Sectors
Groups of companies listed on a particular stock exchange that carry out the same activity (e.g. electrical engineering, property construction or financial services).

Looking at the correlation between returns shows that there are different levels of portfolio diversification. The first is to spread the portfolio across a number of shares, say UK shares listed on the London Stock Exchange, typically spread across a number of different **sectors**. The next stage is to widen the portfolio to include overseas investments. The idea is that the US stock market is less correlated with the UK stock market than, say, BP and Vodafone are in the UK. The final stage is to include emerging stock markets, which are even less likely to be highly correlated – for example, the Chinese and Indian stock markets can be argued to have 'decoupled' or disconnected from developed economy markets. In building portfolios of shares, fund managers work through these levels of portfolio diversification on behalf of their investors.

Activity 2

Foreign & Colonial Investment Trust (F&C) still exists, with a slight change of name, more than 140 years after it was founded. Go to its website, by inputting 'Foreign and Colonial Investment Trust' into a search engine, and see how many shares it currently has in its portfolio. Using Figure 7, what can you say about its specific and systematic risk?

As of September 2009, F&C stated that it held shares in more than 600 companies in 30 different countries. It also stated that it invested in another asset class, private equity funds – that is, funds that buy whole companies rather than just shares. International diversification will reduce risk by more than just diversifying across companies in the same country. However, 600-plus companies is a large number when it comes to monitoring and management costs, and it may be that these costs outweigh the diversification benefits of holding such a large number of shares.

International diversification is good for you

4 Balancing risk and return

Thus far we have looked at diversification across shares, and how this can be achieved by collecting shares in funds. But compared to other assets, shares can involve high levels of both risk and return. In this section, we will consider how a less risky portfolio can be put together by combining shares with a risk-free asset.

4.1 The Capital Asset Pricing Model

A key model in investment analysis is the Capital Asset Pricing Model (Sharpe, 1964), also called the CAPM. It makes three additional assumptions to those assumed thus far in our development of portfolio theory, and leads to some pretty startling conclusions for fund management. The additional assumptions are that:

1   All investors are looking at the same risk–return diagram.

2   There is a risk-free asset that is risk-free for us all. Chapter 2 showed that a truly risk-free asset is hard to find, but there are some close equivalents in short-term government-backed bonds.

3   Investors can borrow and lend at the same risk-free rate. We know that this has to be unrealistic, but allowance for differences in borrowing and lending rates makes the model that much more complicated.

These assumptions are captured in Figure 8. As before, this is a diagram showing combinations of risk and return associated with different portfolios. The risk-free rate of return is represented by R_F. This could, for example, be a yield of 3 per cent on a government bond. Note that there is no risk attached to this investment, hence its location on the vertical axis. An investor could choose to put their entire portfolio into the risk-free asset, yielding the return R_F at no risk.

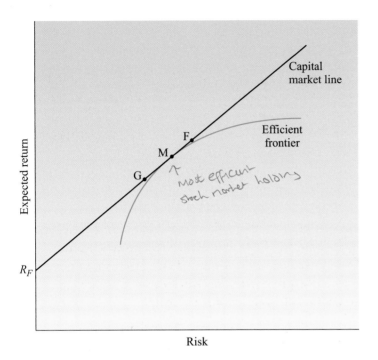

Handwritten annotations on figure:
R_F = risk free rate of return
↳ no risk assed

M. ↑ Most efficient stock market holding

Figure 8 Introducing a risk-free asset

Notice also that a straight line has been drawn on Figure 8 that starts at R_F. This is called the **capital market line**. As we move along the line, risk-bearing shares (in proportions to be explained shortly) are added to the portfolio. Assume that the investor has £100 to invest at the outset. At R_F, the investor puts all of the £100 into a portfolio made up of only the risk-free asset. But at G, the investor holds only £20 in risk-free government bonds, and the other £80 in shares. This increases both the expected return and risk associated with the portfolio.

The investor could alternatively put all of the £100 into shares at M, which is a point on the efficient frontier that touches the capital market line in Figure 8. Now, it has been assumed that all investors are looking at the same diagram, which leads them to reach the same conclusion: that the most efficient combination of shares is to hold M since it is a point on the efficient frontier. Since all investors will hold M in some proportion in their portfolios, and for the economy as a whole investors hold all shares in the stock market, the portfolio M must include all shares in the stock market in proportion to their market value. This is called the **market portfolio**. By choosing this efficient outcome the investor diversifies away all specific risk associated with shares held in the portfolio, as discussed in Section 3. Only systematic (market) risk is incurred.

Capital market line
A line representing combinations of the market portfolio and the risk-free asset.

Market portfolio
A portfolio of all the shares in the market, in proportion to their market value.

At M the investor does not hold any of the risk-free asset: all of the £100 is invested in a market portfolio of shares. Hence the line between R_F and M represents combinations of the risk-free asset and the market portfolio of shares. Under the CAPM, investors choose the combination between these assets that most suits their appetite for risk and return. The choice is between zero risk at R_F or full exposure to market risk at M.

It is important to emphasise that even at G, where only £80 is invested in shares, these shares will consist of the market portfolio (based on the stock market as a whole), in which there is only systematic risk. All that varies, at this stage in our analysis, is the amount of money invested in this market portfolio, and hence the amount of systematic risk.

Activity 3

Using the earlier example considered in Figure 5, assume that the market portfolio M is made up of 62 per cent Gelato shares and 38 per cent Hotchoc shares. Given £100 to invest, how much will be allocated to each share at point G in Figure 8?

The £80 invested in shares will consist of £49.60 allocated to Gelato (62 per cent of £80) and £30.40 allocated to Hotchoc (38 per cent of £80). This is the most efficient (optimal) combination of shares.

The CAPM also allows for the investor to borrow. Assume that the investor could borrow £10 and use this to buy more shares: an expanded market portfolio of £110. Moving further along the capital market line to point F in Figure 8, the investor has further increased expected return and risk. By borrowing money to invest in shares, the investor has taken on more systematic risk.

What the CAPM essentially says is that investors get rewarded only for taking on systematic risk. So, provided that all the assumptions underlying the model hold, investors can only expect a return for bearing systematic risk. There is no point in taking on specific risk, as there is no expectation of any additional return for this. According to the CAPM, investors should hold efficient portfolios made up of M and the risk-free asset. Unlike the Markowitz approach, which leaves it open to each investor to hold their own tailor-made portfolio, the CAPM says that we should all hold different proportions of the risk-free asset and of the same risky portfolio of shares (that is, the market portfolio, M).

4.2 Market sensitivity

For fund managers there is a shorthand way of applying the principles of the CAPM. They can compare the risk of any share or portfolio to that of a benchmark that is represented by the market portfolio. This is achieved using a measure called **beta**. Beta measures the sensitivity of returns on a share or portfolio to those of the market (or any other benchmark).

Figure 9 shows how beta is used in a simple example. At the market portfolio M, the value of beta is set equal to 1 by definition. But consider point F, in which beta is equal to 1.1. This portfolio will be more sensitive to market fluctuations than M. It will rise by 11 per cent if the market rises by 10 per cent, and fall by 11 per cent if the market falls by 10 per cent. When its beta is more than 1, a portfolio tends to outperform the market in both directions.

Beta
The beta of a portfolio (or an individual share) measures the sensitivity of its return to changes in the return from the market portfolio.

what do we mean by this

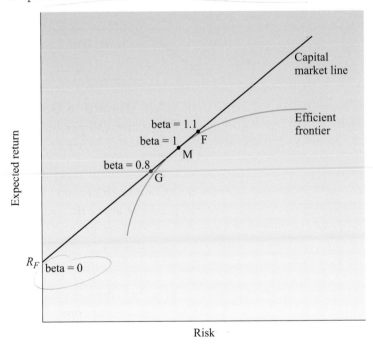

Figure 9 Choosing a market-related portfolio

Activity 4

Now consider point G at which the beta is equal to 0.8.

With a beta of 0.8, what is the likely impact on a portfolio if there is a 10 per cent fall in the market?

The portfolio is expected to fall back by 8 per cent. This is calculated by multiplying 10 per cent by 0.8. When a portfolio's beta is less than 1, the portfolio will tend to underperform the market in both directions. If at the extreme the portfolio is all held in the risk-free asset, to give a return of R_F, the beta is equal to zero. This portfolio is not at all sensitive to market fluctuations.

In the risk–return diagram in Figure 9, beta can be adjusted by varying the amount invested in the market portfolio. Consider again what happens if, instead of investing £100 in M, an investor borrows £100 and invests £200: an extra £100 worth of shares added in the same proportion to the portfolio. This will make their portfolio twice as sensitive to the market and so they will have a beta of 2 – taking on twice as much market risk but with twice the expected return. So if the market does well, then they will do very well. On the other hand if, say, the market falls by 20 per cent, their portfolio is likely to fall by 40 per cent. These are the extreme highs and lows associated with leverage (borrowing), as discussed in Chapter 2, Section 5.

Passive investor
An investor who seeks to track, and not outperform, a specified investment benchmark.

Investors who believe in the CAPM and whose portfolios consist only of the market portfolio M and the risk-free asset, are called **passive investors**. In Chapter 4 you will also be introduced to the Efficient Markets Hypothesis (EMH) that makes the same recommendation. Such investors do not believe that it is possible to consistently outperform the market and so do not try. In the next part of this chapter we will consider how performance benchmarks can be established that may be tracked by passive investment.

A passive investor

4.3 The market and stock-market indices

We now turn to the question of how to invest in the market portfolio. In practice, investors tend to buy investment products linked to a stock-market index, which represents an underlying market, through the medium of **index funds**. These have become widely used by investors partly due to the implications of the CAPM. Economic and financial theories do matter! These index funds are investment trusts or unit trusts designed to track an index as it moves from day to day. Index fund managers do so either by 'full replication', buying shares in proportion to their importance in an index, or by sampling, buying the larger shares and a sample of the smaller ones, to reduce transaction costs while still getting a close replication of the movements of the index. **Exchange-traded funds (ETFs)** are index funds that are listed on the stock exchange as shares but are essentially funds. (Note that the word 'exchange' here has nothing to do with currency exchange.) ETFs allow low-cost investment in market portfolios.

Index fund
An index fund is a fund that aims to track rather than outperform a particular stock market index.

Exchange-traded fund (ETF)
A fund that typically tracks market indices.

Box 3 What do we mean by 'the market'?

The Capital Asset Pricing Model assumes that the market portfolio M includes all investible assets. This would include stocks, shares, works of art, commodities, property, and even our future earnings if these could be traded. This would be impossible to value in practice, so investment managers choose to represent the market by a stock-market index. Of course, different investors of different nationalities will look at different indices: the CAC40 for France, the S&P500 for the USA, for example. But even within countries there are a number of indices to choose from.

For example, in the UK, the index most cited on the news is the FTSE100, which tracks the change in value of the top 100 shares listed on the London Stock Exchange weighted by market value. Every quarter, those companies that have fallen out of the top 100 are thrown out of the index and new large companies are included. In the USA, the most popular indices are the S&P500, a market-value-weighted index of 500 large US shares, and the NASDAQ Composite Index, a market-value-weighted index of all shares listed on the National Association of Securities Dealers Automated Quotation system, which consists primarily of shares in technology companies.

But the object of the CAPM is to represent the market as a whole and not the top 100 shares only. So, for our purposes, a more appropriate UK index would be the FTSE All Share Index, which in 2009 included 619 shares, weighted by market value, and these shares represented in value terms around 98 per cent of the value of all the shares listed on the market.

For a more global perspective, there is the MSCI World Index, but even this is designed to measure the equity market performance of only developed and not emerging markets. As of 2009, it consisted of the following 23 developed market indices, also weighted by market value: Australia, Austria, Belgium, Canada, Denmark, Finland, France, Germany, Greece, Hong Kong, Ireland, Italy, Japan, The Netherlands, New Zealand, Norway, Portugal, Singapore, Spain, Sweden, Switzerland, the UK, and the USA. You can see how difficult it is to define 'the market'.

Investing in index funds is a passive investment strategy aiming to track an index rather than outperform it. But what this has meant for traditional fund managers is that they now have a benchmark strategy against which they can be judged. They have to try to outperform the index by following an *active* investment strategy.

Investors who do not believe the assumptions underlying the CAPM and think that they have superior investment skills can take on specific risk in the hope of achieving positive returns that beat the market. This is called an **alpha** investment strategy. It is the holy grail for investors seeking to earn superior returns. And this type of investor is called an **active investor.**

Alpha
The amount by which a portfolio has outperformed (or underperformed) its benchmark by taking on specific risk.

Active investor
An investor who seeks to outperform a specified investment benchmark.

An active investor

Fund managers who are active investors can try to outperform the market portfolio, or an index, by one of two strategies. One is to take on more specific risk by selecting companies in different proportions to their weighting in the index, so that the portfolio will be overweight in those companies that are expected to do well and underweight in those that have poor prospects. This strategy is called **stock selection**.

The other way to try to outperform an index is to try to forecast the movement of the market by adjusting the beta of the portfolio. This can involve increasing the amount of shares in the portfolio when the market is expected to rise, and reverting to cash just before the market goes down. By varying beta, fund managers are trying to time their entry into the market, and their exit out of the market. They are indulging in **market timing**.

Stock selection
An investment strategy that involves buying shares in different proportions to their weighting in a stock-market index to try to outperform that index.

Market timing
An investment strategy that involves buying and selling a particular portfolio to try to outperform the alternative strategy of buying the portfolio and holding it.

In fact, there are two ways in which active fund managers can attempt to time the market. The first is by varying the amount of leverage in a passive portfolio, moving up and down the capital market line and varying the beta of the portfolio according to whether they think the market will rise or fall (as shown in Figure 9). The second way is to alter the composition of the portfolio by increasing the proportion of shares that have high beta when the market is expected to rise, and increasing the proportion of low-beta shares when the market is expected to go down.

The investor can choose between different types of shares. An example of a cyclical, or aggressive, share is an airline – which does particularly well in a boom and particularly badly in a recession – giving it a beta of more than 1 (high beta). An example of a non-cyclical (defensive) share is a utility or food manufacturer – people use electricity and water, and eat, regardless of the state of the economy – and these typically have a beta of less than 1 (low beta). Typically, low-beta shares do relatively well in a recession, and high-beta shares do relatively well in boom times. So shares can have high or low betas as well as portfolios. But, if the active fund manager buys a portfolio of shares selected for their high or low betas and not the market portfolio, M, they will no longer have a fully efficient portfolio, and will bear specific as well as systematic risk.

So, whether adopting a stock selection strategy or a market timing strategy, the active fund manager is taking on more risk than the passive fund manager, by varying share beta risk (market timing) and/or through taking on specific risk (stock selection). Active fund managers also reduce the net expected return by charging higher fees than do passive fund managers; the latter run index funds in a competitive market and charge low fees for the replication of indices (essentially because less work is required to seek information about future price changes). Proponents of the CAPM, which assumes no particular investment skill, believe that the active approach is doomed to failure. Active managers argue that since some of them make a good living, some of them must be successful some of the time. Chapter 4 will further explore this tension between active and passive investment strategies.

There is little evidence of market timing skills. A few people have become famous for timing the market correctly – George Soros for selling sterling before sterling left the Exchange Rate Mechanism in 1992 and Jon Moulton of Alchemy Partners for selling securities linked to sub-prime mortgages before that market collapsed – but these are individual occurrences for two particular investors and do not reflect general market timing ability. Indeed, retail investors are often sellers in a **bear market** when prices have already fallen and buyers in a **bull market**, the exact opposite of 'buying low and selling high', which is effectively what a market timing strategy attempts to do.

Bear market
A market where the majority of investors are selling ('bears'), causing overall share prices to fall.

Bull market
A market where the majority of investors are buying ('bulls'), causing overall share prices to rise.

5 Measuring investment performance

5.1 Relative returns

The traditional way in which fund-manager performance has tended to be judged is against the performance of other fund managers with similar investment objectives. So pension fund managers are judged against other pension fund managers, and unit trust managers investing in UK shares are judged against other fund managers investing in UK shares. Table 2 shows how funds are grouped by the Investment Management Association (IMA) to allow performance measures to be applied to peer groups of funds.

The IMA maintains a system for classifying funds, as there are over 2000 investment funds. The classification system contains 30 sectors grouping similar funds together. The sectors are split into two categories, those designed to provide 'income' and those designed to provide 'growth'. The sectors are designed to help investors to find the best fund(s) to meet their investment objectives and to compare how well their fund is performing against similar funds. Each sector is made up of funds investing in similar assets, in the same stock-market sectors or in the same geographical region.

Similar frameworks have been put in place by the Association of British Insurers for life company funds and other groups of investment funds. Whatever the framework, the aim of each fund manager is to be top of the league tables so that new investors will choose them based on past performance. For such managers, success is about *relative* not *absolute* performance, and this can affect fund managers' behaviour.

Peer group
A group of funds with the same investment objectives.

Income fund
An investment fund that favours companies with high dividend yields.

For example, suppose that you are trying to compare funds investing in cash and UK equities (shares). In a bull market, a top performer relative to the **peer group** is likely to be the fund most heavily invested in equities. Because of this, there will be a temptation on the part of all the fund managers in this peer group to increase their equity participation. So, over time, the typical fund's equity exposure will rise, increasing its risk. When the bear market comes, the funds in the group will suffer more than if they had invested relative to a benchmark linked to cash and equity indices, say 50 per cent in each. Staying close to this benchmark would have meant that their equity market risk stayed more or less the same over time.

Table 2 UK fund sector classification

Income funds		Growth funds		Specialist funds
Immediate income	**Growing income**	**Capital protection**	**Capital growth/total return**	Absolute return
Global bonds	UK equity income	Money market	Active managed	Personal pensions
£ Corporate bond		Protected/ guaranteed funds	Asia Pacific, including Japan	Property specialist
£ High yield			Asia Pacific, excluding Japan	Technology and telecommunications
£ Strategic bond			Balanced managed	
UK equity and bond income			Cautious managed	
UK gilts			Europe, including UK	
UK index-linked gilts			Europe, excluding UK	
			European smaller companies	
			Global emerging markets	
			Global growth	
			Japan	
			Japanese smaller companies	
			North America	
			North American smaller companies	
			UK all companies	
			UK smaller companies	
			UK zeros	

(Source: Investment Management Association, 2009)

Retail funds can also be judged against a suitable benchmark index, say an Indian stock-market index for an Indian equity fund, or the MSCI global equity index for a global equities fund. This makes it easier to measure that all-elusive outperformance, as it is a specified, calculable benchmark return, and allows funds to be judged relative to an established alternative investment strategy.

Growth fund
An investment fund targeting capital appreciation by selecting companies tipped for above-average earnings growth and reinvesting dividends.

The further away from the benchmark, therefore, the greater the risk taken on by the fund manager. And individual funds deviate from the benchmark to try to outperform in different ways. As you have already seen, some take on more beta, others more specific risk, in order to earn what is called 'positive alpha'. Box 4 shows which performance measures can be used when comparing performance against a peer group or when comparing against the performance of a benchmark index.

Box 4 Performance measures

(a) Peer group performance measures

Peer group performance measures can be used when there is no benchmark index available and allow comparison of funds within an appropriate peer group. The key measures of peer group performance are:

Sharpe ratio

This measures how much is earned per unit of total risk taken on by the fund (the standard deviation of its returns). The ratio consists of two elements. The first element (the numerator) is the excess return of the fund relative to the risk-free rate. So if the return is 13 per cent and the return to the risk-free asset is 3 per cent, this means that the excess return is 10 per cent. The second element (the denominator) is the standard deviation of returns to the fund. If, say, the standard deviation is 10 per cent, then with an excess return of 10 per cent this gives a Sharpe ratio of 1, considered to be a good performance. If the excess return is only 2 per cent, the Sharpe ratio would be a less impressive 0.2. Earning less than the risk-free rate, as fund managers did in 2008, would give a negative Sharpe ratio!

R^2 (R-squared)

This is the percentage of the total risk of a portfolio that can be explained by market risk. The remainder is the percentage represented by specific risk. A high R-squared, say 90 per cent or

---

more, means that the fund closely resembles an index fund and is not following an active outperformance strategy.

(b) Index benchmark performance measures

Where an index or other benchmark is specified, the following measures are used to judge performance relative to that benchmark:

Alpha

The difference between the return on the portfolio and the return on the benchmark, positive or negative, that can be derived by taking on specific risk – for example through stock selection.

Beta

A measure of the fund's sensitivity to market movements. Fund managers use beta to engage in market timing. In a bull market, a fund with a beta of more than 1 will be expected to do well relative to the market; in a bear market, a beta of less than 1 will be expected to do less badly than the market.

Tracking error

This measures the volatility or standard deviation of the alpha over time. The larger the tracking error, the more likely is a high outperformance or underperformance relative to the benchmark in any one period.

Information ratio

This is a risk-adjusted performance measure, that is, the alpha divided by the tracking error. This measure prefers funds that earn consistent, positive alphas, rather than higher but more volatile alphas over time.

Box 5 Performance statistics for the Newton Balanced Income fund

Measures compiled by fund-rating agency Morningstar as at 25/05/09.

The objective of the Newton Balanced Income fund is to achieve a balance between capital growth and income predominantly from a portfolio of UK and international securities.

3-year standard deviation	13.72%
3-year mean return	3.60%
3-year Sharpe ratio	−0.10
3-year R-squared	82.87%
3-year beta	1.06
3-year alpha	4.94%
Tracking error	5.73%
Information ratio	0.76

(Source: Fidelity International, 2009)

Using the internet, you can find performance measures based on portfolio theory and the CAPM to analyse funds such as the Newton Balanced Income Fund in Box 5. This particular fund achieved a three-year positive mean return, but a negative Sharpe ratio over three years, meaning that it returned less than the risk-free rate over the period. The beta is 1.06 compared to a benchmark index which is 40 per cent UK equities and 60 per cent global equities excluding the UK. The positive alpha means that the fund has been rewarded for taking on specific risk through stock selection and not just mirroring the benchmark index. The tracking error is relatively low – meaning that the alphas are not very volatile over three years, and the information ratio quite good, with 0.76 per cent alpha return for every unit of tracking error.

Beating an investment benchmark is not always easy

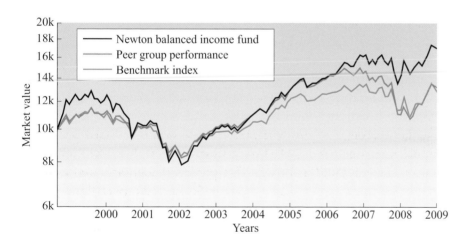

Figure 10 Historical performance of Newton Balanced Income versus peer group and benchmark index

(Source: Morningstar, 2009)

Figure 10 shows the ten-year performance of £10,000 invested in the Newton Balanced Income relative to the chosen peer group and the chosen benchmark index. The peer group included several hundred other income funds with the same investment objectives. This shows the fund's superior performance, also shown in Box 5, over the period 2004–09 compared to both the index and the average performance of the peer group. The fund-rating agency Morningstar awarded the fund its top five-star rating for three and five years – but not for ten years as it did not do well in 2002.

So, for the period from 2004 to 2009 we would have been happy to have invested in the Newton Balanced Income Fund instead of another fund in the same peer group or even an index fund tracking the chosen benchmark index. But the problem is how to identify such funds *before* the event and not *after*. Figure 10 shows that the average peer group performance was about the same as that of the benchmark index over the period from 1999 to 2003. Furthermore, some funds would have performed worse than the peer group since this is an indicator of average performance. So only if we were lucky, and had picked a fund manager who did well, would we have achieved our target return – as measured by the index – or more. Tracking the benchmark index offers a strategy of avoiding investment in the weaker performing funds.

But by far the most common indicator of performance is simply returns over the past year, three years and five years. Since markets may well experience a bull or bear phase over more than five years, aggressive funds will look good in the good years and defensive funds will look good in the bad years. An example of an aggressive fund is a growth fund, a fund that looks for companies with growth potential but may be expensive in earnings terms (that is, have high price–earnings ratios, P/E), as did internet companies in the late 1990s (see Chapter 6). An example of a defensive fund is a **value fund**, which invests in companies that look relatively cheap on fundamental ratios such as P/E, dividend yield or Tobin's q (see Chapter 2).

Value fund
An investment fund that focuses on stocks believed to be undervalued, seeking investment returns through capital gain, when undervaluation is corrected, as well as dividends.

Indeed, some fund management groups make sure that they have a wide range of different types of fund to make sure that they always have at least one or two near the top of the league tables, whatever the state of the stock market. This is another example of how diversification informs investment strategy.

5.2 Absolute returns

The relative approach to peer groups or to benchmarks does not always work well. For example, in the dot-com crash of 2000, when pension funds suffered badly as the equity market fell, pension fund managers argued that they had all lost money, so it didn't really matter. This included even those who outperformed the benchmark (which in this case means that they lost less than the benchmark). But this was a matter of concern to company directors, who found that their company pension funds had to be topped up to cover the stock-market losses. They decided to turn to fund managers who promised absolute returns – that is (hopefully), positive returns whatever the economic situation. So, for example, the fund might promise not to outperform the FTSE All Share Index by 2 per cent – a 10 per cent fall in the index would still mean a loss of 8 per cent – but rather to earn, say, 4 per cent more than the risk-free rate. Two types of investment that promise absolute returns are some types of hedge fund and **structured products**.

Absolute return hedge funds

A hedge fund is a fund that is allowed to use aggressive investment strategies through high leverage (borrowing). This is unavailable to unit trusts (which cannot borrow) and investment trusts (whose leverage is normally capped). Hedge funds are exempt from many of the rules and regulations governing unit trusts and investment trusts, which allows them to invest large amounts at any one time. Retail investors can invest in so-called funds of funds that are unit trusts or OEICs investing in a number of hedge funds with varying investment strategies. As with traditional funds, investors in hedge funds pay a management fee; however, hedge funds also collect a percentage of the profits (usually 20 per cent).

Unlike the managers of unit trusts and investment trusts, hedge fund managers can sell shares short. So, for example, managers of a 'long/short' hedge fund will buy shares that they like and sell those that they don't, in equal amounts, so netting out the market exposure and keeping specific risk relatively low. In such a case, the risk of the hedge fund will be uncorrelated with market risk and will offer pension funds, and other investors seeking to diversify away from equities and bonds, a positive expected return. However, in practice, such hedge funds use a lot of leverage to enhance expected returns and many suffered from the lack of liquidity during the credit crunch and were forced to sell shares into a falling stock market. Their returns turned out to be more positively correlated with market returns than investors had anticipated.

Structured products

A typical capital structured product is one that will offer, as a minimum, return of the original capital invested at the end of a period of, say, three years and any upside of, say, the FTSE100 stock index.

Structured product
An investment product that guarantees the investor either a minimum capital amount at the end of the product life or a minimum income over the product life.

This would mean that if, at the end of three years, the FTSE100 was lower than the index value at inception, customers would receive £100 per £100 invested. If, on the other hand, the FTSE100 had risen by 20 per cent by the end of the three-year period, the investor would receive £120 per £100 invested.

Guaranteed products are typically put together by investment banks or other investment institutions by using combinations of bonds, shares and derivatives. As a result, guaranteed products are called structured products. Structured products are exposed to the counterparty risk (see Chapter 2) of whichever banks or other institutions supply the underlying guarantees. Counterparty risk was not considered to be significant until 2008, when Lehman defaulted on a number of guarantees underpinning structured products, although some of these guaranteed products have since been honoured by the banks that had marketed them.

It is worth pausing to ask how the client is paying for having the best of two worlds – limited downside risk and yet upside potential. The answer in the case of capital-guaranteed products is in foregone income. For the whole of the three-year period, no interest is paid and the rise in the index excludes dividend income. Depending on the size of the dividend foregone, this can be equivalent to quite a high annual charge.

6 Investment in practice

In this final section of the chapter, we look at a few practical matters that arise when one puts together an investment portfolio. In particular, we look at cultural differences, diversification in practice and performance measurement in practice.

6.1 Cultural issues

Portfolio theory suggests that diversification is good for investors and it seems logical to suppose that investing internationally will improve the risk–return trade-off. Indeed, if we follow the Capital Asset Pricing Model to its logical conclusion, we should all be investing in the global equity markets in proportion to their market value. Since the USA has by far the largest market capitalisation, investors, whatever their home country, should in theory be putting most of their money in the USA. But in practice, there is home bias. For example, US investors tend to invest in US stocks, with very little overseas, and even the more internationally focused UK investor will typically invest the majority of their funds in UK equities. Part of the reason is that it is more difficult to invest overseas – some brokers will not let investors buy overseas stocks in small amounts, and information on shares is not so readily available, not to mention the fact that transaction costs are typically higher – and also one would need a lot of money to gain exposure to all the major stock markets. As a result, small investors typically gain access to international markets through pooled funds such as OEICs or investment trusts.

Another difference is the span of investments that investment advisers typically cover. In the UK, investment advice is mostly on equities, pooled funds and some bonds. In France, however, the investment adviser will consider investment in property and stock-market investments as part of one portfolio. This is because tax advice is part of the investment adviser's role and property can be a tax-efficient investment. In the UK, although tax advice is also important, stock-market investment and property tend to be kept separate.

Some investors like to carry their investments with them at all times

Some countries also have more of an 'equity' culture than others. British investors have been happily investing in global equities since well before the First World War. Bonds also fell out of fashion after the high inflation of the 1970s and 1980s. As a result, British investors have been relatively happier to invest in shares than have other nationalities.

When comparing countries, there are important differences in how assets are combined into funds. Figure 11 shows the asset mix in 2008 for pension funds surveyed in the UK, Germany and France. Whereas on average pension funds in the UK had 58 per cent of assets allocated to shares, in Germany only 19 per cent had shares, and in France only 22 per cent had shares. A much higher proportion was invested in bonds: 76 per cent in France and 71 per cent in Germany, compared to only 38 per cent in the UK.

U.K.

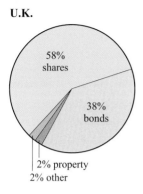

58%
shares

38%
bonds

2% property
2% other

Germany

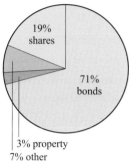

19%
shares

71%
bonds

3% property
7% other

France

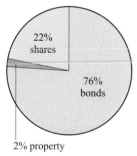

22%
shares

76%
bonds

2% property

Figure 11 The asset mix of pension funds in three European countries
(Source: Mercer, 2008)

6.2 Diversification in practice

Portfolio theory offers the investor the ability to create efficient
portfolios from a selection of investment alternatives, ranging from
choosing a portfolio of UK equities, or choosing a set of overseas
markets in which to invest, to making an asset allocation choice
between UK equities, overseas equities, cash and bonds, say. In each
case a set of efficient portfolios can be created provided that the

investor has a database of the expected returns, risks and correlation coefficients.

In practice, investors tend to use historical data to estimate in particular the risks and correlations. Expected returns chosen are more likely to be subjective estimates. The risks and measures of correlation might be calculated from, say, the past 12 monthly periods, the past 20 quarters, or the past 10 annual periods. The financial publication *Money Management*, for example, publishes the standard deviation from the most recent 36 monthly periods. Each choice of data will give a different answer. And, to make matters worse, the efficient frontier portfolios that the analysis provides may be difficult to sell to clients in practice. Suppose that an international equity market analysis suggested that US investors should place 50 per cent in Belgian equities, 5 per cent in the UK and the remainder in Chile. This might appear too different from a market-capitalisation-weighted global equity index to please. So analysts tend to play it safe and constrain their models to give answers that are not likely to change too much and that are not that different from a popular benchmark index.

The CAPM is also based on assumptions that do not hold in practice. Investors based in different currencies will not all be looking at the same opportunities; investors cannot in practice both borrow and lend at the risk-free rate; and the market indices used to represent the market are not very good approximations to estimates of all marketable assets.

However, the conclusions that the CAPM reaches – that there is, for passive investors, an investment alternative based on index funds and cash, that active managers can be judged relative to that passive investment alternative, and that investors can analyse what kinds of risk investment funds are taking on – have meant that investment managers have to be very careful to implement the investment strategies that they put in their marketing literature.

6.3 Performance measurement in practice

The level of performance measurement varies from cursory to detailed depending on the size of the investment. Managers of large pension funds have to provide their clients with detailed breakdowns of the risk-and-return characteristics of their portfolios, and there are a number of consultants who specialise in such analyses. They also use the key measures such as tracking error and alpha.

When it comes to funds, such as investment trusts, OEICs and life assurance funds, more complex measures tend to be combined into a star-rating or number-rating system. This allows investors to identify good recent performers and high- or low-risk funds relatively easily.

It is rare to find a fund that significantly outperforms an index benchmark over the long term. We saw in Figure 10 that Newton Balanced Income outperformed its peer group and a benchmark index over five years, but it did not do this over ten years. It is very difficult to spot future winners, and past performance – as the adverts say – is not a guarantee of future performance. But analysing performance can and does say something about how the performance was earned and what kinds of risk an investor in the fund is likely to be taking on. It can also force investors to face the truth of their investment performance.

Activity 5

Suppose that you were asked to judge the performance of your trading portfolio, which you have run with an internet broker for the past five years. Suggest how you would go about this.

Most retail investors or traders judge performance against the cost of the shares that they have bought, ignoring the opportunity cost of their money – what they would have got from investing in an equivalent-risk investment, including dividends, for the whole five-year period. You can only really judge performance relative to a benchmark. This might be buying an index fund linked to the FTSE All Share index and holding it for five years untouched. But if you included non-UK shares in the portfolio, a more international benchmark would be appropriate. It is all too tempting to set yourself an easy benchmark and to forget the bad investments that you have made, concentrating only on the successes. This type of investing behaviour will be discussed further in Chapter 6.

7 Conclusion

In this chapter, you have looked at ways in which the trade-off between investment risk and investment return can be improved. You first looked at the role of tax in increasing the net return after income and capital gains taxes, through tax-exempt investments and so-called tax wrappers. You then looked at how lower costs for buying and selling shares and lower investment management charges could also improve returns without adding risk.

However, the main way in which the risk–return trade-off can be improved is through diversification. This is called portfolio theory. There are two types: naïve diversification, which essentially boils down to investing equal amounts in a number of different shares, and Markowitz diversification, which takes into account the risks and expected returns of different shares, plus the correlation between the returns on different shares. Efficient portfolios are defined that offer the highest expected return for a particular level of risk or the lowest risk for a particular level of expected return.

You then considered the introduction of a risk-free asset and the assumption that all investors have the same expectations. In that case, investors will hold different proportions of the same two investments – the market portfolio, called M, and the risk-free asset. They will reduce the market exposure of their portfolio, called the beta, by holding more of the risk-free asset, or increase their market exposure by borrowing and buying more of M. This theory is called the Capital Asset Pricing Model or CAPM.

The final sections of the chapter were concerned with active and passive portfolio management – with active investors trying to outperform an index or market strategy either by market timing or by stock selection. Positive outperformance is called alpha. You looked at a number of performance measures that attempt to identify whether active fund managers have outperformed either their peer groups or the passive but equal-risk alternative. Finally, you looked at a number of topics to do with investment in the real world: cultural factors, diversification and performance measurement in practice.

References

Clark, R. (2008) 'The unravelling of the great buy-to-let scam', The Spectator

Department for Work and Pensions (DWP) (2006a) *Personal Accounts: A New Way to Save,* White Paper, December [online], www.dwp.gov.uk/ pensionsreform/new_way.asp (Accessed 3 December 2009).

Department for Work and Pensions (DWP) (2006b) *Attitudes to Saving for Retirement Among Adults Under State Pension Age* [online], http://research.dwp. gov.uk/asd/asd5/summ2007-2008/434summ.pdf (Accessed 3 December 2009).

Evans, J.L. and Archer, S.H. (1968) 'Diversification and the reduction of dispersion: an empirical analysis', *Journal of Finance*, vol. 23, no. 5, pp. 761–7.

Fidelity International, Performance statistics for the Newton Balanced Income Fund [online], www.fidelity.co.uk/investor/research-funds/fund-supermarket/ factsheet/performance.page?idtype=ISIN&fundid=GB0006778574&UserChannel =Direct (Accessed 3 December 2009).

Foreign & Colonial Government Trust (1868) *Prospectus*, ms14235, London, London Guildhall Library.

Institute for Fiscal Studies (2009) 'The IFS Green Budget', London, Institute for Fiscal Studies.

Investment Management Association, *UK Fund Sector Classifications* [online], www.investmentuk.org/statistics/sector_definitions/fund_class.asp (Accessed 3 December 2009).

Markowitz, H. (1959) 'Portfolio selection: efficient diversification of investment', *Cowles Foundation Monograph*, issue 16, New Haven, CT, Yale University Press.

Mercer (2008) *European Asset Allocation Survey* [online], www.mercer.com/ referencecontent.htm?idContent=1301240 (Accessed 3 December 2009).

Moneysavingexpert.com, *Full ISA Guide* [online], www.moneysavingexpert. com/savings/ISA-guide-savings-without-tax (Accessed 3 December 2009).

Morningstar, Historical performance of Newton Balanced Income Fund versus peer group and benchmark index [online], www.morningstar.co.uk/uk/ snapshot/snapshot.aspx?tab=7&id=F0GBR04RQD (Accessed 3 December 2009).

Office for National Statistics (2009) 'Attitudes to saving for retirement among adults under state pension age, 2006, wealth and assets survey (experimental data)', *Social Trends*, vol. 29, p. 80.

Sharpe, W.F. (1964) 'Capital asset prices: a theory of market equilibrium under conditions of uncertainty', *Journal of Finance*, vol. 19, no. 3, pp. 425–42.

Further reading

Howells, P. and Bain, K. (2007) *Financial Markets and Institutions*, Harlow, Financial Times Prentice Hall.

Rutterford, J. (2007) *An Introduction to Stock Exchange Investment*, Basingstoke, Palgrave Macmillan.

Chapter 4
Markets and players

Alan Shipman

1 Introduction

Learning outcomes

After reading this chapter, you will:

- understand why financial markets are important for investors
- be aware of different types of markets and market players
- understand the role of information in markets
- understand the efficient markets hypothesis.

> All it took was finance ministers of the Group of Eight raising the subject of 'exit strategies' in their final communiqué Saturday, and the global rally in shares and commodities such as oil hit a wall. Yesterday was the worst drop for world share prices in two months, showing just how shaky confidence is.
>
> (Erman, 2009)

> I used to think if there was reincarnation, I wanted to come back as the president or the pope ... But now I want to come back as the bond market. You can intimidate everybody.
>
> (Carville, 1993)

Bond and share markets constantly raise or lower the value of our savings and investments. When confidence is shaken, as in the example of the Group of Eight decision, this has the direct impact on the value of investments in shares. And as James Carville (a political strategist for Bill Clinton) argues in relation to bonds, investors can be intimidated by the power of markets, which seem to have influence equivalent to that of a dominant leader.

The purpose of this chapter is to explore how financial markets work. You will be introduced to the reasons why markets are so important to investors, and the key market players and types of markets. The role of information is of particular importance, since markets provide vital signals to investors about risk and return. Some of the strategies that you have been introduced to in previous chapters, such as passive and active strategies, are further explored as part of this discussion.

Section 2 of this chapter looks at the role of financial markets, and how vital they are to investors and the wider economy. Section 3 introduces forward contracts and other derivative instruments, and examines the capacity for pricing and trading risk that underlies their rapid growth in recent years. Section 4 sets out the efficient markets hypothesis that has been advanced to explain the movement of asset prices, and Section 5 assesses its implications for portfolio selection strategy. The importance of accurate information for setting prices and strategy leads, in Section 6, to consideration of key information sources for personal and professional investors.

2 What financial markets are intended to provide

Likening the market to a dominant individual leader, as Carville does in the second opening quote, contradicts conventional assessment of how it operates. According to its admirers, a free market achieves the best coordination of economic activity without any influential individual or central agency having to exert power. Since Adam Smith (1979 [1776]), economists have argued that markets remove the need for central coordination of resources. The best use of resources is by producers and consumers responding to the price mechanism, as introduced in Chapter 1, Section 4.1. Markets will guide behaviour towards this outcome, so long as we put the right price on things, including our work time and leisure time. The pursuit of profits by trading in free markets can promote **allocative efficiency**: putting resources to best use.

Allocative efficiency
The allocation of resources to their best possible use.

Markets rely on money to facilitate trade between buyers and sellers. Money makes multiple trades far easier than if we had to barter one product directly for another. But money can also be a store of wealth – resources that we do not want to spend immediately – and a means of borrowing if we need to spend more resources than we currently have. So as well as goods and service markets lubricated by money, there are financial markets where money is bought and sold. When someone puts money into a bank account or pension fund, or buys insurance, or tells a broker to buy shares, this money flows into a financial market where it is used to buy assets. When someone borrows to buy a house or car, or puts their shopping on a credit card, their loan flows out of a financial market, where it comprises part of someone else's investment.

Shares and bonds, being divided into small units suitable for portfolio building, can be traded on organised markets where the large volume of traders and daily transactions ensures competitive pricing. The main forum through which shares and bonds are traded is in a **stock exchange**. In recent years, even the biggest stock exchanges have internationalised in order to widen their depth and coverage. So, for example, the New York Stock Exchange (NYSE) has merged with Euronext, an alliance of the Paris, Brussels and Amsterdam exchanges; and the London Stock Exchange (LSE) with Italy's Milan exchange.

Stock exchange
An organised market on which shares and bonds are traded

Box 1 Conditions for a free market

A free market, for financial instruments or any other tradable product, requires:

- large numbers of competing buyers and sellers, none large enough to affect the market price through the amount they trade (making the market 'competitive'), or the potential for new entrants to compete away any monopoly profits (making the market 'contestable')

- products that are standardised, or similar enough for buyers to identify many of similar quality and choose the cheapest

- legally protected property rights, which ensure that one person can acquire a product from another only through a voluntary sale at the current market price

- free flow of information, about what's being bought and sold, and for what price.

In Chapter 2, Section 4, you learned that the price of a financial asset can be related to its intrinsic value, based on expected future earnings after discounting, to allow for the preference of current over future income. However, prices are actually set by the interaction of buyers and sellers, and the balance between the market demand and supply for each asset that results from this. So the efficiency of markets depends on their ability to adjust prices towards those underlying values. Advocates of free markets say that they can do this better than any system of planning, whether by government agencies or large companies. The existence of competitive markets for bonds, shares and other financial assets can raise the returns and lower the risks on these investments compared with what would happen if such markets did not exist.

Key advantages ascribed to free markets are low transaction costs, liquidity, incentives for efficient management of resources, and instantly available valuation. Each will now be considered in turn.

Low transaction costs

A transaction for buying and selling a financial product involves four stages:

- *Execution*. Buyer and seller agree the price and quantity.

- *Registration.* The transaction is recorded and legally authorised.
- *Clearing.* Funds are transferred from buyer to seller.
- *Settlement.* Ownership of the asset is transferred from seller to buyer.

At each stage, someone has to be paid for professional services (such as the broker who lines up a buyer for the shares that a client wants to sell) or the use of a proprietary system (such as a stock exchange's automated settlement program). But competitive markets work to minimise transaction costs. Organised exchanges check the integrity of traders and maintain automated systems for trading, quotation, clearing and settlement, recovering these costs through membership fees and commission on each transaction. Because investors can choose between them, exchanges compete to reduce cost through better organisation and technology. The internationalisation of exchanges (widening the choice of markets in which to trade) and the growth of electronic communication (enabling cheaper virtual trading) have given larger investors more scope to shop around, and drive down financial transaction costs. As most governments view the growth of financial market activity as beneficial for households, enterprises and the economy, they have encouraged markets' technological change and internationalisation by removing regulations that previously restricted product innovation, separated national markets, and prevented competition to lower transaction costs (see also Chapter 1, Section 3).

Liquidity

The value of the investments profiled in Chapter 2, and the portfolio-building strategies outlined in Chapter 3, depend on financial products being easy to buy and sell. When functioning normally, markets allow an asset to be quickly sold (liquidated) at a price close to the one at which the assets have been valued. The opportunity for quick sale reduces the risk of buying the asset. Without markets, the only way for an individual or financial institution to be liquid is to hold a stock of cash. Markets make it possible to invest, securing a return, without losing the liquidity advantage of cash.

For example, the capital subscribed to a government bond will not be repaid until it reaches maturity. But this asset is treated as liquid because it can be resold through the stock market. For a bank, a 25-year mortgage loan used to be a highly illiquid asset, but it can be quickly turned back into cash provided that there is a market for securitised debt (see Chapter 1, Section 3.3). For a company, a newly received order is an illiquid asset if the client has three months to pay, but it can quickly be turned into cash by selling it to a specialist collector of trade debts. When financial markets are functioning well, assets can become liquid that would normally involve a significant locking-up of capital.

Activity 1

Arrange the following in descending order of liquidity:

- small company share
- rare Penny Black stamp
- your car
- block of Sainsbury's cheese
- Sainsbury's share
- private pension scheme
- the house you live in

Liquidity is always a matter of some debate, and assets that normally guarantee high liquidity can sometimes lose it. The Sainsbury's share is in principle highly liquid, as it is traded in high volumes in a market with many buyers and sellers – though you might have difficulty buying one on a day that another company makes a takeover bid for the store chain. The small company's share, even if traded on an exchange, is likely to have fewer buyers and sellers, so it might take longer to get the price you want. The Penny Black, though it appeals only to stamp collectors and a few specialist investors, is known to have high rarity value, and has become more easily retradable as its traditional auction markets are augmented online. The car is saleable second-hand, but this is likely to take more time, and some models suffer rapid depreciation (even if well preserved) so won't fetch anything near the previous purchase price unless they are veteran or vintage. Your house is resaleable (if you own it) and may have appreciated since it was bought, but selling it can take weeks or months even when the market is buoyant. The block of cheese has no organised market, so an investment in it can be liquidated only by finding someone else who is willing to buy it. The pension scheme has limited liquidity unless the holder is about to retire, since it is not transferable to anyone else and so can't be resold (unlike some other long-term investments, like endowment policies, which are not person-specific).

Box 2 Marketmakers and liquidity

Most of the time, there are plenty of buyers and sellers for any bond, share or other financial asset. Active investors (see Chapter 3, Section 4.3) disagree in their evaluation of an asset, with some viewing it as undervalued (a 'buy') and others as overvalued (a 'sell'). And because a share's value to any investor depends on what else is in their portfolio, some will be selling it while others will be buying it even if they agree on its valuation. Prices tend to fall when there is more supply than demand, and rise when there is more demand than supply; and these changes bring demand and supply into balance, ensuring equilibrium (see Chapter 1, Section 4.1). At certain times, however, buyers may greatly outnumber sellers, or sellers outnumber buyers. The market can then become unstable, with prices rising or falling unusually rapidly. And this may mean that it ceases to be liquid, with investors able to buy only at an unaffordable high price or sell at a ruinously low price.

The risk to liquidity from clustering on one side of the market can be greatly reduced by the presence of marketmakers (see Chapter 3, Section 2.2). These are intermediaries who buy when most others are selling and sell when most others are buying (or holding), thus ensuring that there is still liquidity for those going against the majority. Marketmakers expect to make a profit in the long run, by buying low and selling high, and also make a profit on each transaction through the spread between buying (bid) and selling (ask) prices (see Chapter 3). But as they will often be in a loss-making position for long periods, they need large capital reserves, long lines of credit and access to support from bodies such as a central bank, first introduced in Chapter 1. For this reason, large investment banks have tended to take on the marketmaking role.

Incentives

Because share prices give the market's verdict on a company's future profitability, and corporate bond prices indicate the state of confidence in its debt repayment, financial markets impose discipline on company management. Managers who raise the productivity of their company and open up new sources of profit will, if the market works correctly, be rewarded with a rising share price. Less competent managers will see share prices fall until the company becomes vulnerable to takeover by acquirers who believe that they can make it more profitable by bringing in new managers.

As companies grow, and their ownership becomes more dispersed, shareholders may find it more difficult to get up-to-date information on performance and corporate strategy, and to take coordinated action. In the past, this weakening of shareholder power may have enabled managers to follow strategies that did not deliver the high profits and dividends that shareholders demanded. Shareholders are forced to delegate decisions to managers, and may find it difficult to get managers to act on their behalf. Many companies have tackled this problem by linking managers' pay to profit, or to share prices, giving them more incentive to earn company profits in line with shareholders' interests.

Valuation

Even when they are not intending to buy or sell, investors can use the market to find out how their assets are valued. The market price of a share or bond is a continuously updated average of all traders' valuations. Individuals can reach different judgements about the current value of a bond (e.g. because of different evaluations of future inflation, interest-rate movements and default risks), and of a share (e.g. because of different evaluations of future profitability and takeover prospects). That is, although investors might be using the same dividend valuation model (Chapter 2, Section 4.3), each is likely to be inserting different expected earnings into the model, so coming out with different prices. Markets pool each individual evaluation to arrive at a single price.

Prediction market
A market created to predict outcomes of an event, by inviting people to place bets on it.

This average of many opinions often turns out to be more reliable than one opinion, even if the many are mere amateurs and the one is an expert. Financial markets work in a similar way to **prediction markets**, in which large numbers of people predict an event and are rewarded for being closest to the outcome. Prediction markets have been found to perform at least as well as expert predictions on events ranging from elections to films' box-office success (Surowiecki, 2004, pp. 3–39). Financial markets can, likewise, get closer to the correct valuation than most of the individuals within them, provided that they reach their judgements independently. (Because the prices of shares and bonds depend on expectations of future variables, it's possible to see if the market priced them correctly when these variables become known.) The accuracy of prediction markets can break down at times of economic change, when people fail to foresee the extent of change or differ too widely over its direction; and it can also decline if traders' judgements start to be influenced by the ideas and actions of other traders, as will be explored in Chapter 6. But the parallel is a close one. Indeed, art now imitates financial life in the case of the Hollywood Stock Exchange, in which people use free Hollywood Dollars to buy and sell shares in their favourite film actors, and in the process help producers to gauge their next movie success.

3 Derivative markets

Stock markets on which bonds and shares are traded are examples of **spot markets**, in which buyers and sellers agree a price and exchange money for assets in an immediate exchange. Shares in a big company such as British Telecom, for example, are traded each day at a spot price listed at the London Stock Exchange. Buying these shares at this spot price, on a particular day, would involve an immediate exchange of the asset to the purchaser.

However, these and many other assets are also traded in forward markets. Here, investors agree to buy or sell an asset on or before a specified future date, at a specified price. A forward contract is one of the simplest forms of a **derivative**: a contract to trade one or more underlying assets (such as a bond, share or commodity). The price paid for the contract is derived from the present or future price of the underlying asset, but the contract can be traded independently of that asset; and some investors buy and sell derivatives purely to make profit from the trade, without the intention of acquiring the assets underlying them.

This section introduces several key types of derivative. You will see that these have been introduced by financial players as a way of managing risk. This introduction will give you a sense of what kinds of services the financial services industry provides for its clients. It will also consider some of the system-wide risks associated with derivatives, in the light of the 'credit crunch' that began in 2007.

3.1 Futures and option contracts

A futures contract makes it possible to reduce uncertainty about future prices by setting them here and now. For example, a company that has to buy raw materials now, but can only sell the resultant product in six months' time, can minimise the risk of price movement by 'selling the output forward': it finds buyers who will agree now to pay a specified price in six months' time. Similarly, if the company must buy oil or another commodity in a year's time, and doesn't want to be caught out by unpredictable price movements, it can 'buy the input forward' by agreeing right now what price it will pay at the end of the year. The futures market is also an important source of information for those trading in spot markets, since it indicates where investors believe the

Spot market
A market in which transactions are agreed for immediate exchange and settlement.

Derivative
A contract on one or more underlying assets, whose price is derived from the spot-market price of such assets.

Futures contract
A contractual right to buy or sell a quantity of an asset at a specified price at or before a future date.

price of commodities and other assets will have moved by specified future dates.

Futures contracts have the drawback that if the price moves in the 'wrong' direction, the investor can get locked in to an unfavourable price: buying for more or selling for less than if they had not signed the contract and had just waited to trade at the spot price. For example, between 2008 and 2009 the global oil price fell sharply but the price of many food products continued to rise. A farmer who played safe by agreeing to buy their fuel and sell their processed crop in 2009 at 2008 prices would have done worse than one who decided to leave these transactions until 2009.

To overcome this problem, risk-averse traders can make use of **options**, futures contracts that needn't be exercised if spot-market prices turn out to be more favourable than the price in the contract (known as the strike price). A **call option** gives the right to buy at a specified future price, and will be exercised only if this is below the spot price. A **put option** gives the right to sell at a specified future price, and will be exercised only if this is above the spot price. If the spot price is below

Option contract
An optional futures contract.

Call option
An option to buy an asset at a specified future time and price.

Put option
An option to sell an asset at a specified future time and price.

the strike price for a buyer, or above the strike price for a seller, the option contract is 'out of the money' and need not be exercised. Buyers of options thus get insurance against adverse price movements, but can still gain from beneficial price movements, paying only the cost of the option contract. A European-style option can be exercised only on a specified expiry date, whereas a US-style option can also be exercised ahead of that date.

Non-financial companies have an interest in buying options (to buy or sell) in order to reduce their risk. The financial institutions that sell (write) these options are, correspondingly, taking on that risk. Like an insurance company, they take a fixed fee (the premium) in return for meeting the cost of a specified adverse event, if this occurs during the lifetime of the contract. In the case of a call option, the adverse event is a rise in the spot price above the strike price. The institution (usually an investment bank) that writes the option 'pays out' by buying the item at the spot price and selling it to the option holder at the lower price specified in the contract. In the case of a put option, the adverse event is a fall in the spot price below the strike price. The option writer, who is a counterparty to the option, 'pays out' by buying the item from the option holder at the specified price and reselling it at the lower spot price.

3.2 Swaps

Under a swap arrangement, two investors holding different assets agree to exchange the income streams that they generate. This can be advantageous, compared to a situation in which each has to buy the assets held by the other, due to reductions in transaction cost, tax liability or risk. Under an interest rate swap, two parties borrow on different terms and then arrange payments of interest to each other. Commonly, one party who would like to borrow at a fixed rate, but can obtain a loan more cheaply at a variable rate, swaps with another who can borrow more cheaply at a fixed rate but does not mind variability. The first makes fixed-rate payments to the second, who reciprocates with variable-rate payments to the first; and both obtain their funds at a lower interest rate than without the swap.

Under an exchange rate swap, a company that wants funds in one currency but can borrow more cheaply in another (usually that of its home country) swaps with another that can borrow more cheaply in the target currency. Exchange-rate swaps can encompass interest-rate swaps, where one party borrows at a fixed rate and one at a variable rate. Under a credit default swap (CDS), the holder of a risky loan makes regular payments to a counterparty, which agrees to repay the loan if the borrower defaults. The CDS works like an insurance policy against default. But whereas insurance is only sold to those who own the insured asset, CDSs on a bond can be bought by people who don't own the underlying bond.

Table 1 Growth of interest-rate swaps, currency swaps and CDSs, 2001–08, US$bn

	Interest rate and currency swaps	% change year-on-year	Credit default swaps (CDSs)	% change year-on-year
2001	69 207.3		918.9	
2002	101 318.5	46.4	2 191.6	138.5
2003	142 306.9	40.5	3 779.4	72.4
2004	183 583.3	29.0	8 422.3	122.8
2005	213 194.6	16.1	17 096.1	103.0
2006	285 728.1	34.0	34 422.8	101.3
2007	382 302.7	33.8	62 173.2	80.6
2008*	464 695.0	33.9	54 611.8	20.1

* Jan–Jun

Source: ISDA, 2008

Issuance of swaps grew rapidly worldwide over the period 2000–08, as shown in Table 1. There was a seven-fold increase in the number of interest-rate and currency swaps, from $69,207 billion in 2001 to $464,695 billion in 2008. Annual rates of growth in these swaps were as high as 46.4 per cent in 2002. The increase in credit default swaps was even more pronounced, increasing at an annual rate of over 100 per cent in 2004, 2005 and 2006. A sea change appears to have taken place in the use of derivatives during this period.

3.3 Securitisations

Any asset that produces a regular, predictable stream of income can in principle be securitised. This involves issuing bonds secured against the asset, whose interest is then repaid from the income that the asset generates. Securitisation can make an asset work harder by releasing the capital tied up in it. The income stream is diminished, because the issued debt must now be serviced, but the deal can still be profitable provided that the rate of return on the securitised asset stays above the interest rate on the bonds. During the 1990s and 2000s, for example, several UK hotel and pub chains securitised their estates, pledging their freehold properties as security for loans that enabled them to expand and diversify their businesses.

Securitisation is an extension, into longer-term borrowing, of the technique that companies have long used to speed up their collection of income from customers. When goods or services are delivered in advance of payment, companies speed up the flow of cash (and reduce the risk of customer default) by selling their order book to a specialist financial institution. This institution (often called a forfaiter or discounter) buys the orders for a discount, in return for providing their value up-front, and then takes on the right to collect customer payments along with the risk of some of those customers failing to pay.

Banks also became heavily involved in securitisation after 2000 – securitising customer debts, their principal asset, as well as generating fees from arranging securitisations for others. Commercial banks issued bonds secured against their loan books, often known as mortgage-backed securities (MBSs) or collateralised debt obligations (CDOs). Of particular importance has been the securitisation of mortgage debts (see Chapter 1, Section 3.3) into CDOs.

Those who oversaw this process regarded it as an example of innovation in financial market and product design. This can be seen as part of a profound economic change that took place in the 2000s. Commercial banks could focus on arranging and pricing loans, leaving specialists to diversify and manage the risk. Table 2 shows the rapid growth in securitisations at the start of the century. Within Europe, the UK was the main source, accounting for 38 per cent of all new securitisations in 2008 (European Securitisation Forum, 2008, Tables 1.5, 2.3).

Table 2 Issuance of securitised debt, 2000–08, billions of euros

	Europe	Annual % change	USA	Annual % change
2000	78.2		1088.0	
2001	152.6	95.1	2308.4	112.2
2002	157.7	3.3	2592.7	12.3
2003	217.3	37.8	2914.5	26.3
2004	243.5	12.1	1956.5	−32.9
2005	327.0	34.3	2650.6	35.5
2006	481.0	47.1	2455.8	−7.3
2007	453.7	−5.7	2147.1	−12.6
2008	711.1	56.7	933.6	−56.5

Source: ESF, 2008, Tables 1.1, 1.2

Table 2 reveals a sharp increase in securitised debt in 2001. It increased by 95.1 per cent in Europe, and 112.2 per cent in the USA. The USA started from a higher base, since mortgage-backed securities had been introduced there ahead of Europe. The reduction in the use of these securities also started first in the USA, in 2006 (by 7.3 per cent), although Europe was still increasing its usage in 2008 (by 56.7 per cent), the second year of the credit crunch that began in 2007.

3.4 Spread betting and contracts-for-difference

Instead of trading in assets, an investor can place bets on price movement (in a share, bond, commodity or market index such as the FTSE100), with a specialist company taking the role of bookmaker. These spread bets resemble derivatives, being contracts on which payment is determined by price movement of an underlying asset. A bet is placed on an asset or index moving above the offer price or below the bid price set by a spread betting firm. Bettors win (or lose) the amount of the bet multiplied by the scale of price movement, in the predicted direction (or the other direction). Unlike trading in actual derivatives, spread betting is available to retail investors using comparatively small sums. The initial outlay can be kept down, and the potential profits (and losses) multiplied, by betting 'on margin', using funds borrowed from the betting firm. Spread betting has itself spread into non-financial areas, such as election and sports results. Because it is widely used by financial professionals and other experts, spread-betting odds have, like futures and option market prices, become an important indicator of asset-price, interest-rate and exchange-rate expectations for traders in spot markets.

Contracts for difference (CFDs) also give investors a chance to seek profit on price movements without the expense of buying and selling options, or their underlying assets. If the price is expected to rise, the CFD allows an investor to 'borrow' a quantity of the asset, in the hope that the profits from the price rise will exceed the interest cost of the loan. If the price is expected to fall, the CFD allows the investor to 'lend' a quantity of the asset, receiving interest that they hope will outweigh the amount that they must pay out to compensate for the price fall. Although CFDs can be of any duration, they are usually kept short (because of the daily cost to holding them), and taken out just before a price is expected to move.

3.5 Derivatives and the transfer of risk

Options, swaps and securitisations all provide ways to transfer risk. In Chapter 3, Section 3.3, you saw that diversifying an investment portfolio can only remove the unsystematic risk that is specific to an asset's future earnings as reflected in its price. Even a well diversified portfolio still encounters systematic risk, due to unpredictable factors affecting all prices in the system. But where risk cannot be reduced, derivatives enable it to be sold to someone else with a greater risk appetite. A risk-averse investor can use options and swaps to pay a fixed cost to avoid the prospect of buying or selling at a loss, or securitisation to turn an uncertain stream of income into a certain one. A lender can use credit default swaps to protect against default.

Traditionally, retail financial institutions such as commercial banks, building societies and pension funds sell risk so as to protect the capital of small-scale savers and investors. Investment banks, hedge funds and other wholesale institutions are willing to buy risk, in pursuit of higher returns for bigger investors who can afford to expose some of their capital to it. For large banking groups that include commercial, investment and fund-management operations, this means that risk is traded internally (between departments) as well as externally (with other groups).

Risk-seeking investors, often investment banks, can take on risk by:

* *Being a counterparty* to a future, option or swap contract. When the holder of the option chooses to exercise it, because the strike price

is below the current market price, the counterparty must buy at the higher market price and sell to this client at the lower strike price. Similarly, when the holder of a put option exercises it because the strike price is above the market price, the counterparty must buy from this client at the strike price and resell at the lower market price. The counterparty must charge a fee that covers their risk of having to buy high and sell low.

- *Underwriting* an issue of debt or other securities. The underwriter pays the issuer the amount that they are expecting to raise, and takes over the task of finding buyers for the issue. Underwriters seek to profit by taking fees, and by reselling the issue for more than they bought it, often buying it at a discount to face value.

- *Marketmaking*: committing to providing a liquid market in a particular asset or asset type, by offering to buy when most others want to sell, or sell when most want to buy. By going against the market, the marketmaker sometimes gets the opportunity to buy at very low prices and sell at very high prices. But they must also hold stocks on their books for long periods, awaiting favourable price adjustment, so the high reward again comes with high risk.

Box 3 Over-the-counter contracts: expansion and risks

Some futures and option contracts are standardised, and traded on exchanges in a similar way to shares and bonds. The London International Financial Futures and Options Exchange (Liffe), Frankfurt's Eurex and the Chicago Board of Exchange (CBOE) are among the largest exchanges. Exchange trade lowers investors' risks by assembling large numbers of buyers and sellers, ensuring a liquid market at most times. Exchange-traded contracts also have a clearing system to oversee exchange and settlement, minimising counterparty risk.

However, most of the recent growth in derivatives, especially in the UK, has been in **over-the-counter** (OTC) issues. These can be specially designed to fit the buyer's particular requirements; but as they are not standardised, they cannot be traded through an organised exchange. They therefore transfer risk from the contract holder to one individual or institution as the counterparty, with limited protection against counterparty risk if the other side pulls out. The September 2008

Over-the-counter
Trade in a non-standardised contract, away from an organised exchange.

bankruptcy of Lehman Brothers, a US investment bank that was counterparty to many derivative contracts, seriously damaged the finances of many other banks and investment funds that had been counting these now-worthless derivatives as assets or insurances.

Compared to exchange-traded contracts, OTC contracts may also run greater liquidity risk because of the absence of marketmakers, and lack a continuous flow of price information because of deals being struck bilaterally. Some OTC markets, such as that set up by the US NASDAQ (National Association of Securities Dealers' Automated Quotation), have tackled the liquidity problem by introducing marketmakers, and the information problem by using electronic systems to display information prices and quantities traded. Despite this, one effect of the credit-derivative problems that began in 2007, and consequent regulatory tightening, may be to slow the growth of OTC derivatives and shift more trade onto the exchanges.

Electronic trading

3.6 Option valuation and the pricing of risk

Futures and options contracts remove the uncertainty over future prices, while swaps and securitisations turn uncertain future income and cost streams into predictable ones. But to provide risk-averse investors with such instruments, the banks that underwrite them or serve as counterparties to them have to know what price to put on them – just as an insurance company must know what premium to set on each policy. Futures contracts are relatively easy to price: their present value is simply the value at maturity, discounted at the risk-free rate of interest, using the present-value method that you were shown in Chapter 2, Section 4.1. But valuing option contracts presented more difficulties, especially of determining the contract's value on expiry and the appropriate rate at which to discount this to the present, and an accurate formula only appeared in 1973.

Fischer Black and Myron Scholes (1973), followed by Merton (1973), built the first option-pricing formula. This was based on the Capital Asset Pricing Model (CAPM) introduced in Chapter 3. The Black–Scholes formula links the price of a call option to its strike price, the time to expiry, the spot-market price of the underlying asset, the risk-free rate of interest, and the volatility of the underlying asset. All of these can be ascertained from the contract terms or from past market data. The Black-Scholes formula assumes, like the CAPM, that prices adjust so that all assets (on spot or forward markets) give investors the same expected return per unit of risk. Its introduction was followed by rapid growth of options trading as previous regulations were relaxed and new exchanges set up.

Although Black–Scholes was only a model of how traders set option prices, it was soon found to predict the prices set in the market with great accuracy. This wasn't surprising, because a model designed to be predictive quickly became prescriptive – traders started using Black–Scholes as their guide in pricing options and derivatives based around them (MacKenzie and Millo, 2003, pp. 121–5). The widespread adoption of a reliable option-pricing formula, which could be speedily implemented as computers became faster and cheaper, was an important step in persuading regulators to relax previous restrictions on the issuance and trading of derivatives. These now became viewed as respectable investments that could correctly align spot and forward prices and promote the efficient trading of risk, rather than a form of speculation that could destabilise prices and add to risk. The Chicago

Board of Exchange was thus founded in 1973, and other exchanges soon after, to accommodate the newly legitimated trade.

3.7 Are derivatives risky?

Discovery of the Black–Scholes formula can be likened to a technological innovation that revealed substantial demand for derivatives (from corporations and commercial banks) and a willingness to supply them (by investment banks), once appropriate pricing of the instrument had been worked out. There are sound economic reasons for the growth in demand and supply of derivatives, once constraints due to contract design and regulation are removed. For example, more companies do business internationally and need to protect themselves against currency risk through options and swaps. Pension funds are responsible for the incomes of a growing retired population and need to protect against fluctuations in interest rates, exchange rates and equity prices. Such fluctuations would disrupt the flow of income from the assets that pension funds have built up.

Despite these reasons behind derivatives, their growth has also been argued to cause systemic risk. In 1998, a precursor to more recent problems with derivatives was the demise of Long-Term Capital Management (LTCM), a US-based hedge fund. The fund had been set up by no less than Scholes and Merton, two of the architects of the Black–Scholes model. Billions of dollars were borrowed and made in profits by trading derivatives, which included interest-rate swaps on government bonds. What the mathematical equations could not take into account, however, was the crisis of the Russian economy that led to a collapse in the price of bonds issued by the Russian government. Derivative trades on these bonds became worthless, and since LTCM had borrowed so much to finance these trades, it became insolvent.

An intricate network of relationships emerged between LTCM and other financial institutions: a myriad of brokers and investment banks that were counterparties to its over-the-counter trades. In the crisis that ensued, these parties were unwilling to lend to either LTCM or each other. The US Federal Reserve was forced to implement a rescue package for the hedge fund. The consequent systemic risk to the financial system (see Chapter 1, Section 1) was too great to allow LTCM to go under.

For *The Economist* (2009, p. 12), 'LTCM's collapse was the credit crunch in miniature'. But calls to regulate over-the-counter derivatives were resisted, and their issuance continued to grow rapidly. The credit crunch in full, as experienced in the global financial downturn that started in 2007, was amplified by miscalculations of the extent to which financial institutions had transferred risk through derivatives, which had also grown more complex. This was illustrated in Chapter 1, Section 3.3, in relation to the effect of mortgage-backed securities, such as collateralised debt obligations (CDOs), on the global banking system. When house prices started to fall, the value of CDOs fell, and banks became uncertain about how much debt was held by other parties. The threat of systemic risk forced intervention by central banks throughout the world.

4 Financial market efficiency

The theory of options pricing, supplied by the Black–Scholes model, filled in an important information gap for investors. Spot-market prices could now be informed by forward prices that indicated expectations of future price movement, formed on an accurate assessment of risk. With forward markets accurately pricing options, and improving the flow of information to spot-market traders, financial markets moved closer to **informational efficiency**: when prices reflect the best information available in the market. It is only if markets are informationally efficient, as well as competitive and contestable (see Box 1), that resources traded through them can be expected to attain the allocative efficiency defined in Section 1.

Informational efficiency
When prices reflect the best information available in the market.

Even before this gap was filled, many economists had come to see financial markets as a uniquely efficient allocator of resources through informed, competitive price setting.

4.1 Contributors to efficiency: arbitrage and short-selling

Arbitrage
The pursuit of profit from price misalignment by buying the underpriced asset and/or selling the overpriced asset.

This confidence is based on **arbitrage**: the pursuit of risk-free profits arising from identifying price differences between assets that should be identically priced. Consider the simple example of two assets. The trader can either buy the lower-priced asset or bet against the higher-priced one. In so doing, traders put upward pressure on the underpriced asset and downward pressure on the overpriced one, and so close the price gap. Swift action by arbitrageurs ensures that there can be no lasting price differences for the same product in different locations, except for any cost (of transport, transaction or tax) of moving it from one place to the other. It also ensures that all new information that reveals past prices to have been mistaken – such as good or bad news about a company that changes the outlook for its shares – will be quickly learned and incorporated into market prices.

The impact of the Black–Scholes model on options markets is itself an example of arbitrage. It enabled traders to recognise where their intuitions or simplified calculations had been mispricing options in the past. Black–Scholes showed, in particular, that options markets had tended to set too high a price for contracts whose underlying assets showed low price volatility (as measured by standard deviation, as in Chapter 2, Section 4.4), and too low a price for contracts on underlying assets with high price volatility. It was not impossible that the markets were right, and the modellers wrong; but traders saw no problem with Black–Scholes mathematics, so they started to trade using prices derived from the model. Fischer Black was soon making extra money selling lists of calculated prices to options traders, who could use them to arbitrage between the underpriced and overpriced options, and make extra money of their own. But as more did so, market prices converged to those predicted by the model, and the easy arbitrage profits disappeared.

Because it led to trading strategies that guided prices in the predicted direction, it is possible that the formula has succeeded through 'self-fulfilling expectation', causing traders to standardise their expectations on an incorrect model. But if that were the case, financial theorists who identified the error could have put forward another model that revealed misalignments under the Black–Scholes approach, and caused market behaviour to change again. There has, indeed, been a succession of refinements to the Black–Scholes model, and a movement of prices away from those that it originally predicted, by for example designing new types of call options. But these refinements have not involved corrections to the central formula.

The power of arbitrage is increased when rules allow the **short-selling** of assets as well as their ordinary purchase and sale. Short-selling involves borrowing the asset from someone who previously bought it, and selling it into the market. The short-sale will be profitable if the price drops, so that buying and returning the borrowed stock costs less than was raised from selling it. When two prices are out of line and expected to converge, the arbitrage can be quickened by buying the lower-priced asset and short-selling the higher-priced asset. Hedge funds have been especially active users of arbitrage trading strategies: the price gaps that they exploit are often very small, but they can multiply the profits by borrowing to buy and short-sell very large quantities of the mispriced asset – regarding such leverage as relatively risk-free because of the high degree of certainty that the two prices will converge. In a competitive market, no trader affects the price through their buying or selling. But if many traders engage in arbitrage, or if one trader achieves a very-large-volume trade through leverage, their expectations of price convergence can be self-fulfilling, since sales at the higher price and purchases at the lower price will push prices in the anticipated direction.

Short-selling
Borrowing and selling an asset on the expectation that it will fall in price before the loan is repaid.

4.2 The efficient markets hypothesis

As financial markets have grown, and as regulatory and information barriers to arbitrage and short-selling have fallen away, economists have been more confident about the efficiency of markets. This greater informational efficiency has led some theorists to go as far as supporting the efficient markets hypothesis (EMH). The EMH states that market outcomes – the prices set and the volumes traded – are efficient in the sense of immediately and accurately incorporating all relevant information. There are different versions of the EMH, each with striking implications for the behaviour of market prices and for appropriate investment strategy.

Technical analysis
The use of regularities or trends in past price data to predict future prices. Closely related to chartism, which seeks repeated patterns in charts of price data.

A *weak form* of the EMH acknowledges that traders may not be able to obtain or process all publicly available information, and that current prices only contain all the information conveyed by prices in the past. This form denies the effectiveness of **technical analysis**, by which some investors study past patterns of price movement and look for signs of their repetition that will indicate the next price movement. If all information from past prices is already priced-in, any apparent patterns will have arisen by chance and cannot be expected to recur.

The *semi-strong form* of the EMH holds that prices contain all relevant publicly available information, but leaves open the possibility of some traders gaining an advantage through inside information. This form denies the effectiveness of fundamental analysis (see Chapter 2, Section 4.3), by which some investors study published information on the issuers of shares and bonds, and on commodities, to identify those that are underpriced and can be expected to rise in price. If the market price already reflects this publicly available information, there will not be undervalued or overvalued instruments as the fundamental analysts assume.

The *strong form* of the EMH holds that market prices contain all relevant information. This includes inside information – held by a small number of market players – as well as information publicly available to all, such as business and economic news and published company accounts. It is assumed that people holding privileged information will, through their trading behaviour, cause it quickly to be captured in the price, which then transmits the information to everyone.

The type of information that is relevant to the EMH depends on what model of asset price determination is being used. For example, if this is the dividend valuation model, as used in fundamental analysis (Chapter 2, Section 4.3), the model will incorporate all relevant information regarding the expected earnings of a company. So prices will only move on the arrival of genuinely new information that changes the assessment of these earnings. The impact of this news and the direction of price movement will not be predictable, otherwise those who predicted it would already have carried out trades that incorporate the information into the price.

The EMH does not rule out the possibility of different traders working with different models, or inputting different data (especially on expected variables) into the same model. However, it does implicitly require traders to believe that assets have a value set by factors that are independent of other traders' behaviour and beliefs. Problems arise for market efficiency if there is **momentum trading**, with the expectation of asset prices based on recent movements in the price. Such traders use technical analysis of stock market charts to treat previous price movements as containing relevant information, which the EMH denies.

Momentum trading
Buying assets whose prices are moving, in order to profit from further movement; sometimes termed 'noise trading' because it pays attention to (and may amplify) unexplained price movements that other traders call noise.

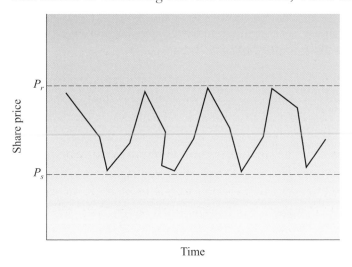

Figure 1 Charting in a price channel

An example of how charts are analysed in technical analysis is provided in Figure 1. A trader might look at the cycle in share prices as taking place in a price channel, as shown by the two horizontal dashed lines. If enough traders believe that there is a support level for the share price, as represented by the price level p_s, their belief in the support level price ensures that this price is supported in the market. Similarly, when the share price breaks through the resistance level p_r, this will also lead to a reaction that pushes the price back into the price channel. Technical traders monitor the pattern of prices using this type of charting analysis.

Technical traders are anticipating that others will make the same trade later, and 'because their speculation in the stock market is based on what they think other people wish to do, they are working from a slightly different set of information than those who buy or sell based on a firm's long-term earnings prospects' (Peters, 1999, p. 81). This potentially undermines the EMH assumption that everyone works from the same information. Although technical traders typically work on very short time-horizons, their behaviour can amplify price movements, causing these to overshoot beyond fundamental values even if they began with arbitrage correcting misalignment – sometimes contributing to 'bubble' episodes, which are examined further in Chapter 6.

4.3 The random walk prediction

Random walk
A journey in which the direction of the next step is not influenced by the direction of the previous step.

The EMH makes the powerful prediction that prices of shares and other financial assets will follow a **random walk**. The next price movement, up or down, will be unrelated to any of its previous movements. If the hypothesis is correct, there is little scope for investment experts to achieve better returns than others through stock picking and market timing. The EMH suggests that there is no reason for such expert investment strategies to work any better than buying stocks in proportion to their weighting in the market index, or even buying a random selection of stocks.

Activity 2

Which of the following events would you expect to follow a random walk, and why?

- Heads or tails when tossing a fair coin
- A football team's pattern of wins and losses
- Sunny or cloudy days during the summer

Tossing a coin is an example of a random walk – whether it turns up heads or tails next time is in no way related to the result of the previous toss, or any that went before.

In contrast, a football team's pattern of wins and losses need not be entirely random, as its chances of success in the next game may be related to its previous result. Several consecutive wins (or losses) may make another more likely, signalling the relative strength (or weakness) of the team, which could be self-sustaining because of soaring (or sagging) morale.

The summer weather is likely to be intermediate: many weather systems are durable enough for one sunny (or cloudy) day to raise the likelihood of another, but they change often enough (at least in the UK) for today's weather to be a poor predictor of tomorrow's, which is why weather forecasters remain in strong demand.

Malkiel (2007) carried out an experiment with his students in which they were asked to toss a coin. The experiment started with a share price of $50. If the coin came out as a head, they were told to add half a point to the share price; a tail would result in a half point cut in the price. Figure 2 is a chart of the stock price for one of these experiments. You can see that it looks like the type of cycle in share prices that we see all the time for companies and stock market indices. Yet this pattern is derived from a purely random event, the tossing of a coin. This argues against the use of technical analysis to look for patterns in stock-market data.

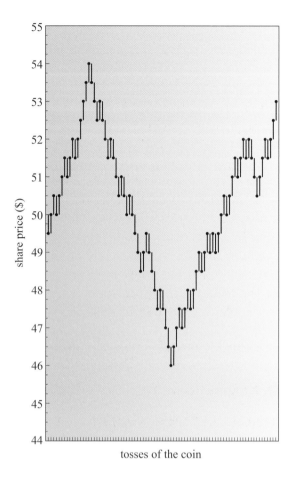

Figure 2 Stock market chart derived from random tossing of a coin
(Source: Malkiel, 2007, p. 130)

Many empirical tests of the EMH have been made because of its bold prediction about the randomness of price movements. Most tests are of the weak form, as this requires only past price data, which are readily available on the world's main exchanges. In general, these tests have shown some degree of price predictability, even on the largest and seemingly most efficient exchanges (e.g. Jarrett and Kyper, 2006). If prices can be predicted on the basis of previous prices, this means that the EMH fails. This predictability can extend to individual asset prices, as well as market indices, although it has been argued that individual prices could remain random even if there were predictable movements in the market as a whole (Jung and Shiller, 2005). There often appear to be seasonal, weekly and even daily patterns in the movement of price indices and of individual stocks (especially smaller firms), which contradict the EMH even in its weakest form.

5 Active investment management in the light of the EMH

Despite these caveats, the EMH remains a powerful influence on investors' choice of strategy because of the doubts it raises over whether even the best-informed can 'beat the market'. As we saw in Chapter 3, Section 4.3, active managers can potentially outperform a passive portfolio in two main ways. They can use stock selection to raise the weighting of assets that are expected to do better than average, and lower the weighting of those expected to do worse; and they can use market timing to switch into high-beta stocks (those that vary more than the index) when the market is rising, and low-beta stocks (those that vary less than the index) when the market is falling. In practice, it has been difficult to find clear evidence of actively managed funds consistently outperforming passive funds over long periods.

The EMH offers a theoretical foundation for doubts about the superiority of active management. Even in the weak form of the hypothesis, it rejects the value of stock selection based on chartism, technical analysis or other methods of extrapolation from past values. Even if a share price has increased steadily in the past, for example, this does not provide a guide to its future price. All information that caused the share price to increase in the past is already captured by the current price. On this basis, there is no point in charting past values of share prices.

The EMH also challenges the effectiveness of market timing, since the determination of a stock's beta depends on the pattern of past prices. If this pattern contains no information useful for anticipating future prices, then computing beta (and choosing high- or low-beta stocks in anticipation of market movements) will be no help. Since values of beta are published, they are part of the information that is already incorporated into market prices.

The semi-strong form of the EMH rejects fundamental analysis, based on studying publicly available information about companies, product markets, economic developments and technological changes that might impact the future value of a share or other asset. Any announcement by a company that might augur well for its future performance has already been incorporated in the share price. In the strong form of the EMH, even inside or private information about a company will be captured by the price.

If, as the EMH suggests, all public and private information is already captured in market prices, there is nothing to be gained from gathering and processing this information. Indeed, since such analysis costs time and effort, it would be better to assemble and manage a portfolio passively, buying and holding a selection of stocks in proportion to their market capitalisation, as given in a stock-market index. Such index funds have the added advantage of much lower management charges, reflecting the passive role of managers. Some studies find that active managers can outperform passive peers in the same market, but the problem is converting this into superior investment returns for fund members, largely because of higher charges (as shown by de la Bruslerie, 2004).

Total expense ratio
The annual cost to a client of an investment fund, including all management fees and charges, but excluding dealing costs.

The lower costs associated with passive funds are indicated by comparisons of the **total expense ratio** (TER). This expresses the managers' annual fee, and any other charges that they make (such as passed-through costs of auditing or share registration), as a percentage of the asset value under management. TERs for active funds have typically been in the 1–2 per cent range, whereas those for passive funds are generally less than 1 per cent. Moreover, the gap appeared to widen in the 2000s, in Europe and the USA. Index funds' management fees were pushed downwards by the arrival of new competition (especially from exchange-traded funds), while managed funds' charges were pushed upwards by their greater use of hedge funds and other vehicles that charge higher fees on the promise of higher absolute returns.

TERs for all fund types have historically been lower in the USA than Europe. For example, a study by Lipper Fitzrovia (2005) found average TERs of 0.92 per cent for a US equity fund, compared with 1.68 per cent for a UK fund and 1.79 per cent for a pan-European fund. For bond funds, the respective TERs were 0.86 per cent, 1.24 per cent and 1.35 per cent (McDermott, 2005). This is mainly due to Europe's smaller national markets, and the smaller average size of funds, which gives them higher average overhead costs. Both sources of higher cost have been tackled by the EU's integration of financial markets and adoption of the euro. But with some index-tracking funds dropping their annual fees to less than 0.5 per cent in the 2000s, active funds on both sides of the Atlantic continued to charge significantly for their services – perhaps motivated by the expectation that equity markets, after recovering from their 2001 crash, would reach another of the turning points at which those trying to beat the index would be rewarded compared to those merely tracking it.

As shown in Chapter 3, management fees and charges can significantly erode the rate of return for investors in an active fund. 'The expense ratio of the average fund has doubled, from 0.77% in 1951 to 1.54% [in 2007] … this rise in costs constitutes a major negative for … the returns earned by fund investors' (Bogle, 2008, p. 97). However, active managers still operate, despite their higher fees and frequent inability to outperform the passive over long periods. And many of these managers believe in the EMH. They argue that an index-tracking benchmark can be regularly beaten because of the reasons argued below.

Efficient markets still make mistakes

The EMH assumes only the accurate use of all relevant information in whatever valuation model the traders are using. Given that some agents – sometimes even a majority of agents – may adopt models that others consider irrational: 'Markets can be efficient even if they sometimes make egregious errors in valuation' (Malkiel, 2007, p. 246). US and European equity markets experienced this during 1998–2001 when many traders abandoned traditional valuation methods when assessing high-technology (dot-com) stocks. The presence of traders who apply an inappropriate model can create profit opportunities for others, even if all are using information efficiently. The causes and consequences of markets departing from traditional valuation models are examined further in Chapter 6.

Efficiency isn't instantaneous

Because prices take time to adjust even in the most efficient markets, it is still possible for stock selectors to profit on the adjustment if they move fast enough. This is especially possible for investment banks that make trades for others as well as on their own account. When they know that a big buy or sell order from another fund is likely to move the market price, the bank's traders can position themselves to gain from the price change before it happens. With modern trading technology, 'high-frequency traders' can buy or sell an asset fractions of a second before the big fund buys or sells it. 'They can spot trends before other investors can blink, changing orders and strategies within milliseconds … high-speed investors [get] an early glance at how others are trading, and their computers can literally bully slower investors into giving up profits' (Duhigg, 2009).

Tracking goes off-track

Studies showing indexed funds to deliver the best of both worlds – performance no worse than most active funds, and much lower charges – were mostly conducted when there were relatively few passive funds in most markets. But over time, doubts about the effectiveness of active management have led index-tracking investment and exchange-traded funds to grow in number and raise their share of total managed investment. Active managers argue that this can restore their advantage. Indexed funds can distort market pricing, overvaluing assets represented in the index compared to those that fall outside, and making price movements predictable because then movement of passive funds is dictated by changes in the index.

6 'Infomediaries' and the problem of unbiased information

Informational efficiency – the capture of assets' fundamental (present discounted) value in their market price – is essential for the allocative efficiency that markets are argued to promote. Investors therefore rely on a continuous flow of information-providing intermediaries, often called infomediaries. While some of these are public agencies, such as central banks and regulators, most are private, profit-driven companies. For example, stock exchanges and other markets provide information on the assets listed on them, the traders operating in them and the prices that they arrive at. Large accounting firms draw up and audit the accounts of banks and other publicly listed companies. Other companies provide calculations that add value to these data, and some use it to make investment recommendations.

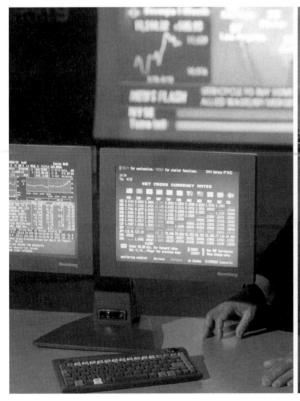

Individuals and companies that inform and advise others on investing in financial markets, while also making their own investments, are in principle at risk of a *conflict of interest*. Such conflicts are avoided by keeping own-account and advisory operations separate. Through this separation, for example, investment banks seek to avoid any suspicion that their proprietary traders might benefit from the market impact of the advice that they give to clients, and accounting firms seek to allay any danger that their opinion on a company's accounts might be influenced by other advisory business that they do with that company.

Traditionally, these separations have been upheld through self-regulation by industries or professions working in them. The professional *ethics* of bankers, accountants and others compelled them either to declare an interest (and opt out of decision making) if their prospective gains from one activity threatened to limit their neutrality in another, or to structure their business in such a way that conflicts were avoided. More recently, dissatisfaction with self-regulation – fuelled by instances where conflicts of interest arose to the detriment of clients – has led to an increase in external regulation, in financial and other professions. For example, politicians have been made answerable to a Parliamentary Commissioner for Standards, and academics have been subjected to quality assessments for teaching and research. In financial services, the UK has followed a strategy of strengthening professional standards through external regulation. The Financial Services Authority's (FSA) Retail Distribution Review proposes new training and qualifications 'to achieve by the end of 2012 a step change in standards of professionalism of advisers in the retail investment market' (FSA, 2009).

Despite efforts at stronger professional ethics and self-regulation, troubling episodes at the start of the century – including the dot-com share price boom and bust of 2000–01, and the wider collapse of major banks and equity markets in 2007–08 – highlighted some potentially unresolved conflicts of interest that might require more external regulation.

6.1 Credit rating agencies

Issuers of bonds commission assessments from a credit rating agency (CRA) to assure investors about their creditworthiness. CRAs assign ratings that indicate the likelihood of the debt being serviced and repaid; a typical rating scale is illustrated in Chapter 2, Section 4.2. Ratings are regularly reviewed, and upgraded or downgraded if the issuing company or government changes in its ability or willingness to repay. A positive or negative outlook is often posted if a CRA is considering changing its rating.

CRAs are licensed as 'nationally recognised statistical rating organisations' by the US Securities and Exchange Commission, and by equivalent regulators in the EU. As of 2009, three – Standard and Poor's (S&P), Moody's and Fitch – were licensed to provide ratings in the USA and widely quoted elsewhere. Most of the investment and pension funds handling ordinary households' investments are mandated only to buy debt that is rated 'investment grade' by one or more CRAs, avoiding lower-rated 'speculative' issues. A conflict of interest concern arises because CRAs are commissioned by the borrower, rather than the investors who must decide if the bond is worth buying. While CRAs say that this ensures that they get access to otherwise confidential company information, and keeps down the information cost to investors, critics fear that it may lead to their assessments being too lenient. Many CRAs are part of consultancy groups that offer other services to the same companies, including advice on how to improve future ratings.

These fears intensified in 2007–08, when leading CRAs conferred investment grade status on collateralised debt issues that, as we have seen, later proved to be highly speculative. Critics suggested that CRAs, keen to retain borrowers' business, had been biased in their favour and unwilling to dig deeply into the income and profit projections that they had supplied.

> To achieve a triple-A rating, especially from lower rated sub-prime mortgages, often requires a degree of financial engineering … enabling the creation of at least one class of securities whose rating is higher than the average rating of the underlying collateral asset, with the end result that AAA security tranches are often backed in part by BBB securities … The relatively recent innovation of tranching, whereby a pool of assets is converted into low-risk, medium-risk and high-risk securities, has led to a mushrooming of triple-A securities available for investment. Rating these securities has been an increasing source of income for the CRAs.
>
> (Treasury Select Committee, 2008)

The UK Treasury Select Committee, having observed this, expressed itself as 'deeply concerned' about CRAs' conflicts of interest, demanding regulation or fuller disclosure if the agencies could not demonstrate their impartiality. In late 2008, authorities in the USA and the EU, after investigations of the 'Big Three' rating agencies, issued recommendations for stronger regulation. This required clearer disclosure of methodologies and results, separation of ratings research teams from those who agree the ratings contract, and a right for all agencies to view any data disclosed to one agency.

6.2 Financial analysts

Analysts assess shares, bonds and other financial instruments with a view to determining whether they are worth buying, holding or selling from a portfolio. As more basic data become freely available, due to reporting regulations and online information sources, analysts have been forced to 'add value' to the information that they present. Some, for example, devise ways of forecasting future price–earnings ratios and other key ratios, rather than just computing the historical ones, by building predictive models or by detailed probing of companies' executives and their plans. Most analysts specialise in either shares or bonds ('fixed income'). Some equity analysts also specialise in particular industrial sectors, and some bond analysts look exclusively at sovereign bonds (issued by governments) or corporate bonds. Their usual strategy is to predict future earnings in order to work out an intrinsic present value for an instrument, and compare it with the present market price to determine whether an investor should buy, hold or sell it.

Activity 3

When analysts classify shares and bonds as 'undervalued' or 'overvalued', is this a contradiction of the efficient markets hypothesis?

For analysts to be correct in judging that an instrument is overvalued or undervalued, and destined to fall or rise in price, there must be inefficiency in the market that prevents other traders from making the same calculation and instantly selling or buying so as to move the instrument to its intrinsic price. Analysts can only work with publicly available information, since using undisclosed proprietary information would risk a charge of insider trading. So their employment can be justified if they are capable of using superior knowledge or calculation to identify a price misalignment ahead of the crowd.

6.3 Financial advisers

Advisers are private profit-making businesses: the independent ones must generate revenue above the costs of people, equipment and buildings that they employ, and the ones employed by banking and insurance groups are usually 'profit centres' within them. Whether independent or in-house, an adviser can generate revenue in three main ways:

- a *commission* arising from the sale of a financial product, usually linked to the amount of money that the client puts into the product
- a *flat fee*, based on the time and level of service given to the client
- a *performance-linked fee*, based on the value of financial products in the client's portfolio (often a percentage of the annual valuation).

Commission-based selling has been a popular model for financial advice in the past, but there have been questions around the ethics of how such advice is provided. It has been criticised for causing potential conflict with clients' interests, because advisers are given incentives to:

- sell the client a product, even if none is particularly appropriate, because sales are needed to generate commission
- sell the type of product that generates the most commission, or a product from the supplier that gives most commission, rather than choosing the product and supplier that is likely to perform best for the client.

In the UK, the Financial Services Authority (FSA) steadily tightened the rules on commission-based selling, forcing advisers to publicise the commission that they would receive on the product (and to point out that the cost would ultimately be charged to the client, not paid by the supplying company). But after failing to stop periodic outbreaks of 'mis-selling', involving commission-driven sales of inappropriate products, the FSA in June 2009 proposed an outright ban on independent advisers receiving commission after 2012. You will learn more about the regulation of financial advisers, and other FSA interventions, in Chapter 7.

Despite widespread reaction against commission-based selling, the other methods of rewarding financial advisers are also open to criticism. The flat fee forces clients to pay even if they make no changes to their strategy as a result of advice, and may give the adviser an incentive to schedule long or frequent meetings in order to earn more fees. The performance-based fee encourages advisers to seek higher returns, which may entail higher risks than the client wishes to run, and it may bias the adviser towards using actively managed funds despite their unclear performance advantage over passive funds.

7 Conclusion

In this chapter you have looked at how financial markets work, from the most simple demand and supply for assets in spot markets, to more complicated derivative products. You have been introduced to derivative markets that provide new vehicles for managing the risk–return balance for fund managers and can enhance the efficiency of financial markets. Such innovations have led economists to become more confident about the validity of the efficient markets hypothesis (EMH), in which markets efficiently process all available information.

You have seen that when the EMH holds, this has profound implications for personal investment. In its three forms (weak, semi-strong, strong), the EMH shows that a number of investing strategies will not work. Whether you carry out a technical analysis of past share prices, or a fundamental analysis of future returns, your approach will fall foul of the EMH. You have seen that the EMH provides a theoretical underpinning of the passive investment approach, which was introduced in Chapter 3, Section 4.2. Active investors are warned that under informational efficiency it is impossible to beat the market. Passive investment also has its advantages because of the lower transaction costs involved in, for example, investing in index funds, rather than paying for active investment strategies.

In this chapter you have also considered some of the problems with the EMH. Markets are not always efficient, and high-speed investors can at times capitalise on inefficiencies that might arise. Inefficiencies can arise because analysts use different financial models, and if so many investors now track market trends, this can lead to markets amplifying and distorting such trends. And if markets are so efficient, why are so many infomediaries – analysts, credit rating agencies and financial advisers – employed in the financial services industry? You have explored some of the conflicts of interest associated with these types of market player.

Financial markets cannot, however, be fully understood without examining their wider social and economic context. Financial investors and providers are both enabled and constrained by the income generated by households and producers in other markets. In Chapter 5 you will be introduced to economic fluctuations of the economy as a whole, and how this relates to personal investment.

References

Black, F. and Scholes, M. (1973) 'The pricing of options and corporate liabilities', *Journal of Political Economy*, vol. 81, no. 3, pp. 637–54.

Bogle, J. (2008) 'A question so important that it should be hard to think about anything else', *Journal of Portfolio Management*, vol. 34, no. 2, pp. 95–102.

Carville, J. (1993) interview in *Wall Street Journal*, 25 February, p. A1.

de la Bruslerie, H. (2004) 'Active bond strategies: what link between forecasting ability, excess return and performance?', *Journal of Asset Management*, vol. 5, no. 2, pp. 105–19.

Duhigg, C. (2009) 'Traders profit with computers set at high speed', *New York Times*, 23 July.

Economist, The (2009) 'Greed – and fear, a special report on the future of finance', 24 January.

Erman, B. (2009) 'A fragile confidence is shaken', *Globe and Mail*, 19 June.

European Securitisation Forum (ESF) (2008) *Securitisation Data Report Q4* [online], www.europeansecuritisation.com/Market_Standard/ ESF_Data_Report_Q4_2008.pdf (Accessed 29 March 2009).

Financial Services Authority (FSA) (2009) *Qualifications Update and What You Can Do Now* [online], 25 June, www.fsa.gov.uk/pages/About/What/rdr/ qual_update.shtml (Accessed 26 July 2009).

International Swaps and Derivatives Association (ISDA) (2008) *Market Survey Results* [online], www.isda.org/statistics/pdf/ISDA-Market-Survey-historical-data.pdf (Accessed 28 January 2010).

Jarrett, J. and Kyper, E. (2006) 'Capital market efficiency and the predictability of daily returns', *Applied Economics*, vol. 38, pp. 631–6.

Jung, J. and Shiller, R. (2005) 'Samuelson's dictum and the stock market', *Economic Inquiry*, vol. 43, no. 2, pp. 221–8.

Lipper Fitzrovia (2005) *A Comparison of Mutual Fund Expenses Across the Atlantic*, Insight Report, September, New York, Lipper.

MacKenzie, D. and Millo, Y. (2003) 'Constructing a market, performing theory: the historical sociology of a financial derivatives exchange', *American Journal of Sociology*, vol. 19, no. 1, pp. 107–45.

Malkiel, B. (2007) *A Random Walk Down Wall Street* (9th edn), London, Norton.

McDermott, R. (2005) 'Fitzrovia finds fund fees almost double in Europe', *Money Management Executive*, 3 October.

Merton, R. (1973) 'Theory of rational option pricing', *Bell Journal of Economics*, vol. 4, no. 1, pp. 141–83.

Peters, E. (1999) *Complexity, Risk and Financial Markets*, New York, Wiley.

Smith, A. (1979 [1776]) *The Wealth of Nations*, London, Penguin.

Surowiecki, J. (2004) *The Wisdom of Crowds*, London, Little, Brown.

Treasury Select Committee (2008) *Sixth Report. Section 2 Changes in Financial Markets* [online], www.publications.parliament.uk/pa/cm200708/cmselect/cmtreasy/371/37105.htm#a15 (Accessed 26 July 2009).

Further reading

Lefevre, E. (2006) *Reminiscences of a Stock Operator*, London, Wiley.

MacKenzie, D. (2008) *Material Markets*, Oxford, Oxford University Press.

PART THREE: BUBBLES AND THE ECONOMY

Clearly, sustained low inflation implies less uncertainty about the future, and lower risk premiums imply higher prices of stocks and other earning assets. We can see that in the inverse relationship exhibited by price/earnings ratios and the rate of inflation in the past. But how do we know when irrational exuberance has unduly escalated asset values, which then become subject to unexpected and prolonged contractions as they have in Japan over the past decade? And how do we factor that assessment into monetary policy? We as central bankers need not be concerned if a collapsing financial asset bubble does not threaten to impair the real economy, its production, jobs, and price stability. Indeed, the sharp stock market break of 1987 had few negative consequences for the economy. But we should not underestimate or become complacent about the complexity of the interactions of asset markets and the economy.

Greenspan, A. (Ex-Chairman of the US Federal Reserve) (1996) Speech at the Annual Dinner and Francis Boyer Lecture of The American Enterprise Institute for Public Policy Research, Washington, DC, 5 December [online], www.federalreserve.gov/boarddocs/speeches/1996/19961205.htm (Accessed 15 October 2008).

Thought-provoking questions for Chapters 5 and 6:

- What is the relationship between financial markets and the real economy i.e. consumers' spending decisions and businesses' investment decisions?
- Why are financial investors subject to 'false optimism' and irrational exuberance – or what Keynes called *animal spirits*?

Chapter 5
Economic fluctuations

Andrew Trigg

1 Introduction

> ## Learning outcomes
>
> After reading this chapter, you will:
>
> - be able to describe how economies fluctuate
> - understand key macroeconomic categories and indicators
> - be familiar with debates about the self-correcting properties of market economies
> - understand fiscal policy, monetary policy and exchange rates.

Les Thain, 53, a credit manager for a human-resources firm, has three personal pensions which have fallen in value by a total of £40,000, or about 45%, since the outset of the downturn.

(Hussain, 2009)

Cynthia Bartrop, 79, will have to make some tough sacrifices because of the latest interest rate cuts. She used to get £250 a month from her life savings to supplement her state pension. But she expects her savings income to drop to £83 a month after yesterday's cut.

(Barrow and Brogan, 2009)

These are just two of the millions of people whose personal investment portfolios were affected by the downturn of the world economy that began in 2007. The first individual, who is still working, had suffered losses 'on paper' from investing in shares as part of his pension plan, and was left hoping for a rise in share prices to retrieve his loss before he came to retire. For the second, already in retirement, the loss was immediate, due to low interest rates on the cash savings that were part of her income in retirement.

But consider a different scenario, reported in *The Times* on 22 November 1985: 'The gallop towards the 1,200 points mark was underway in earnest yesterday when shares climbed 15.6 points. Buying was heavy. Institutional investors, spurred on by year-end performance considerations, piled into the market' (Pain and Feltham, 1985). This was a period of upturn in the economy characterised by profitable companies and a booming stock market.

Individuals compelled to engage in personal investment have to take into account the state of the economy, and how it fluctuates. In an economic downturn there is the possibility that share prices will crash; in (or before) an upturn, share prices often increase. Big market movements can also feed back into the state of the economy. For example, a stock and bond market crash can worsen the downturn by making it more expensive for firms and households to borrow; or it may force the central bank to cut interest rates sharply, so that investment and consumption spending recover. The movements of other key assets, such as returns on property, are also closely related to the state of the economy. Economies have been observed to go through a regular business cycle, despite the efforts of governments to keep activity stable or to ensure that free markets do so.

This chapter will introduce some of the ways in which economists try to understand fluctuations in economic activity. Why do economies fluctuate, and how are these fluctuations measured? Are economies self-correcting, or do they require government intervention? This chapter provides an introduction to the economic landscape in which personal investment plans are carried out.

Section 2 introduces two ways in which economic fluctuations can impact on personal investment plans: through inflation eating into the real value of savings, and via economic recession disturbing the value of shares. Section 3 then examines some of the explanations that economists provide as to why economic fluctuations take place, and Section 4 gives some of the key economic indicators that are used. For personal investment, a judgement has to be made on the impact of economic policy, and this provides the focus of Section 5. Finally, in Section 6, the wider impacts of exchange rates are explored.

2 Economic fluctuations

The main indicator used to measure economic fluctuations is the level
of national output. During an economic recession the level of output
will contract, and during a period of expansion it will increase. Other
indicators, such as the level of employment, can also be used to
measure fluctuations, but the most commonly used indicator is output.

Activity 1

What examples are there in recent years of periods in which output has
contracted?

The most recent example (at the time of writing) is the recession in the
world economy in 2009, with UK national output contracting by 2.4 per
cent in the first quarter and 0.8 per cent in the second, leaving it 5.6
per cent lower than a year before (ONS, 2009). Previous recessions
occurred in 1991 and 1980. Figure 1 shows fluctuations in real output
for the UK over the period from 1962 to 2009. Output is measured by
Gross Domestic Product (GDP), first introduced in Chapter 2, and
represented here by its annualised real rate of growth. A 2 per cent rate
of growth, for example, measures an increase of £2 for every £100 of
output.

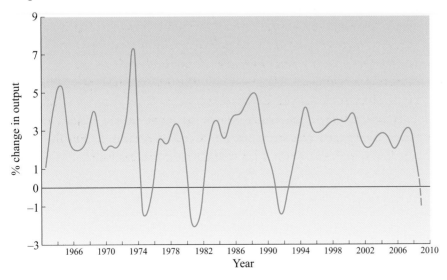

Figure 1 The rate of growth of output in the UK, 1962–2009

(Source: Office for National Statistics, 2009)

The vertical axis shows the rate of growth of real output, and the horizontal axis the relevant time periods. The horizontal line represents a zero growth rate of output. If the curve that tracks the growth of output falls below this line, then there is negative output growth. The fall in output in 1991, for example, is shown by the rate of growth of output falling to −1.4 per cent. Other contractions in output are in 1980, where output fell by 1.9 per cent, and in 1974, where it fell by 1.4 per cent. These can be contrasted with periods of expansion, such as in the Lawson boom in 1987 and 1988 (named after the Chancellor Nigel Lawson), where the economy grew at over 4 per cent each year. It should be emphasised that Figure 1 also shows positive growth to be the norm. The UK economy tends to grow at about 2.5 per cent per year on average in the long term, but you can see from Figure 1 that there is much variation around this average.

There are two main ways in which economic fluctuations impact on personal investments, each involving types of risk that were introduced in Chapter 2. First there is the problem of inflation risk. Periods of expansion in economic activity can be associated with inflation of prices. This eats away at the cash value of income from bonds and other assets. There is also capital risk associated with economic recession. Contractions in economic output reduce profits made by companies, which reduces share prices. Some companies also go out of business, which threatens all of the capital held by shareholders.

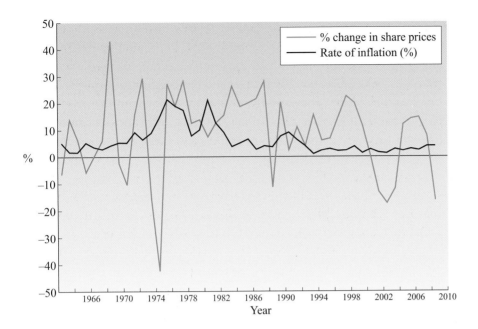

Figure 2 The rate of inflation and growth of share prices in the UK, 1962–2008

(Sources: ONS, 2009; OECD, 2009)

To illustrate these two types of risk consider Figure 2, which shows the fluctuations in two indicators for the UK economy. The first is the rate of inflation of goods and services; it measures the rate at which the price index changes from year to year. The second is the rate at which the index of all share prices changes each year.

Box 1 UK inflation measures: CPI and RPI

The UK Office for National Statistics (ONS) publishes every month two measures of inflation in the prices that most affect households.

The Consumer Prices Index (CPI) measures the average price of a range of goods and services consumed by a typical household; it gives the measure of inflation that is targeted by the Bank of England, and used for comparisons by international organisations such as the Organisation for Economic Co-operation and Development (OECD) and the European Union (EU).

The Retail Prices Index (RPI) measures the average price of a slightly different range of goods and services and gives the measure of inflation used to adjust state benefits, pensions and

---

interest on index-linked gilts. The RPI differs mainly by the inclusion of housing costs.

Because of the sharp fall in mortgage interest rates in 2008, the RPI fell – indicating **deflation** – in early 2009, whereas the CPI continued to record positive (though low and declining) inflation. Note that on both measures the inflation rate can stay positive even if prices fall during some months of the year, because it measures the year-on-year price change.

Deflation

Falling prices, shown by a negative inflation rate.

Activity 2

Comparing Figure 2 with Figure 1, identify what has happened to share prices in periods of economic recession.

Periods of recession can be associated with a downturn in share prices. In 1974, for example, the value of shares fell by 42.1 per cent, at a time of falling output. But note also that share prices tend to move before movements in output. The fall in share prices by 13.6 per cent in 1973 preceded the contraction in output the year after. Similarly, the contraction of output in 2009 was preceded by a reduction in share prices of 16.1 per cent in 2008. And although share prices did not fall in 1990, they did slow down to a relatively low 2.4 per cent rate of growth, ahead of the 1991 contraction of output. Share prices are referred to as a **leading indicator**, a measure of economic or financial activity that moves ahead of other indicators. (Other leading indicators are considered in Section 4.)

Leading indicator

A measure of economic activity that tends to change before other measures change.

Further illustrating this characteristic, share prices can recover while the national economy is still contracting. In 1975, for example, investors enjoyed a 27.3 per cent increase in share prices while output contracted by 0.6 per cent. Share prices also increased by 10.9 per cent in 1991, alongside falling output. As a leading indicator, prices and returns on shares can precede a recovery in output, as investors anticipate higher profits due to cost-cutting during the downturn and recovering sales at the end of it.

Note also, in comparing Figures 1 and 2, that movements in share prices are often not related to movements in real output. The reduction in share prices over the period 2001–03, for example, was during a period of modest growth in UK output. This was a period in which investors thought a recession was likely; US economists often joke that their stock market 'has predicted five of the last three recessions'. Share prices also increased throughout the 1980s, despite the recession that took place in the first two years of that decade. Investors have to monitor the progress of economic conditions, but are also faced with uncertainty about the impact on share prices.

Share price indices move in response to any change that affects investors' future profit expectations for a large number of companies. These can include major changes in technology, social trends, the natural environment, national and international politics, as well as economic developments. Moreover, globalisation means that the London Stock Exchange trades an increasingly high proportion of shares of companies based outside the UK, such as mining and banking conglomerates. This weakens the relationship between share prices quoted in London and the UK economy.

Figure 2 shows several periods in which inflation risk came to the fore. Over the period 1974–77, for example, inflation ran at more than 15 per cent. Savings of £100 were eroded by at least £15 each year – a catastrophe for any saver who kept this money under the mattress! Inflation is closely related to economic fluctuations, not least because of its importance to policymakers. Consider again the Lawson boom of the late 1980s. Inflation rose from 3 per cent in 1986 to a peak of 9.4 per cent in 1990. The government's efforts to slow the inflation rate also reduced the level of demand in the economy, and may have led to the recession of 1991.

Similarly, the fall in retail prices (deflation) that took place in 2009 was associated with a slowdown in production that started at the end of 2008 and led to national output falling sharply in the first half of 2009. The spectre of deflation forced a policy reaction by governments in response to the recession. One major task for investors is to try to anticipate what policymakers will do about inflation and the strength of demand in the economy. A key indicator, which will be considered later in this chapter, is the rate of interest. This is a major policy tool used by governments and central banks to control inflation, and is critical to the return on investments in cash and bonds.

3 Are economies self-correcting?

Economists strongly disagree about why economic fluctuations can be so pronounced. On the one hand, some blame 'Big Government', arguing that market economies will be less prone to fluctuations, and faster-growing, if unencumbered by government intervention. On the other hand, market economies can be viewed as fundamentally unstable, prone to continual instability due to 'shocks' from the business, financial and natural environment, which can be tempered only by government intervention. 'If only I could get advice from an economist with one hand,' US President Harry Truman is said to have complained.

A key difference between these two economic approaches is their interpretation of demand and supply. In what has been called the *demand-side* approach, it is argued that government intervention is required to regulate demand, ensuring that there is enough to prevent an economic downturn but not so much as to cause shortages and inflation. In the alternative, *supply-side* approach, entrepreneurs should be free to decide on the supply of goods and services in answer to consumers' wishes expressed through the market. Each of these approaches will be introduced in turn.

3.1 The supply-side approach

To explain the basics of the supply-side approach, consider a simple economy in which there are only two groups: firms and households. The role of government is left out of the picture for now, and we assume that the economy under consideration is closed, taking part in no trade with other countries. Economists frequently make this kind of simplifying assumption, since market economies are such complex systems. By constructing a simplified model of the economy, we are able to understand some relationships among key variables. A warning sign should be attached, of course, since the choice of assumptions will have an impact on the outcome of the exercise.

Figure 3 is a basic model of the circular flow of income between households and firms. There are two sets of exchanges to consider. First, households provide labour services to firms as their employees, and they receive consumption goods from firms. These physical flows, of labour and consumption units, are shown by the solid lines, with arrows pointing in the direction of these flows.

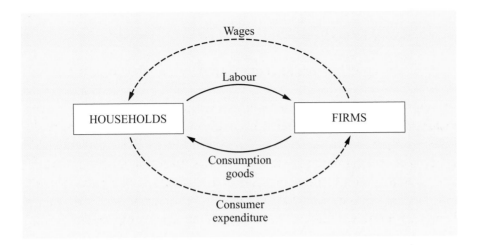

Figure 3 The circular flow of income

Second, the dashed lines indicate the direction of money flows between households and firms. In return for their labour services, households receive money incomes (wages) from firms; and to pay for consumption goods, households return (money) consumption expenditure to firms. Another simplifying assumption is that these households don't save any money, but spend all of their income from wages on consumption. There is no room for credit cards and savings accounts in this model.

Households and firms depend on one another. Firms need households to buy their outputs of consumption goods; households need the products of firms in order to live. Households rely on the income from labour services that firms require in order to engage in production.

The model of circular flow can be used to illustrate the supply-side approach to economics. To do this we set out a key plank of supply-side theory. This theory is associated with what historians of economic thought call classical economics, which can be traced back to the eighteenth century.

Consider an economy in which firms produce five bushels of corn, and corn is the only good consumed by households. To do this, firms hire five workers (working one year each) from the household sector, and in return five bushels of corn are consumed by households. As shown in Figure 4, these five workers together receive £10 in wage income, all of which is spent on bushels of corn.

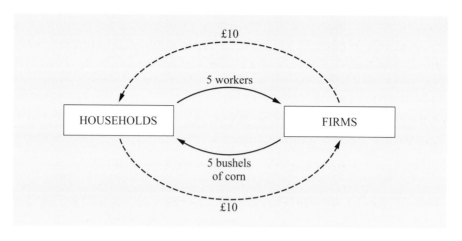

Figure 4 A corn model of supply

From a supply-side perspective, the firms in this example are guaranteed to sell their corn to households. They decide how much corn to supply, and how many workers they need to meet this supply. And these workers are able to purchase all of the corn produced by firms. This is a demonstration of **Say's Law**, the proposition that supply creates its own demand. The early classical economist and French businessman Jean-Baptiste Say (1767–1832), whose name is given to this law, was an early advocate of the supply-side approach. Its implication is that there should not be any shortage of demand for goods produced by firms, since they create this demand through the supply of goods and the hiring of labour. Since all labour is hired, there is also no unemployment in this supply-side model. If any new workers arrived, they would find employment, and there would be extra output that they could consume with the wages that they received.

Say's Law
Usually expressed as the idea that supply creates its own demand.

In the real world, of course, the balance between demand and supply is regularly disturbed. But under Say's Law, the economy should not experience serious shortages or gluts that disrupt economic activity. Any temporary imbalance between supply and demand is quickly corrected. In classical economics, there are three key arguments as to why a market economy is self-correcting, which are explained below.

Flexible prices

Say's Law assumes that prices will adjust to ensure that supply and demand are in balance. This equilibrium between demand and supply is established through the operation of a price mechanism, as introduced in Chapter 1. To illustrate this argument, we can make further use of Figure 4 by noting that the price per bushel of corn is £2, since £10 buys 5 bushels of corn. Consider what would happen if there were a bumper harvest, with firms producing 10 bushels of corn. How can this excess supply of corn be sold? The classical response is that the price of corn will fall, in this case to £1. The workers earn £10 in wages, with which they can now purchase 10 bushels of corn at this lower price. Say's Law is upheld, with the new level of supply met by an equivalent level of demand. The glut in the supply of corn was only temporary, with the market adjusting to ensure that all produce is sold.

This simple example illustrates the extraordinary power of a market economy. Without any intervention by government, the market has the power to correct an imbalance between supply and demand. Adam Smith, the founder of classical economics, saw this as part of an invisible hand directing the behaviour of actors in a market economy.

Adam Smith

This supply-side view leads to a defence of the free movement of prices. Policymakers are particularly concerned about inflation, because, when all prices are rising, it's harder for people to make the right relative price adjustments that balance supply and demand in each market. The European Central Bank (ECB), for example, has as its primary objective keeping the inflation rate below 2 per cent. One of the main reasons given is that near-stable prices improve the transparency of the price mechanism. 'Under price stability people can recognise changes in relative prices (i.e. prices between different goods), without being confused by changes in the overall price level' (ECB, 2009).

Flexible wages

The supply-side view also depends on the flexibility of wages. One recurring problem of a market economy is unemployment, which can be interpreted as an excess supply of workers. The classical response is to let employers reduce wages so that all workers can find jobs, if they accept the market wage.

Activity 3

Assume in Figure 4 that there are five new workers looking for employment – an oversupply of workers. The existing wage rate (wages per worker) is £2 per worker. At what new wage could all ten workers be employed?

If the wage rate were cut to £1 per worker, then all of the ten workers could be employed, earning a total of £10. The logic of this classical view is that bodies such as trade unions or minimum-wage setters frustrate the free movement of wages and actually create unemployment. Whereas workers in existing jobs enjoy the protection of trade union rights, and artificially high wages, workers looking for jobs are priced out of work.

Flexible interest rates

Thus far the unrealistic assumption has been made that individuals cannot save. Relaxing this assumption creates problems for the classical model, since savings represent a leakage from the system. Consider again the example shown in Figure 4. If workers suddenly decided to save £2 out of their wage income of £10, this would lead to a shortfall of £2 in expenditure on bushels of corn. To allow for this possibility, a more realistic model of the economy is required in which people can save.

We also know that firms do not just produce consumption goods, as Figure 3 assumes. Some produce physical investment goods, such as raw materials and machinery that are not directly consumed by households; and all firms have to buy investment goods in order to produce. This 'physical investment' should not be confused with 'financial investment', the type of personal investment considered in other chapters of this book. Note that when economists discuss 'investment', it is this type of physical investment that they are usually referring to.

A modification can therefore be made to the circular flow to include savings and physical investment. Figure 5 focuses on the circular flow of money in this more sophisticated (but still very simple) economy. All income is still directed to wages, but out of these wages workers can now save. Savings are a leakage from the system, since they are withdrawn from the household sector. Investment expenditure, on the other hand, is an injection, bringing additional expenditure to the system. These money flows are, as before, represented by dashed lines. The real flow of physical investment goods between firms is represented by a new solid line.

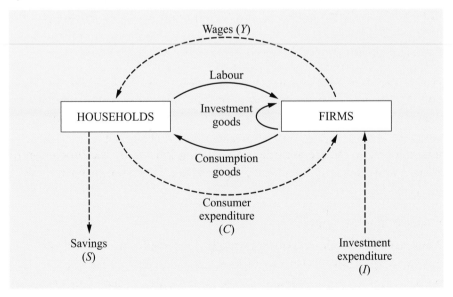

Figure 5 The leakage of saving from the circular flow

For Say's Law to hold, the introduction of savings must be matched by an increase in investment. In our example, the shortfall in expenditure generated by £2 of savings must be matched by £2 of investment in (for example) agricultural machinery.

How can we be sure that savings (*S*) will always be matched by investment (*I*)? The classical defence is that any savings will be automatically channelled into investment via the market for money. In addition to the market for goods, and the market for labour, there is a market for money, in which the 'price' is the rate of interest charged for lending and borrowing. If savings temporarily increase, the excess supply of savings induces a fall in the rate of interest, which then leads to an increase in investment, since firms can now afford to borrow more. Say's Law holds once again, with the market (in this case the money market) generating matching demand for any excess supply.

Box 2 Defining national income

A key economic indicator can be defined for Figure 5. The closed economy can be summarised using a simple equation:

$Y = C + I$

The income of the economy (*Y*), which is shown at the top of Figure 5, is equal to expenditure on consumer items (*C*) and investment goods (*I*). This is a basic model of national income: the income earned by residents of a nation from producing investment and consumption goods. National income can be looked at either as the national output of all goods produced or as the income generated from their production.

Now we know that savings (*S*) are the difference between income and consumption $S = Y - C$. It follows that savings must equal investment:

$S = I$

Imagine an economy has a national income of £100 billion, and £70 billion is spent on consumption. The savings of households in this economy would be £30 billion. This leakage from the system is matched by £30 billion of physical investment. Economists refer to this equality as the savings–investment identity.

3.2 The demand-side approach

The classical model was very influential, especially in persuading governments to remove restrictions on the setting of prices and wages. But its suggestion that supply will always be matched by demand, if prices adjust, has not always been supported in practice. And its theoretical assumption, that savings will always be matched by investment through adjustment of interest rates, has been particularly challenged. Economists have more recently recognised the importance of demand for investment goods by firms, and the impact on that demand of factors other than the interest rate on borrowing. Firms are faced with uncertainty about how successful their investments might be, and can on occasions decide not to make physical investments even when interest rates are low, opting instead for liquidity. This section will consider these two aspects of the demand-side approach.

Uncertainty and investment

The demand-side approach first came to prominence in the wake of the Great Depression of the 1930s. Before this prolonged period of high unemployment, the economic establishment in the UK was committed to the precepts of classical economics. So long as wages, prices and interest rates were allowed to vary, the market economy would be self-stabilising, with full employment and low inflation. The only seriously dissenting views had come from radical groups such as Marxists, who rejected markets as a way of distributing resources. But, as the depression worsened, this argument was attacked by a core member of the economic establishment itself. John Maynard Keynes, educated at Eton and Cambridge University, and closely connected to the British civil service, wrote a book that was intended to revolutionise how we think about economics. In his *General Theory of Employment, Interest and Money*, first published in 1936, Keynes argued that market economies are prone to slump, with high unemployment persisting even if prices and wages are completely flexible.

The problem in a market economy is that investment is highly sensitive to fluctuations in the confidence of decision makers. Keynes emphasised the importance of 'animal spirits': psychological traits that make people act in a spontaneous way and be influenced by the behaviour of others. Lack of information and uncertainty about the future can leave agents paralysed with doubt, but animal spirits help to overcome this doubt.

Keynes argued that the profit or yield from investment is extremely difficult to predict:

> The outstanding fact is the extreme precariousness of the basis of knowledge on which our estimates of prospective yield have to be made. Our knowledge of the factors which will govern the yield of an investment some years hence is usually very slight and often negligible. If we speak frankly, we have to admit that our basis of knowledge for estimating the yield ten years hence of a railway, a copper mine, a textile factory, the goodwill of a patent medicine, an Atlantic liner, a building in the City of London amounts to little and sometimes nothing.
>
> (Keynes, quoted in Walsh, 2008, p. 63)

In the face of such uncertainty, decision makers fall back on their gut instincts, based on their interpretation of market sentiments.

For Keynesian economists, animal spirits provide an explanation as to why real investment is subject to such pronounced fluctuations. Consider the rate of growth of physical investment in the UK, as represented in Figure 6. This is presented for the period from 1962 to 2009, alongside the rate of growth in output of the UK economy. Fluctuations in investment are much more pronounced than fluctuations in output. At the peak of the Lawson boom in 1988, output increased by 4.9 per cent, but investment raced ahead at 14.8 per cent. In the subsequent recession in 1991, the reduction in output by 1.4 per cent coincided with an 8.1 per cent fall in investment. From a Keynesian perspective, these fluctuations are driven by animal spirits, with the market veering from terrific confidence about the prospective yield from investments, as in 1988, to a collapse in collective confidence, as in 1991.

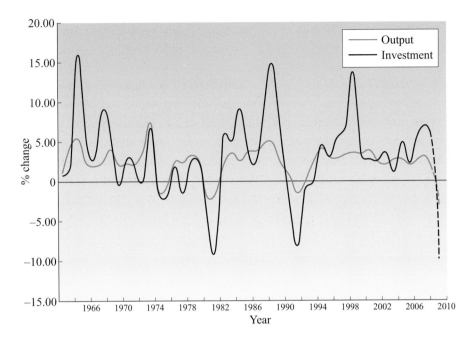

Figure 6 Rate of growth of output and investment in the UK, 1962–2009
(Source: ONS, 2009)

Note: Output is GDP; investment is Gross Domestic Fixed Capital Formation, the amount spent on new capital goods plus depreciation and amortisation.

Keynesians view investment as the key driver of the circular flow of income, as considered in Figure 5. As Box 2 shows, in this simple model, investment (*I*) and savings (*S*) are identical: *I* = *S*. What is at stake in economics is the direction of causation between the two. The classical approach treats savings as the driver for investment. Keynesians give investment an independent status, as a key economic activity that is determined by animal spirits. From a Keynesian perspective, it does not matter how much households save, and how far the interest rate falls, if the collective confidence of the market is negative. What matters is the demand for investment goods by firms, as determined by their animal spirits. If investment rises, it will generate more income from which households can produce the matching savings; but if investment falls, there'll be a matching fall in savings caused by shrinking national income, which leaves some people out of work.

Uncertainty and interest rates

This emphasis on uncertainty has particular importance for the functioning of interest rates. Recall that for the classical approach, interest rates bring Say's Law into the financial market. Savings are channelled into investment through the signals provided to physical investors by interest rates. If savings increase, for example, this induces a cut in the rate of interest, resulting in more investment. For Keynes, uncertainty brings this classical mechanism into question. If firms are very uncertain about the future, they may not want to invest however low the interest rate goes.

A second key problem is that interest rates may not fall far enough, because individuals speculate about their level. In the *General Theory*, Keynes (1936) examined how speculation takes place on the price of government bonds, which you saw in Chapter 2 are intimately related to the rate of interest. Given a fixed coupon on a bond, the rate of interest is the ratio of the coupon to the bond price.

Activity 4

Suppose that a government bond pays a fixed coupon of £1. Calculate the rate of interest (in percentage terms) with:

1   a bond price of £5

2   a bond price of £10.

For 1, the rate of interest at a bond price of £5 is 20 per cent; for 2, the rate of interest at a bond price of £10 is 10 per cent. An increase in the price of bonds reduces the rate of interest (also called the bond's interest yield, recalling Chapter 2, Section 2.4). This is because the fixed coupon on the bond is now a smaller proportion of the price. It follows that for the rate of interest to fall, there must be an increase in bond prices. But investors may be uncertain as to what will happen to the price of bonds, and to the prices of other assets (such as shares) that they could hold instead. If investors fear that they will lose money on bonds, they may hold their money in cash, so bond prices stop rising and their yields cease to fall.

Consider, for example, a debate that took place in *Investors Chronicle*, in January 2009, between John Redwood (MP for Wokingham) and David Kauders (partner of Kauders Portfolio Management). They were each asked, 'Is there a bubble in gilts?' (Redwood and Kauders, 2009, p. 17).

In response to the financial crisis at the time, bond prices were increasing since they were regarded as a safe haven compared to the volatile stock market. Redwood argued that the bubble in bond prices would eventually burst. Kauders, on the other hand (again we see the two-handed economist in action here), thought that bond prices were not yet near their peak. Bonds would continue to be a safe haven for investment on the anticipated deepening of the financial crisis. What is clear, as Keynes argued, is that there is uncertainty about what will happen to bond prices and hence the rate of interest paid on government bonds, which sets the minimum for the interest rate that corporate borrowers must pay.

This key role for uncertainty brings into question the classical mechanism for channelling savings into investment. The rate of interest may not drop if savings increase, since individuals will speculate on how this impacts on the demand for bonds. If the rate of interest does not drop because of speculation, this will prevent the recovery of investment.

Keynes argued that at times the economic system could be stuck in a **liquidity trap**, where there is a mass scramble for liquidity, and no one wants to channel their savings into long-term physical investment. The 'credit crunch' that started in 2007 has also been described in this way. On this occasion the key problem was that banks withdrew into liquidity, unwilling to lend to firms, or even to each other. A *Financial Times* headline read: 'Interbank lending grinds to near-standstill' (Mackenzie and Oakley, 2008). Because of a fear that banks or companies might become insolvent, banks held on to cash. Interest rates to household and corporate borrowers levelled off, or even increased, despite the Bank of England steadily reducing its base rate from 5.75 per cent in July 2008 to 0.5 per cent in March 2009.

Liquidity trap
A situation where low or even zero interest rates fail to revive an economy, because investors refuse to buy non-liquid assets.

Households also held on to cash. Having engaged in a consumer boom before 2007, they became worried about their future employment prospects and started to spend less. In such circumstances, especially with the downturn keeping inflation low, the safest thing to do is hold cash. Whatever happens to the economy, households can limit their losses, and have a chance to go back into more risky assets at the bottom of the market. Supply-side economists question the existence of liquidity traps, some arguing that the problem arises from banks being unwilling to lend at low interest rates and could be solved if these were allowed to rise. But in a liquidity crisis as serious as that which began in 2007, central banks actually tried to stop commercial banks raising their

Interesting thought, not sure I agree

233

lending rates, as you will see in Section 4.3. For the financial commentator Martin Wolf (2008): 'The ghost of John Maynard Keynes, the father of macroeconomics, has come back to haunt us.' He may even be laughing at us from his grave!

We can therefore introduce two alternative approaches to understanding how economies work. In the supply-side approach, economies are regarded as self-correcting; in the demand-side approach, problems of uncertainty bring into question these self-correcting mechanisms. In the analysis that follows, we will explore the role played by government policy, according to these contrasting perspectives. For investors, government policy and its impact on the economy is important for understanding what might happen to inflation, interest rates and demand – all of which directly affect the returns from assets. To understand how and why policymakers react to events, we first need to look at some more of the key indicators that economists employ.

4 Economic indicators

The focus of this chapter is on a particular type of economic analysis. We have been looking at the economy as a whole, concentrating on economic activity at the national level, as captured by measures of aggregate output, investment and inflation. Instead of looking, for example, at the output of individual firms, which would be a concern of **microeconomics**, the focus here is on **macroeconomics**, which looks at the output of all firms in the economy. This section introduces a further selection of economic measures and indicators, used by macroeconomists, that are of particular relevance to personal investors.

4.1 National income

In Section 3, the national income was defined for a closed economy, with no government sector and no foreign trade. In this most simple model, national income (Y) consists of household consumption (C) and real investment (I). To make the model more realistic, government expenditure, denoted by G, can now be introduced. Government expenditure can consist of any expenditure by the public sector that generates output. The building of a new hospital, for example, requires the output of all the materials supplied by the private sector. (Note that state pension and welfare payments, though the biggest component of the budget, are not 'final' government expenditure, since they flow as income to households and so will turn into household spending or saving; they would therefore be found in C rather than G.)

We also need to introduce foreign trade, which consists of exports (X) and imports (M). Exports require output by the national economy, since goods and services are produced domestically and sent abroad. Imports represent negative output, since they substitute for output that could have been produced domestically.

The full equation for calculating national income is therefore

$$Y = C + I + G + X - M$$

All of the elements on the right-hand side of this equation represent macroeconomic expenditure. The term Y represents the income

Microeconomics
Analysis of an economy's constituent parts, e.g. firms, consumers and particular markets, and especially the role of prices and wages as incentives for efficiency.

Macroeconomics
Analysis of whole-economy features such as national output, inflation rates, interest rates and growth rates.

received from agents that sold these goods and services – to other private firms and households, to the government or abroad. Y also represents the output of the national economy, since it provides an indicator of the value of all goods and services produced.

Table 1 shows how the national income of the UK economy was calculated in 2006. The estimate of national income of £1,301,914 million is calculated by adding up the elements of our national income equation. This particular measure is referred to as Gross Domestic Product, or GDP for short (as first introduced in Chapter 2, Section 2.3).

Table 1 Composition of GDP for Great Britain, 2006

	£m	%
Consumer expenditure (C)	828,691	63.7
Gross investment (I)	234,814	18.0
Government expenditure (G)	285,925	22.0
Exports (X)	369,247	28.4
Imports (M)	−417,616	−32.1
Statistical discrepancy	853	0.0
Total: GDP at market prices (Y)	**1,301,914**	**100.0**

Source: OECD, 2009

By far the largest proportion is represented by consumer expenditure, which makes up 63.7 per cent of national income. Investment and government expenditure are of similar importance, at around 20 per cent of national income. Since the UK is such an open economy, exports are also very important, representing 28.4 per cent of national income.

4.2 The official rate of interest

An institution that is key to the macroeconomy is the central bank. The central bank is the official bank to the government, its historical role being to raise money to pay for government expenditure. As you saw in Chapter 2, governments that want to spend more than they can raise in tax obtain extra money by issuing bonds. In Europe, government bonds can be traced back to the wars that took place around the fourteenth century between Tuscan city-states: Florence, Pisa and Siena (see Ferguson, 2008, p. 69). Mercenaries were hired to fight these battles, at great cost to the state treasuries. To finance their expenditure, over and above tax revenues, these states innovated by issuing bonds. The Bank of England secured its status as the UK central bank in 1694 by offering the government a large loan for its wars against Spain.

The government can raise aggregate expenditure in the economy by spending more than it taxes and issuing bonds, or reduce aggregate expenditure by taxing more than it spends and paying its debt back. This financial innovation has been critical to regulating demand and managing the modern economic system.

The other main role of the central bank is to ensure stability of financial markets. Money flows between banks, firms, households and government, with the central bank as the lender of last resort (see Chapter 1, Section 1). Figure 7 shows some, but not all, of the money flows between these institutions. The banks, for example, make loans to firms as represented by the arrow pointing from banks to firms. Firms also hold any spare cash with banks, as represented by the arrow in the opposite direction. Now, the provision of loans by banks may at times result in a shortfall in their reserves (which banks must hold to be viable). This is where the central bank comes in, allowing the injection of new cash into the system, to ensure that the banks have sufficient reserves.

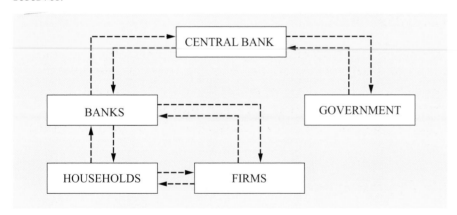

Figure 7 The monetary system

How does the central bank inject money into the banking system? The short answer is by using government bonds. The Bank of England, the central bank for the UK, makes loans that are backed up by government bonds (the European Central Bank uses a similar system). This type of loan is referred to as a repurchase agreement, or repo for short. Suppose that Lloyds Bank wants to borrow £1 million from the

Repo rate
The interest rate at which a central bank makes short-term loans to commercial banks (sometimes called the 'official rate' or 'policy rate').

Bank of England. This loan is set up as a repurchase agreement: the Bank of England buys £1 million of government bonds from Lloyds, injecting £1 million into its reserves, but sells the bonds back to Lloyds after a short period of time. Of critical importance is the rate of interest that the Bank of England charges for the repo. If, for example, it charges 5 per cent, this means that the **repo rate**, the official rate of interest, is set at 5 per cent. This is the rate of interest set each month in the UK by the Bank of England's Monetary Policy Committee.

The official rate of interest provides the main tool by which the Bank of England intervenes in the money market. To increase the amount of money in the system, the central bank will make it easier for commercial banks to borrow (by reducing the repo rate). To reduce the amount of money available, the central bank can make it more expensive to borrow, by increasing the repo rate. The central bank makes use of commercial banks' very low liquid assets ratios (see Chapter 1, Section 3.4), which keep their finances sufficiently tight so that they are regularly in need of short-term funding.

4.3 The inter-bank rate of interest

Loans are made at many different interest rates, depending on their purpose, the period of the loan, and the players involved. Of particular importance is the way in which banks take out loans with one another. In the example above, Lloyds would not usually have to borrow money directly from the Bank of England; its first call would be to the inter-bank market, where banks take out loans from and make deposits with other banks. The role of the Bank of England is to act as the lender of last resort, stepping in to supply liquidity when there is a shortfall of funds in the inter-bank market, or to 'soak up liquidity' if the market is overflowing with funds.

The inter-bank market has its own rate of interest. In the UK this rate is the LIBOR (the London Inter-bank Offered Rate), which sets the cost of borrowing funds (or making deposits) on the inter-bank market. The importance of this rate is that it is used as the benchmark for setting many other interest rates throughout the financial system. Similarly, in France, the inter-bank rate is called the PIBOR; the nearest US equivalent is the Federal Funds Rate. Historically, the LIBOR is slightly higher than the official repo rate, reflecting in part the higher rate of return required to place deposits with banks other than the central bank. In normal times, lending to other banks is not backed by the security of government bonds.

To ensure that it has monetary control, the Bank of England tries to ensure that repo and LIBOR rates are closely related. In April 2006 it introduced a corridor aiming to constrain the LIBOR rate to no more than 1 per cent above or below the repo rate (Howells and Bain, 2008, p. 317). Exceptional conditions can arise, however, as during the credit crunch that began in 2007 when inter-bank lending became frozen (see Section 3.2 of this chapter). On this occasion the Bank of England, and other central banks, were unable to control what happened to inter-bank rates, which failed to fall in line with repo rates.

4.4 Mortgage rates

Building societies originally started, in the late eighteenth century, with small groups of people joining together to help each other to build houses. If there were (for example) 20 people in a society, each would contribute a certain amount of savings to be members; and each year a house would be built for one of the members. Building societies were based on the principle that individuals save to finance the building of houses in association with other savers.

However, members who had to wait too long for their house to be built became frustrated with the process. In response, a system of mortgages became the standard model for the purchasing of property by individual members. With the growth of private housing, mortgages have increasingly been underpinned by the inter-bank money markets. Building societies have borrowed in these markets, as have banks following their expansion into the provision of mortgages. Chapter 1 discussed the case of one of the largest mortgage lenders in the UK, Northern Rock (a former building society), and how it could no longer raise finance from securitisations or the inter-bank markets. The inter-bank rate of interest can therefore have a key role in determining the rate of interest paid by mortgage holders, especially those on 'floating' rates that lenders adjust in line with their own cost of borrowing.

4.5 Confidence indicators and house prices

For investors, various confidence indicators are available as a way of assessing economic conditions. Surveys of managers, for example, provide information about how confident they are about the prospects for their own businesses, whether they expect sales to rise or fall and whether they plan capacity expansion. Investors also monitor the confidence of consumers, since this provides evidence of a future market for goods and services produced by companies. Various lenders and business associations sponsor regular surveys asking households about their confidence and spending intentions, and retail sales are often taken as a more direct gauge of consumer sentiment.

Alongside measures of consumer confidence, the trajectory of house prices can also be important. Rising house prices can reflect consumer confidence by indicating households' willingness to borrow in order to buy them; they can also boost this confidence by making homeowners feel wealthier and more able to spend. Figure 8 displays the annual inflation rate in house prices for the UK over the period 1985–2009. This is displayed alongside an index of consumer confidence put together by the European Commission. This index is positive when consumers are optimistic and expecting their situation to improve, and negative when they are pessimistic. The rate of output growth, which you first saw in Figure 1, is also included here for purposes of comparison.

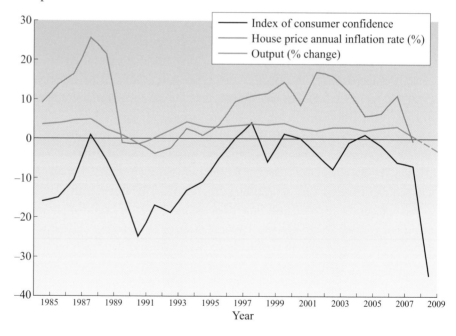

Figure 8 UK consumer confidence and house price inflation, 1985–2009

(Sources: Office for National Statistics, 2009; European Commission, 2009; Communities and Local Government, 2009)

The most startling observation is the collapse in consumer confidence that took place in 2009, with the index falling to −35, from a value of −7 in 2008. A similar level of −25 was reported in the recession of 1991, when output also contracted. Both these recessions provide some evidence that consumer confidence worsened before the contraction in output. From a positive consumer confidence index of +1 in 1988, the index fell to −14 in 1990, prior to the fall in output in 1991. Similarly, the confidence indicator was equal to +1 in 2005, before it fell slightly to −7 in 2008. These falls in confidence are small compared to the eventual reduction during recession, but can provide a leading indicator of the direction in which the economy is travelling.

House prices also reached a peak rate of annual growth of 25.6 per cent in 1988, then fell by 1.3 per cent in 1990, the year preceding the recession. In 2007, however, house price inflation reached a peak of 10.9 per cent, giving little indication of the impending recession. As with the collapse in consumer confidence that year, the contraction in house prices seemed to have been sudden, and not easily predicted. Investors should be careful in how they use these types of indicator, in view of the uncertainties that can engulf a macroeconomy.

5 Fiscal and monetary policy

We are now ready for a consideration of government economic policy, which investors often try to anticipate so that they can forecast market reactions. Governments operate two main types of economic policy: fiscal policy (linked to the budget) and monetary policy (linked to management of financial markets via the central bank). How these policies are framed depends closely on whether policymakers adopt the demand-side or the supply-side perspective. Very few economists are ambidextrous!

5.1 Fiscal policy

As we saw in explaining how national income is defined, government expenditure has a key role to play in the economy. National income is generated by government expenditure on items such as transport, health, education and defence. This expenditure is financed in the main by taxation, including taxation on personal incomes (income tax), on products and services (value added tax), and on company profits. **Fiscal policy** involves decisions about taxation and public expenditure.

Fiscal policy
Decisions by government on public expenditure and taxation.

From a Keynesian perspective, fiscal policy can fill the gap when private investment fails to provide sufficient demand in the economy. In a recession such as that which followed the 2007 credit crunch, lack of confidence can cause firms to cut back their investment plans. A Keynesian response is for government to give the economy a fiscal boost. This can consist of more government expenditure and/or a reduction in taxes. The gap between expenditure and taxation (the **fiscal deficit**) tends automatically to rise when the economy goes into recession, and Keynesians argue that this can help to get the economy growing again. In November 2008, as an additional temporary measure, Chancellor Alistair Darling cut value added tax in the UK in order to stimulate consumer spending.

Fiscal deficit
The excess of government spending over the revenue that it receives, usually expressed as a proportion of national income.

In the 1930s, US President Roosevelt introduced his New Deal, a massive programme of government spending to combat the Great Depression. The federal government assigned $3.3 billion in 1933 for the Public Works Administration – amounting to 5.9 per cent of the US economy's national income (Rauchway, 2008, p. 65). Public buildings, highways and other infrastructure were built throughout the USA in an attempt to get the economy working again. Inspired by the New Deal,

President Obama came into office in 2009 with a similar package of around 5 per cent of national income (Buiter, 2009).

Workers employed under Roosevelt's New Deal

Keynes recommended a similar programme in the UK during the 1920s and 1930s. In the pamphlet *The Means to Prosperity*, Keynes (1933) argued that a fiscal injection would in part pay for itself. But there are limitations and risks associated with fiscal injections. Keynes recognised that a fiscal stimulus will open up, or widen, the fiscal deficit, at least for a time. Critics argue that the government may have difficulty funding such a deficit without crowding (squeezing) out private sector expenditure as its borrowing needs force it to raise interest rates, and that the extra expenditure may result in higher inflation rather than extra output. Whereas the supply-siders argue that government spending crowds out the private sector, the Keynesians argue that government spending can increase the level of national income, generating more activity in both the state and private sectors.

The UK government of the 1930s was determined to balance its budget. Ramsay MacDonald, the Labour Party's first prime minister, formed a National Government with the Conservatives and Liberals, with the explicit aim of avoiding a fiscal deficit. Similar worries were voiced about whether the Obama fiscal stimulus could be paid for without getting the US economy into permanently higher debt.

Belief in balanced budgets now tends to be associated with a supply-side perspective. The argument is that taxation eats into the amount of savings that the private sector can supply for investment purposes. Keynesians tend to be less concerned about fiscal deficits, arguing that the government has a responsibility to ensure that there is sufficient demand for goods and services in the economy, and that the deficit will close once the fiscal stimulus has re-started economic growth, which raises tax revenue. When announcing his record fiscal deficit in 2009, President Obama published forecasts that showed the US federal budget back in balance by 2013; and Chancellor Darling, announcing record UK government borrowing in 2009–10, also maintained his commitment to balancing the budget over the business cycle.

5.2 Monetary policy

Monetary policy
The control by central banks of money supply and interest rates.

Economists of a supply-side persuasion tend to favour **monetary policy**. This involves keeping aggregate demand and prices stable through the control of the supply of money in the economy and the setting of interest rates. The rate of interest is treated as the price of money. High interest rates make the use of money expensive, reining in consumption and investment that have become excessive; low interest rates make money cheap, reviving demand that has dropped too low.

Hyperinflation
Very high inflation.

The **hyperinflation** experienced by Germany in the 1920s showed what can happen when the supply of money gets out of control. Too much demand, fuelled by too much available money, leads to rapidly rising prices. In extreme cases, inflation erodes the value of money so rapidly that people resort to barter, getting paid in goods and exchanging these directly for other goods. Table 2 shows what happened in Germany to bank note circulation and the index of prices; July 1923 represents a base of 1.0 for each column of numbers. The number 73 in September 1923 therefore represents a 73-fold increase in the volume of notes in circulation compared to the base of 1.0 in July; there is a 207-fold increase in prices from July to September. If these figures aren't astonishing enough, take a look at what happened by November 1923: prices rose to 853,665 above their July level, while the number of bank notes in circulation rose by 131,778. The abiding image of this period is of Germans buying loaves of bread with wheelbarrows full of bank notes. In more recent times, many eastern Europeans suffered hyperinflation when price controls were removed after 1989, and Zimbabwe claimed record inflation rates of over 23 million per cent during 2008.

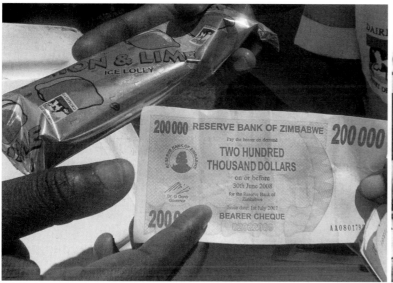

Hyperinflation in Zimbabwe and Germany

Table 2 Bank note circulation and prices under German hyperinflation

1923	Index of bank note circulation	Index of prices
July	1.0	1.0
August	2.7	3.9
September	73	207
October	57,339	109,938
November	131,778	853,665

Source: Kindleberger, 1993, p. 307

A key legacy of this hyperinflation scenario is that German policymakers were subsequently very cautious about inflation. The European Central Bank, with its focus on price stability, has been set up under the influence of German policymakers. Similarly, since the Bank of England Act 1998, an inflation target of around 2 per cent has been set for monetary policy in the UK. 'The Bank's monetary policy objective is to deliver price stability – low inflation' (Bank of England, 2009). In January 2007, for example, interest rates were increased in response to a 2.7 per cent rate of inflation reported the previous November. It was decided at the time that 'the risks to inflation now appear more to the upside' (Bank of England, 2007). During the economic boom that took place in the 2000s, the Bank of England policy/repo interest rate was increased from an average of 3.67 per cent in 2003 to an average of 5.95 per cent in 2007 (OECD, 2009).

These increases may seem tame compared to the interest rate hike carried out by Margaret Thatcher's Conservative government in the early 1980s. From a short-term interest rate of 9.3 per cent in 1978, the rate was increased to 16.6 per cent in 1980 (OECD, 2009). An attempt was being made to purge the UK economy of the high inflation experienced in the 1970s; but at that time, the government was attempting to control inflation by restricting the growth of money supply, and it may not have anticipated how much this would cause interest rates to rise.

There are scenarios, however, in which interest rate reductions are recommended by a supply-side approach. Milton Friedman, an economist central to the supply-side approach, argued that the Great Depression in the 1930s was caused by misjudgements on monetary policy. On this occasion the problem was one of deflation (falling prices). For monetarists, deflation is as damaging as inflation. Anything that threatens price stability requires a monetary response. Under deflation, the monetary authorities are recommended to cut interest rates.

The legacy of this approach was seen in policy decisions of the US Federal Reserve and its long-serving chairman, Alan Greenspan – an economist very much from the supply-side tradition. During his five terms of office, from 1987 until 2006, Greenspan used interest rate reductions on several occasions to avoid the dangers of deflation, especially of asset prices. He did so, for example, in response to the stock market crash of 1987 and the dot-com crash in 2000, helped by the consumer inflation rate (which excludes asset prices) staying very low. These interventions are referred to by Morris (2008, p. 65) as the *Greenspan Put*: 'No matter what goes wrong, the Fed will rescue you by creating enough cheap money to buy you out of your troubles.'

Each time Greenspan managed to steer the US economy out of a potential crisis, he was regarded as a genius by economic commentators. There were some murmurings of criticism in supply-side circles that Greenspan should be wary of increases in asset prices, in particular in share values and property prices. A 2005 address by Jean Claude Trichet, President of the European Central Bank, entitled *Asset Price Bubbles and Monetary Policy*, sounded a note of caution. It warned that 'certain historical episodes suggest that major asset-price escalations can be encouraged by lax monetary conditions' (Trichet, 2005). With hindsight, the argument can be put much more strongly. It is now widely argued that Greenspan gave the US economy one too many doses of medicine (easy money), which led to a 'bubble' in asset prices whose bursting caused the credit crunch that began in 2007. Such 'bubbles' can make life immensely more complicated for personal investors trying to secure future wealth through assets, and are examined in more detail in Chapter 6.

A similar criticism was levelled at Mervyn King, governor of the Bank of England during and after the boom in the 2000s. He, like Greenspan, was accused of being unconcerned with the bubble in asset prices. As we have seen, the remit of the Bank of England's Monetary Policy Committee (MPC) has been to target inflation – measured by the CPI – with its interest rate decisions. In the opinion of Philip Stephens, a columnist for the *Financial Times*:

> Discussion of the wider economic forces shaping output and prices was discouraged in favour of a rigid definition of the MPC's remit to hold inflation at close to 2 per cent. There was insufficient discussion of the dangers inherent in rapid credit growth and soaring asset prices.

(Stephens, 2009)

This approach, which again with the benefit of hindsight can easily be criticised, cannot be understood without examining its supply-side underpinnings. A central bank's primary objective is to maintain a low and stable inflation rate, measured by an index that focuses on consumer prices and does not include asset prices. Keynesians also care about monetary policy, but they are less keen on making the targeting of inflation the primary objective. The tendency is to set low interest rates to encourage investment demand and hence stimulate employment. As we saw in the downturn that started in 2007, this type of monetary policy has its limitations. Keynesians have described cutting interest rates in a liquidity trap situation as akin to 'pushing on a string', and tend to favour fiscal policy over monetary policy.

5.3 Implications of policy for personal investment

The need for personal investors to look ahead, to future economic developments and the way that policy reactions might affect them, is illustrated by an April 2009 *Financial Times* article: 'Even before deflation has fully hit the world's leading economies investors are fretting about inflation' (Oakley and Mackenzie, 2009, p. 37).

This was written at a time of economic recession, in which governments worldwide were engaged in a fiscal and monetary relaxation. We saw earlier that in 2009 both the US and UK governments implemented a fiscal stimulus. Governments also eased their monetary policies, introducing low interest rates and 'quantitative easing': the buying of government bonds by the central bank to make more money available in the economy. (Quantitative easing is more traditionally referred to as 'open market operations'.)

At the time, several judgements had to be made by personal investors. First, would these polices take the world economy out of recession? A recovery would point to a more stable economic landscape for firms, with revived demand and restored confidence, returning them to profit, enabling more dividends to shareholders and probably leading to a rise in share prices. A recovery, or even the anticipation of a recovery, would lead to a revival of shares as an asset class. Second, would the bond market join in this revival, or would governments' deficits force them to issue so many new bonds that their prices fell, causing bond interest yields to rise?

Another important judgement concerned the future path of inflation. At the time, global inflation was very low, with some countries even experiencing deflation – but this did not prevent worries about subsequent inflation. In the same *Financial Times* article, Michael Hartnett, equity strategist at Bank of America Merrill Lynch, said: 'There is nothing more inflationary than a whiff of deflation because the deflationary response in policy terms has to be inflationary' (Oakley and Mackenzie, 2009). Fear of falling asset prices after the stock-market falls of 2001 led the UK and US central banks into an easing of monetary policy, which was later widely blamed for the strong rise in housing and share prices that suddenly reversed in 2008. A return to inflation tends to promote a move by investors into shares, which, as seen in Chapter 2, are usually considered the best asset class to outperform inflation. If bonds are to be purchased, with inflation on the horizon, then they are usually recommended to be index-linked.

A more pessimistic view, in which the recession persists, and even becomes a depression – the doomsday scenario of the Great Depression in the 1930s – may suggest a much more cautious approach to investing. Even cash savings in a bank deposit account that pays little or no interest will increase in real value under deflation. More goods can be purchased with each unit of cash when prices are falling. Deflationary situations have not occurred very often during the last hundred or so years. But at all times, assessments about the future path of inflation are critical to investor decision making.

6 The open economy

We saw earlier that the UK is a very open economy, with a large part of its income coming from exports. In recent years, the degree of openness between countries has increased as barriers to trade and cross-border capital movement are reduced. The exchange rate between national currencies is a central consideration for people trading or investing abroad. In this section, we will examine how exchange rates work and some of the ways in which they are interpreted in economics.

6.1 Exchange rates and policy

When goods are imported to the UK from abroad, the importing country has to use foreign currency. If a supermarket buys corn from the USA, it must pay the grain traders in their own currency, US dollars. To do this, the supermarket must purchase these dollars with British pounds. The **exchange rate** in this example is the amount of dollars that can be purchased with one pound.

Exchange rate
The number of units of a foreign currency that exchange for one unit of home currency (or vice versa).

Activity 5

A supermarket in the UK spends £100 million on the purchase of wine costing €110 million from France. What was the exchange rate between pounds and euros?

By dividing 110 by 100, the exchange rate can be calculated as 1.10. Each pound purchases 1.1 euros.

Exchange rates influence the volume of trade between countries. In the example of wine purchased from France, suppose that the exchange rate falls from 1.1 to 1.0. This would mean that each pound can now buy only €1 worth of wine. The reduction in the exchange rate makes imports more expensive. Conversely, an increase in the exchange rate from 1.1 to 1.2 would make imports cheaper. Each pound would now purchase €1.2 worth of wine.

Economists from a supply-side perspective tend to worry about falling exchange rates because they can lead to more inflation. An increase in the price of imports, particularly of raw materials such as oil and coal, leads to higher costs for industry and higher prices in the domestic economy. Personal investors would be particularly worried by this scenario. In the UK, for example, inflationary worries over a weakening pound might shift the emphasis towards equities instead of bonds – since equities tend, if held over a sufficiently long period of time, to be a better hedge against inflation (see Chapter 2, Table 3).

Economists from a demand-side perspective tend to favour lower exchange rates as a way to combat recession. This is because lower exchange rates encourage higher export demand. If a garage in France wants to buy a car made in Britain and the exchange rate is 1.1, the UK-based car firm can sell £1 worth of car for €1.1. But if the exchange rate falls to 1.0, this means that £1 worth of car can now be sold for €1. The fall in the exchange rate makes it easier for the British firm to export its cars to France, and to displace eurozone imports in the UK marketplace. The demand for exports is stimulated by the fall in the exchange rate. Investors may respond to a weak exchange rate by buying shares in companies that are orientated towards exports.

The rate of interest has a key role to play in determining the exchange rate. Larger investors in the UK and elsewhere can move short-term deposits between different countries, according to which one is offering the highest interest rate. If the Bank of England raises the official rate of interest, foreign money will flow into the UK to buy government bonds. To buy these bonds, foreign investors must exchange their currency for British pounds, which raises the exchange rate. A rise in the rate of interest therefore tends to strengthen the exchange rate. This reinforces the power of monetary policy: a reduction of interest rates can boost demand in the economy, not only by boosting consumption and investment, but also by promoting exports because an outflow of capital lowers the exchange rate, making UK goods and services more competitive abroad.

The targeting of inflation using a high rate of interest includes some control of the exchange rate in order to ensure that the inflation is not fuelled by expensive imports. Conversely, a more Keynesian policy of targeting investment demand using low interest rates can also be complemented by a positive impact on exports via a lower exchange rate.

6.2 Exchange rates and uncertainty

Since 1973 most exchange rates in the world economy have been allowed to fluctuate freely, according to the demand and supply of currencies. A notable exception is in the eurozone, in which (by 2009) 16 former national currencies in Europe (including the German mark and French franc) have been replaced by the euro currency. But between currency blocs in Europe, the USA and the Far East (often called the euro, dollar and yen zones), there have been flexible exchange rates. By 'flexible', economists mean that there are no formal restrictions on the extent to which exchange rates can fluctuate.

After the Second World War, however, for two decades the world economy operated with fixed exchange rates. At the end of the war, Keynes represented the UK in negotiating the Bretton Woods Agreement, in which the pound had a fixed exchange rate against the US dollar. The British government was only allowed to change this exchange rate under exceptional circumstances. A key part of this agreement was the setting of limits on the amount of money capital that could flow between countries. Keynes was concerned that a free flow of capital would lead to more uncertainty in the world economy, allowing speculation against currencies that were perceived as misaligned (because trade flows between nations were out of balance). The collapse of Bretton Woods in the 1970s enabled governments to remove their capital controls, but this may have led to an increase in instability.

Particularly startling since 1989 has been the growth in currency trading not linked to underlying imports and exports. The Bank of International Settlements has carried out a regular survey of exchange-rate trading between 54 major countries. Its key indicator has been the level of turnover: the average amount of each currency that has been traded on a daily basis. Figure 9 shows the increase in turnover over the period 1989–2007. It increased from $680 billion per day in 1989 to $3210 billion in 2007. Saccomanni (2008, p. 63) estimates that this is 'one-fourth larger than the annual GDP of Germany'. As foreign exchange turnover has grown much faster than the value of international trade, the implication is that an increasing proportion of currency trade is detached from underlying transactions and may be speculative.

A major part of this increased foreign exchange trading arises from the spectacular increase in holdings of financial derivatives, especially by hedge funds. As Chapter 4 observed, the previously restricted derivatives market was allowed to grow because regulators viewed it as a method of risk transfer, perhaps substituting for the protection against exchange-rate risk that had previously been given by fixed exchange rates. But speculation against exchange rates is also widespread, because many traders believe that they can predict currency movements, and some can buy or sell currency in such large quantities that they can move exchange rates in the predicted direction. On 16 September 1992, hedge-fund investor George Soros is believed to have made up to $10 billion by correctly anticipating that the UK would abandon its attempt to fix the pound against other European currencies and allow it to fall. Keynesians have argued that the movement of global capital should be restricted in order to curtail the extent of this speculation, to temper the amount of uncertainty in the world economy.

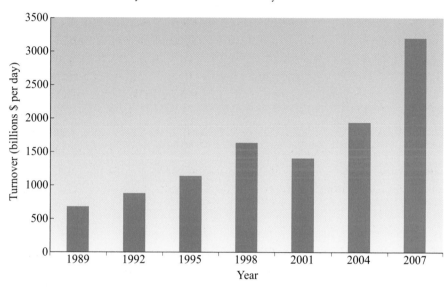

Figure 9 Global foreign exchange market turnover

(Source: Saccomanni, 2008, p. 64)

Note, however, that derivatives are used by fund managers to protect their portfolios against the risk of exchange rate fluctuations. Investors seeking high returns often look to shares in companies located in emerging economies. Such economies, based in Eastern Europe and the Far East, for example, are thought to contain the potential for high rates of growth. For the personal investor, fluctuating exchange rates increase the potential risk associated with such high potential returns. In assessing the trade-off between risk and return, financial derivatives can be seen either as a tool to hedge against such fluctuations, or as part of the underlying cause of increasing uncertainty.

7 Conclusion

In this chapter you have examined how and why macroeconomic fluctuations take place. You have considered the anatomy of how economic indicators such as GDP and inflation fluctuate alongside financial indicators such as share prices and interest rates. The trajectory of these financial indicators is critical to the health of personal investment plans, as illustrated by the individual examples given at the start of the chapter.

Investors have to make judgements about the success or otherwise of government policy in the face of economic fluctuations. An evaluation is required of both fiscal and monetary policy, and changes in exchange rates. In this chapter, you have been introduced to some of the main models and arguments used by economists to anticipate developments in the economy and to give policy advice. A contrast has been drawn between economists who emphasise the importance of demand, following in the tradition of Keynes, and those who emphasise supply, drawing on classical economists such as Adam Smith. The chapter has also highlighted the importance of uncertainty to this debate between strands of macroeconomics. In Chapter 6, you will turn to the theme of uncertainty in a more microeconomic setting, focusing especially on financial markets.

References

Bank of England (2007) *News Release: Bank of England Raises Bank Rate by 0.25 Percentage Points to 5.25%*, 11 January [online], www.bankofengland.co.uk/publications/news/2007/003.htm (Accessed 21 November 2009).

Bank of England (2009) *Monetary Policy Framework* [online], www.bankofengland.co.uk/monetarypolicy/framework.htm (Accessed 21 November 2009).

Barrow, B. and Brogan, B. (2009) 'Another blow to savings', *Daily Mail*, 9 January.

Buiter, W. (2009) 'Can the US economy afford a Keynesian stimulus?', *Financial Times*, 5 January.

Communities and Local Government (2009) *Housing Statistics* [online], www.communities.gov.uk/housing/housingresearch/housingstatistics (Accessed 21 November 2009).

European Central Bank (ECB) (2009) *Benefits of Price Stability* [online], www.ecb.europa.eu/mopo/intro/benefits (Accessed 21 November 2009).

European Commission (2009) *Business and Consumer Surveys* [online], www.europa.eu/econom_finance/db_indicators/db_indicators8650_en (Accessed 21 November 2009).

Ferguson, N. (2008) *The Ascent of Money: A Financial History of the World*, London, Penguin.

Howells, P. and Bain, K. (2008) *The Economics of Money, Banking and Finance* (4th edn), London, Prentice Hall.

Hussain, A. (2009) 'Are we right to stick with the stock market?', *The Sunday Times*, 15 March.

Keynes, J.M. (1933) *The Means to Prosperity*, London, Macmillan.

Keynes, J.M. (1936) *The General Theory of Employment, Interest and Money*, London, Macmillan.

Kindleberger, C.P. (1993) *A Financial History of Western Europe*, London, Oxford University Press.

Mackenzie, M. and Oakley, D. (2008) 'Interbank lending grinds to near-standstill', *Financial Times*, 17 September.

Morris, C.R. (2008) *The Two Trillion Dollar Meltdown*, New York, PublicAffairs.

Oakley, D. and Mackenzie, M. (2009) 'Fears of inflation start to surface again', *Financial Times*, 2 April.

Office for National Statistics (ONS) (2009) *The Blue Book*, London, ONS.

Organisation for Economic Co-operation and Development (OECD) (2008) *Annual National Accounts – Main Aggregates*, Paris, OECD.

Organisation for Economic Co-operation and Development (OECD) (2009) *Main Economic Indicators*, Paris, OECD.

Pain, D. and Feltham, C. (1985) 'Stock Market Report: Shares jump again as buying spree continues', *The Times*, 22 November.

Rauchway, E. (2008) *The Great Depression and New Deal: A Very Short Introduction*, Oxford, Oxford University Press.

Redwood, J. and Kauders, K. (2009) 'Is there a bubble in gilts?', *Investors Chronicle*, 16 January.

Saccomanni, F. (2008) *Managing International Financial Instability*, Cheltenham, Edward Elgar.

Stephens, P. (2009) 'Autocratic leadership has failed the Bank of England', *Financial Times*, 30 March.

Trichet, J.C. (2005) *Asset Price Bubbles and Monetary Policy*, European Central Bank [online], www.ecb.int/press/key/date/2005/html/sp050608.en (Accessed 21 November 2009).

Walsh, J. (2008) *Keynes and the Market*, New Jersey, Wiley.

Wolf, M. (2008) 'Keynes offers us the best way to think about the crisis', *Financial Times*, 24 December.

Further reading

Booth, P. (ed.) (2009) *Verdict on the Crash: Causes and Policy Implications*, London, Institute of Economic Affairs.

Skidelsky, R. (2009) *Keynes: the Return of the Master*, London, Penguin Books.

Chapter 6
Bubbles and investment behaviour

Mariana Mazzucato

1 Introduction

Learning outcomes

After reading this chapter, you will:

- understand the definition of an asset price bubble, and importance in the history of market economies
- understand why share volatility and share overvaluation raise questions regarding the rationality by which investors approach investment decisions
- understand key insights from behavioural finance theory
- understand the implications of different theories of investment behaviour for personal investment planning.

When people look back on a bubble, they tend to blame the mess on crookery, greed and the collective insanity of others. What else but madness could explain all those overpriced Dutch tulips? With hindsight, today's mortgage disaster seems ridiculously simple. Wasn't it the fault of barely legal mortgage underwriting, overpaid investment bankers and the intoxication of easy credit? Yet there is an element of the madhouse in that explanation too. Cupidity, fraud and delusion were obviously part of the great bust. But if they are the chief causes of bubbles – which have repeatedly plagued Western finance since its origins in the Italian Renaissance – you have to suppose that civilisation is beset by naivety and manic depression.

(*The Economist*, 2009)

On 24 August 1921 the Dow Jones Industrial Average, the leading index at the time for the New York Stock Exchange, stood at 63.9. By 3 September 1929 it had risen nearly sixfold to 381.2. On 29 October, subsequently known as Black Tuesday, the index fell 38 points to 260, a drop of 12.8 per cent. This spurred a selling spree that, ironically, worsened the problem by clogging the new technologies that stock markets had introduced in the prosperous 'roaring twenties', including the telephone and telegraph. The lack of information led to more panic and selling, with the Dow Jones over two days falling by

23 per cent. It eventually lost 89 per cent of its value between 1929 and 1932 – with the fall encompassing the high-technology, high-growth 'glamour stocks' that had originally got the boom rolling. These price movements are depicted in Figure 1, while the picture on the next page shows the street scenes that resulted in New York.

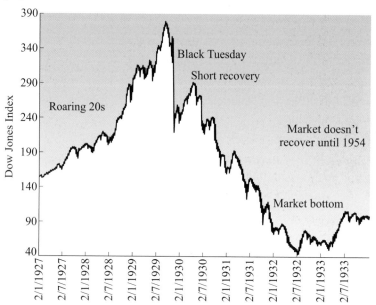

Figure 1 Crash of the Dow Jones Stock Market Index in 1929

(Source: Global Research, 2009)

This chapter asks: what caused this panic selling leading up to the Great Depression – as well as the more recent panic selling and 'madness' in the financial crisis that began in 2007, referenced in the opening quote from *The Economist*? What are the characteristics of investment behaviour, and underlying human behaviour, that can lead to such financial 'anomalies' and take many investors by surprise? And, since they are considered anomalies, what is the normal behaviour that gets contradicted by events such as stock market **bubbles**?

Bubble
The inflation of an asset price, eventually reversed by a sudden burst or a prolonged decline.

Crowds gathered outside the New York Stock Exchange after the 1929 crash

Chapter 5 introduced the demand-side argument that investment under uncertainty is not just mechanically determined by interest rates and the supply of savings. Keynes and his followers argue that investment is governed by 'animal spirits' – the emotion or *affect* which influences human behaviour, especially urging action rather than inaction. This notion of investment behaviour led by animal spirits can help to explain why aggregate business investment (the *I* in the national income equation, which includes spending on physical capital goods) is so volatile. As was discussed in Chapter 5, Keynes used this insight to argue for a greater role for government in the economy, since markets will otherwise generate too little investment when animal spirits are low, leading to periodic economic depressions. Keynes went as far as saying that investment decisions (such as those considered in Chapters 2 to 4) might be better understood through serious examination of such psychological impulses rather than through the sophisticated mathematical models that characterise modern economics.

This insight into psychological aspects driving business investment has also proved very important for understanding fluctuations in financial investment and the periodic build-up and bursting of bubbles, especially in share prices. Research into the psychological foundation of judgements under uncertainty has led to new theories of behavioural finance, which seek to understand individual and collective investment decisions, especially where these involve risk-taking.

Section 2 gives a brief history of financial asset bubbles, revealing some common trends and notable differences that are assessed in Section 3. Sections 4 and 5 look at the degree to which shares can be overvalued and excessively 'volatile', compared to the predictions of asset price models, even in non-bubble periods. Section 6 asks whether these patterns pose problems for some of the theories presented in previous chapters: to what extent are investors rational (as defined in Chapter 2) and markets efficient (as defined in Chapter 4)? Section 7 looks at what behavioural finance theorists have to say about these questions, drawing on the world of experimental economics. Section 8 considers what such insights imply for long-term personal investment planning, and Section 9 concludes.

2 Bubbles in historical perspective

The data in Figure 1, showing share price movements from 1927 to 1933, illustrate a classic bubble pattern. Share prices rise sharply and persistently until the late 1920s, then come crashing down. This sudden burst, revealing the previous expansion to have been built on air, is what earns the name of bubble. The same pattern has been experienced in different markets over the last 200 years: as well as shares, bubbles have been observed in assets as diverse as tulips, sugar, coins, cotton, wheat and land. Sometimes these are limited to a particular country, such as the Dutch tulip bubble discussed below. At other times they start in one economy but then spread to many others. As businesses, banks, financial markets and economies become increasingly interlinked through globalisation, the possibility of such contagion has increased.

Some early bubbles were documented in Charles Mackay's popular 1841 account *Extraordinary Popular Delusions and the Madness of Crowds*. A famous early example was the tulip bubble (1636–37) in Holland. After tulips were introduced from Turkey in the mid-1500s, Holland became the international centre of tulip cultivation, inventing new varieties. Professional growers and wealthy flower fanatics caused the market for rare bulbs to grow very quickly, with bulbs selling at extraordinarily high prices. In 1637, a *Semper Augustus* bulb (with blood-red flames against white) apparently sold for the same price as a large canal-side house in Amsterdam (Walsh, 2008). This price rise later spread to common bulbs. It lasted until bulbs that had sold for 5000 guilders in January 1637 had fallen to 50 guilders just one month later – from gold to onions!

As with many bubbles, the tulip bubble coincided with the introduction of a financial innovation: in this case an early version of futures contracts called *windhandel* (literally, wind trading), allowing traders to sell rights to bulbs that had yet to be planted. This type of trading increased the level of speculation, exacerbating the bubble, as trade became based not only on physical goods but also on abstract goods (Walsh, 2008, p. 72). The tulip crisis is captured symbolically in the painting overleaf by Hendrik Pot (1640), where the goddess of flowers is shown alongside the vices of drinking and money, all in a cart that will soon disappear into the sea. The damage to local industry, which economists refer to as the 'real' economy (as distinct from the abstract economy of asset values), is symbolised by weavers throwing away their equipment.

The tulip mania: *Floras Mallewagen* (1640) by Hendrick Pot (1585–1657)

The 1840s saw a railway bubble, also called railway 'mania', in Britain. There was a speculative frenzy around rail, with many companies (high-tech at the time!) entering the new industry, driven by optimism and confidence of what rail could do for the economy and for individual company profits. Animal spirits soared again, with investors pouring money into the new technology. This caused a fast rise in rail shares, peaking in 1846, when 272 acts of parliament were passed regarding setting up new railway companies. Yet around a third of the railways authorised were never built. Most companies that entered this new industry either failed due to bad business plans or were bought out by a larger competitor before the promised lines were built. In some cases, the companies turned out to be fraudulent, simply transferring investors' money to another business. The bubble burst after 1846.

The 1920s bubble, depicted in Figure 1, became famous due to the stock-market crash of 1929 that sparked the Great Depression. This, like the railway period, was a time of technological fervour, with animal spirits lifted by investors' expectations of how radical innovations would drastically change the way in which people lived their everyday lives. These innovations, which included radio, automobiles, aviation, electrical power grids and the rapid expansion of mass production, drove rapid growth especially in the USA, with a virtuous circle of rising output, incomes and expenditure earning the post-war decade its 'roaring twenties' label. The shares of the main companies that pioneered the innovations, such as General Motors (GM) and Radio Corporation of America (RCA), rose inexorably, becoming 'glamour stocks' that crystallised the optimistic expectations for the new era.

As with the tulip bubble, the 1920s share-price bubble was promoted by financial innovations that responded to, and deepened, public infatuation with the stock market. Pooled investment funds, called investment trusts, took off in the USA in the 1920s. The use of leverage through buying 'on margin' – borrowing part of the cost from the broker – also started in this period and magnified both gains and losses (see Chapter 4, Section 3.4). If an investor bought $100 of shares with only $10 of their own capital, borrowing $90 from a broker, then a 10 per cent rise in the value of their holding to $110 brought a return on their equity of 100 per cent.

Activity 1

What happens if the price in the above example falls by 10 per cent? Or 20 per cent?

In contrast, if the price fell by 10 per cent to $90, the investor lost 100 per cent of their own investment. If the price fell by 20 per cent to $80, the investor not only lost their entire capital ($10), but was now in debt, owing $10 to the broker. Putting some zeros after these figures shows just how serious the bursting of the bubble could become when investors were highly leveraged, with even small price changes potentially leading to bankruptcy.

More recently, the dot-com bubble (1995–2001) was also driven by rapid changes in technology. The internet, and related fields in information technology (IT), saw the rise of many online companies, referred to as dot-coms due to the last letters in their US website addresses. Many of these companies were listed on New York's NASDAQ exchange of shares in technology companies, whose index rose from around 500 to just over 5000 between 1991 and 2000. Figure 2 shows the NASDAQ index as it peaked at 5048 in March 2000, before entering a crash that began on 10 March.

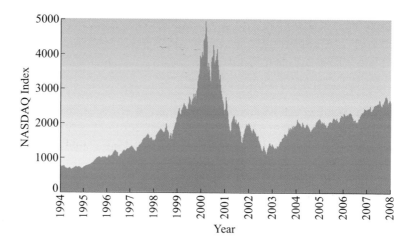

Figure 2 NASDAQ index, 1994–2008

(Source: NASDAQ Composite (^IXIC) Historical series, 1994–2008)

The dot-com bubble exemplifies the effect of animal spirits on financial markets. It is commonly interpreted as having arisen from high expectations about the future growth of the internet, optimism concerning its effect on the firms introducing and using it, and exaggerated expectations about the economic growth that would be enabled by new internet technology. This caused individual and institutional investors to rush to invest in IT-related sectors (manic buying), driving share prices to record high levels – only to come crashing down later (panic selling). The article in Box 1 describes animal spirits at work during this dot-com period and will be referred to again when we delve deeper into the psychological foundations of bubbles in Section 7.

Box 1 Dotcombustion

Twelve months ago, dotcom mania was at its peak. And nowhere was it more obvious than in the panelled rooms of one City investment house. Sitting across the table from two dotcom entrepreneurs, an experienced investment banker was struck by the hideous realisation that the men facing him were trying to float nothing more than an idea for more than £100m. And they had no relevant experience.

'You don't understand,' the ebullient chief executive said. 'This is not about performance, it is about a concept. If we started executing the plan it would lose its purity and investors wouldn't be interested.' The discussion was short and the company never

---

reached the stock market. But, for a few months at the beginning of last year, investors' seemingly insatiable appetite for dotcom companies put normal business rules on hold.

…

Michael Ross, chief executive of Figleaves.com, which sells lingerie online, says: 'You had to be pretty stubborn to sit on the sidelines and predict doom instead of getting involved. People were making real money and many of those who did take the risk still have the fortunes to prove it.' Everybody had a dotcom idea to discuss in the pub. Most never came near fruition. Instead, people ranging from the Queen – who invested in Getmapping.com, an internet mapping company – to housewives, professionals, manual workers and students got involved by investing in dotcoms listed on the seemingly unstoppable stock markets, where demand far outstripped the supply of shares.

…

Michael Jackson, chairman of Elderstreet, the venture capitalist, remains philosophical about the whole experience: 'We all invested in a few [dotcoms]. You look at it now and think you must have been a bit crackers,' he says. 'But at the end of the day you are not paid to sit on your hands while others are making money.'

(Barker, 2001, p. 16)

The railway bubble, 1920s bubble and dot-com bubble illustrate how anticipations about future price increases may be linked to belief in a 'technological revolution', which gives investors exaggerated expectations about how the new technology can create instant fortunes for new businesses and those who back them. These expectations help to mobilise the cheap finance that allows these new technologies to be quickly diffused through the economy. The winners, such as Intel (which supplied key hardware for the internet) and Amazon (which traded successfully through it), owe their survival and much of their growth to these exaggerated expectations, which gave them access to abundant cheap capital. In fact, bubbles often leave a positive legacy in the form of installed technologies that remain after the bubble has burst: the railways and roads that did get built, the high-speed internet. These technologies allow increases in the profitability of current and future firms (through new products and more efficient processes), and in the quality of life (as with the advent of electricity, cheap transport and the internet). Such improvements in the economy's underlying infrastructure and productivity may continue to have positive effects on the stock market in the years after the bubble.

But not everyone can become a millionaire. In fact, most of the firms that are associated with new technologies end up failing very soon. For example, in both the early automobile industry and the early computer industry, almost two-thirds of the hundreds of newly created firms were forced out within the first twenty years, despite a rapidly growing market (Mazzucato, 2002). This is because faith in the profit-making power of these new technologies and industries causes overinvestment in the related firms and infrastructures. Many more automobile and computer companies were launched than could hope to survive, at a cost-effective scale, even if the market fulfilled the brightest growth forecasts. However, as it is impossible to predict which firms will survive, the high failure rate means that many investors will get burned.

In fact, periods associated with major new technologies are often characterised by 'new era' thinking – highly optimistic ideas, so that the period in question represents a turning point for the economy and society. For example, the 1990s dot-com boom was often termed the 'new economy' – suggesting a new era in which intangible knowledge capital (such as software and programming skills) was more important than tangible physical capital and the skills needed to make things. Many researchers believed that the 'new economy' would allow productivity and growth to increase indefinitely, with the business cycle giving way to continuous expansion. This over-optimism was far from new. At the start of the twentieth century, the technological change that led up to the roaring twenties was considered by many to be ushering in a new era of unprecedented growth, as revealed in this quote from the beginning of the century:

> There is nothing now to be foreseen which can prevent the United States from enjoying an era of business prosperity which is entirely without equal in the pages of trade history.
>
> (Sutliff, 1925, p. 3)

Activity 2

Can you think of another major technological change that has produced similar euphoria and overinvestment?

More recently, investors' belief in a 'biotech revolution' has led to similar pronouncements about a possible new era of prosperity, strengthened especially after 2003 by announcements from the Human Genome Project, an international, publicly sponsored programme to map the human genetic code. Box 2 suggests that this led to a bubble in biotechnology, with massive investments in firms, many of which had not yet developed any products and would go out of business very soon. There is a risk that the more recent interest in 'green technologies', designed to reduce and remedy damage to the environment, might see a similar boom–bust cycle, delivering some beneficial innovations but not always rewarding the investors who pour money into them.

Box 2 Is biotech flaming out?

After months of scorching returns, biotechnology investors have been badly burned …

Biotech stocks have been as hot – and volatile – in recent months as Internet stocks. From last July to February 2000, the American Stock Exchange biotech index soared 220 per cent. Protein Design Labs leaped 700 per cent in the three months following Thanksgiving. Cell Therapeutics, trading at $2.75 last September, rocketed to $47 in March of this year – a 1,600 per cent rise.

Investors gleefully piled in. But in March the sector swooned, with stocks like Protein Design Labs, Human Genome Sciences and Millennium Pharmaceuticals losing more than half of their value. The biotech index plunged 35 per cent in just two weeks. The sector had become so speculative that one trigger for this carnage was a relatively innocuous announcement by President Clinton and British Prime Minister Tony Blair that data about human genes 'should be made freely available to scientists everywhere.'

The question for investors now: Is the biotech boom over or is there still serious money to be made here? Some seasoned biotech watchers are clearly sceptical, having previously witnessed the sector's tendency to boom, then bust. In '91 and '92 the biotech

---

index soared 320 per cent, but most biotech stocks went nowhere in the years that followed. By March '99 the index had returned a grand total of just 10 per cent in 6.5 years. Mort Cohen, CEO of Clarion Partners and a long time biotech follower, warns: 'Old biotech investors like myself know it won't be good forever.'

(Moskowitz, 2000)

Some bubbles, like the tulip bubble, involve speculation that may be unconnected with any underlying technological change. The financial crisis that began in 2007 could be traced to a bubble in the US housing market whose impact spread internationally. It had less to do with *technological* innovation than with *financial* innovation, particularly the structured products described in Chapter 3, Section 5.2, and the derivatives outlined in Chapter 4, Section 3.

Similarly, the property bubble in Japan, which saw the residential real estate price index increase by 400 per cent between 1980 and 1989, appears related to neither technological nor financial innovations. The highest peak prices were in Tokyo's Ginza district, with the most valuable properties reaching 100 million yen (approximately £6 million) per square metre in 1989. While the tulip bubble came down with a crash, the Japanese property bubble simply stopped inflating. However, since investors had been speculating on further house price increases, and using inflated property values as security for loans, the end of price rises caused a major crisis in the Japanese banking system. The banks took almost a decade to recover, and Japan had still not regained its buoyant pre-bubble economic growth rates even in 2009. Fears of repeating this experience were one motive for other governments' unusually rapid and extensive fiscal and monetary loosening in response to the bursting of the US housing bubble in 2008, which caused a general stock market crash and international financial crisis.

Given that some bubbles can be traced to major technological changes, and others to pure speculation around the property market with no technological basis, the question arises: what features do bubbles have in common besides the rise and fall of the prices of the assets in question?

3 Categorising asset bubbles

In his book *Manias, Panics, and Crashes*, Kindleberger (1989) defines different stages of bubbles, triggered by a major change (technological or institutional) in the economic system that brings about new hopes for profit opportunities, and how the bubble develops after that. The different phases are illustrated in Figure 3:

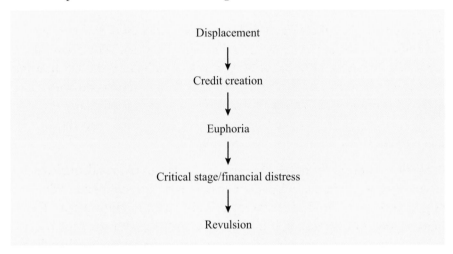

Figure 3 Stages of a bubble

Displacement occurs after an exogenous shock introduces new profit opportunities in a particular sector or in the entire economy. An example is the advent of the internet. Displacement could also be triggered by a new institutional structure, such as monetary policy that suddenly introduces (eases) money into the system. Such relaxed monetary policy is often accused of triggering both the Japanese land and equity bubble in the 1980s and the US housing bubble in 2008. These new profit opportunities cause animal spirits to rise, inducing an increase in both financial and physical investment – potentially leading to an economic boom.

This phase is followed by a credit creation phase, which releases money to finance the investment that is needed to fuel the boom. This part of the bubble is characterised by increased bank lending and the creation of new lending institutions. Increased lending triggers increased investment and income. Figure 4 shows how monetary creation in this period caused household debt, shown as a percentage of household income, to reach record levels during the dot-com boom.

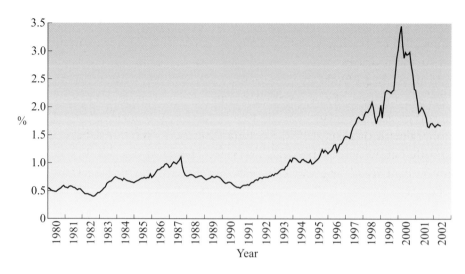

Figure 4 US margin debt as a percentage of household personal income, 1980–2002

(Source: Montier, 2007, Table 38.2)

Overtrading
Moving too frequently between one share or fund and another.

The next phase is one of euphoria, a phase of speculation and **overtrading**. This denotes the placing of excessive bets made on the basis of exaggerated expectations about the future growth potential of particular shares. It is in this phase that the bubble reaches its peak. Euphoria reflects over-optimism about prospective returns, underestimation of the risk (reflected in loans to individuals and companies with inadequate guarantees or collateral), and overconfidence about being able to control the situation (Montier, 2007). The dynamics of overconfidence are further explored in Section 7.

The euphoria phase is characterised by momentum trading (see Chapter 4), where investors try to extrapolate past high rates of growth (past momentum) into the future (future momentum). Fund managers can be drawn into exacerbating the bubble by their need to outperform their peers and their worry about being left behind. Financial investors and company managers are persuaded by 'new era' thinking, often engaging in excessive leveraging, and putting too much faith in mergers and acquisitions to solve structural problems.

The most critical stage in the bubble begins when well-informed 'insiders' start to get worried about the future and decide to cash in their investments before it is too late. Their move out of assets into cash puts downward pressure on asset prices and sends a signal that eventually induces investors as a whole to rush for liquidity. The 'real' economy is doubly hit, by a jump in the cost of debt and equity finance and a fall in sales, as faster-moving investors sit on their cash piles while slower-moving investors absorb their losses. This leads to a period of financial distress when companies begin to default on their liabilities and possibly go bankrupt. Revelation of a 'swindle' or fraud often worsens the loss of confidence (Montier, 2007). Deceits that accompanied the financial crisis that began in 2007 included the concealment of toxic debts at Lehman Brothers investment bank until shortly before its collapse, and exposure of the largest ever US investment fraud by previously respected fund manager Bernard Madoff.

The revulsion phase begins as this process spirals downwards, with banks becoming very cautious, restraining credit even after they regain liquidity. This unwillingness to lend can then lead to a major recession as firms have to cut back production (hence employment) due to their inability to get loans. This may also involve consumers finding it more difficult to borrow.

All this sounds quite negative, but the degree to which, after they burst, bubbles are associated with any positive legacy depends on whether buying behaviour was motivated by fundamentals as opposed to pure speculation. Referring to the dot-com bubble, former US Undersecretary of Commerce Robert Shapiro argued that:

> The American bubble represented an excess of something that in itself has real value for the economy – information technologies. The bubble began in overinvestment in IT and spread to much of the stock market; but at its core, much of the IT was economically sound and efficient. Further, these dynamics also played a role in the capital spending boom of the 1990s, and much of that capital spending translated into permanently higher productivity. The result is that the American bubble should not do lasting damage to the American economy.
>
> (Shapiro, 2002)

The same argument could be made about the railway bubble: a total of 10,010 km of railway line were built in Britain as a result of projects authorised between 1844 and 1846. Only another 8000 km have been built in the century and a half since then. But bubbles that began with other types of shocks, such as financial liberalisation that unleashes cheap credit used in speculation, can exhibit very similar dynamics of overinvestment and rising asset prices without any lastingly positive effects. Once tulips were back to the price of onions, Holland was not measurably better off in terms of national income and productivity. Beneficial legacies from the 1980s Japanese and 2000s US property bubbles may prove equally hard to find.

The time taken for an economy to recover after a bubble bursts might also be related to the source of the initial shock. Bubbles rooted in productive technology appear to allow faster recovery than those with no clear path to the higher returns implied by rising asset prices. Financial regulations, introduced by politicians reacting to bubbles, may also affect this recovery process, as was seen in Chapter 5.

4 Overvalued compared to what?

So far we have referred to the sustained rapid rise and eventual fall of asset prices that define bubbles. These are said to burst because the companies involved are overvalued. But the use of this term suggests that we have some notion of the underlying correct value – with the size of the bubble measuring the distance from that underlying value. So the identification of bubbles must be linked to a theory of asset price determination. Accusations of 'madness' on the part of investors, as in the opening quote from *The Economist*, imply a model of what should be happening when investors are sane. So what is normal investment behaviour that makes stock market bubbles appear abnormal?

Traditional finance theorists, who espouse the efficient markets hypothesis discussed in Chapter 4, offer one definition of the bubble and what it is departing from. Their assessment has been challenged more recently by behavioural finance theorists. The remainder of this chapter is aimed at helping you to understand the ongoing debate among finance theorists about what determines asset prices. For this, we must start by questioning some of the assumptions that have been made up to now about what constitutes a fair price for an asset.

4.1 Bubbles and asset valuation

In any bubble, buying driven by anticipation of future price increases leads to shares or other assets becoming overvalued. In a stock market bubble, excessive demand raises most or all share prices until they bear little relation to the underlying intrinsic value of the share. Recall from Chapter 2, Section 4, that intrinsic value can be calculated through a present value formula, the dividend valuation model (DVM), which links the price of an asset to the present discounted value of its expected future dividends, with a given level of risk. Hence a share is overvalued if its market price exceeds the present value of the future income that would be received by buying and holding it (the intrinsic value). If an asset is overvalued, then investors have inserted cash flow forecasts into this model that are too optimistic and/or excessively weighted future earnings by applying too low a discount rate. This was the case before 2001 with the majority of dot-com companies, which never generated earnings to justify their high stock prices before the crash.

Thus a stock market bubble can be defined more precisely as a type of economic bubble taking place when the price of shares rises to become overvalued when compared to those shares' intrinsic value, based on asset valuation models. Since bubbles can also occur with other types of assets, a similar definition can be applied to these.

Bubbles gain momentum when overvaluation breeds more overvaluation, or undervaluation breeds more undervaluation, with expectations prompting buying or selling decisions that make them self-fulfilling. This momentum may be sector-specific (as when tied to railways, IT or biotech) or index-specific (as with NASDAQ). While some shares are overvalued, others can be undervalued, especially when funds are pulled out of some sectors to pile into others. For example, in the dot-com boom, technology-related shares were overvalued while low-growth, low-risk companies such as breweries were undervalued.

Most of the new internet-based companies in the dot-com boom experienced very large increases in their share prices, based on future cash flow expectations, including now-famous ones like Amazon and eBay. Since most of the highly-valued companies were based on ideas that never came to fruition, such overvaluations are described as a 'madhouse' in accounts such as the opening quote of this chapter or the article in Box 1. In hindsight, Amazon and eBay shares were not necessarily overvalued back in 1999, since they later generated a high stream of cash flows, and many original shareholders became millionaires. But the majority of the other dot-com shares proved to be overvalued, since these companies ultimately earned little or nothing. Those who backed Amazon and made millions may have been unusually far-sighted, or they may just have been luckier than those who bet on equally innovative firms that then went bust. During the railway mania of the 1840s it was common for managers to issue shares in a company, watch them rise, and then sell out before the company had even started to produce, let alone earned any profit. In the end, lines did get built and some railway companies made profit, but most failed to justify their optimistic early valuations.

The biotechnology industry, featured in Box 2, is another example of high expectations about future cash flows leading to overvalued stocks. In 1991–92 the biotech index, which tracks shares in this sector, soared 320 per cent. But most of the companies were virtually just research and development (R&D) labs, without any products destined for the market. Even 15 years later, only around 20 per cent of all publicly held biotech companies had any products on the market or were earning royalties based on products commercialised by partners (Pisano, 2006). However, as with dot-com, some of these companies (like Genentech) did turn out to be highly profitable. It is high expectations around a specific sector, combined with the inability to predict which of the companies will become market leaders, that makes investment in a bubble so risky.

4.2 Detecting a bubble

Overvaluation is easier to detect in hindsight, after a bubble has burst. But there are also various indicators that may signal that an asset is becoming overvalued. Most such indicators compare the price of a share to the underlying intrinsic value of the firm, linked to fundamentals such as its reported earnings and profits. For example, the price–earnings (P/E) ratio will be relatively high when a firm is overvalued. Yet, as discussed in Chapter 2 (Section 4.3), the high P/E ratio may also be a reflection of well-founded investor expectations that a company's earnings will rise significantly, perhaps due to its potential leadership in the use of a new technology. If a high P/E ratio company does become a market leader, it will turn out not to have been overvalued. A high P/E ratio may suggest that investors are expecting higher earnings growth for this company than for others with a lower P/E ratio. In fact, the P/E ratio is relevant only as a relative measure, comparing firms to other firms in a given industry.

Activity 3

Consider why a firm might have a high P/E ratio even though it is not a high technology firm with high expected growth.

Companies that use more traditional technologies may exhibit a high P/E ratio because of unusually low earnings, rather than a high share price. Earnings (E), the denominator of the P/E ratio, may be depressed because the firm has had a recent run of unusually low earnings, or because it has just made some large physical investments, which reduce earnings by increasing depreciation. Another possibility is that a fall in interest rates has lowered the required rate of return on the share and so raised its price, leading to a higher P/E ratio.

5 Volatility and animal spirits

Bubbles are often characterised not only by overvaluation of shares, but also by very volatile share prices. Volatility seems to be a characteristic of stock markets, even in non-bubble times, but it can gain more relevance and impact during bubbles. Here too we must ask: very volatile compared to what? The comparison is with the volatility of underlying fundamentals that prices are, in theory, related to. **Excess volatility** is a specific measure of volatility, showing the degree to which the standard deviation of share prices over time is higher than the standard deviation of the underlying earnings or dividends over time.

Excess volatility
The degree to which share prices are more volatile than the underlying earnings (or other fundamentals).

In an influential article entitled 'Do stock prices move too much to be justified by subsequent changes in dividends?', Robert Shiller (1981) finds that the volatility of share prices is much too high, even in non-bubble periods, to be justified by the volatility of the underlying dividends or earnings. The data in Figure 5, taken from Shiller's (2000) influential book *Irrational Exuberance* illustrate that, over the last 150 years, a main index of US shares (the S&P500) has always been more volatile than the index of underlying earnings of the companies that it represents. This figure reveals that, not surprisingly, the degree of excess volatility is especially high in the periods characterised by technological revolutions, such as in the 1920s and 1990s as discussed earlier.

Another way to look at these data is to compare the actual share price index with the prices that would theoretically emerge if share prices had been driven by the dividend valuation model (DVM, introduced in Chapter 2, Section 4.3); this is done in Figure 6. The flatter line shows the prices that would have occurred between 1871 and 2000 if they had been derived by discounting the historical series of dividends, which we now know. (To derive this, Shiller uses a constant discount rate equal to the historical average real monthly return on the market from January 1871 to June 1999, or 0.6 per cent a month; but this assumption is not key to the results.) By using the *actual* dividend series, which we can now find out, rather than the *expected* ones required by the DVM, we can work out how prices would have moved if investors used this model and knew the entire real series in the future. This is an assumption of perfect foresight, often used in economic models.

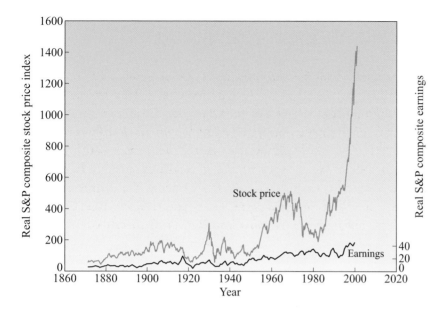

Figure 5 US stock prices and earnings, 1871–2000

(Source: Shiller, 2000, p. 6, Figure 1.1)

Note: Upper series is real (inflation-corrected) S&P Composite Stock Price Index, monthly, January 1871 to January 2000. Lower series shows real S&P composite earnings, January 1871 to September 1999, calculated by Shiller using: S&P Statistical Service; US Bureau of Labor Statistics; Cowles and associates, Common Stock Indexes, and Warren and Pearson, Gold and Prices.

Figure 6 shows that the DVM consistently underestimates the volatility of stock prices. That is, *actual* share prices are consistently more volatile than the theoretical share prices that would emerge using the DVM, if investors had perfect foresight. Although this difference is evident from the figure, the difference in volatility can be more formally measured by comparing the standard deviation of both series over time. When plotted in log-scale (as you learned in Chapter 2, Section 2.1), real stock prices are seen to be on average 2.7 times higher than the intrinsic fundamental share value that emerges from the dividend valuation model (Montier, 2007).

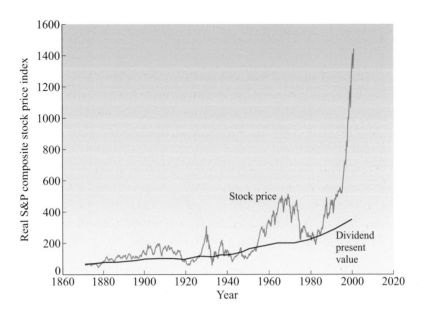

Figure 6 US stock prices and dividend present value, 1871–2000

(Source: Shiller, 2000, p. 186)

Excess volatility suggests that the problem with bubbles is not just one of share price overvaluation. It also means that shares can swing from being highly overvalued to highly undervalued, with the changes having little relationship to changes in the 'fundamentals'. The problem is related to share markets' overreaction to good and bad news, which is examined more deeply in the next section.

6 Efficiency or madness of crowds?

In Section 4 we saw that overvaluation seems to breed more overvaluation. Far from being self-correcting, markets can sometimes swing away from fundamental values as past movement incites expectation of further movement. This also appears in the volatility data of Figures 5 and 6. The high volatility of shares, and its lack of correlation with the volatility of underlying fundamentals, does not appear to decrease over time towards some 'average' level. This not only causes problems for the dividend valuation model set out in Chapter 2, but also challenges the assumptions behind the efficient markets hypothesis (EMH) discussed in Chapter 4.

Recall that the EMH says that financial prices accurately reflect the available data on fundamentals. So prices are the best available forecasts of those variables. Any changes in those prices can only be due to unpredictable news. This is why the EMH holds that share prices will follow an unpredictable, random walk. The random walk means that there are no identifiable structural aspects to price determination that would enable future prices to be predicted from past price data. There is no correlation between past and current prices.

According to the EMH, any mistakes in calculating price are soon corrected by the market. For example, if high-tech shares tend to be overvalued, due to over-optimism about the future growth of high-tech companies, then according to the EMH, investors will over time learn to adjust these share prices downwards. So this information should eventually be incorporated in the correct price. In statistics this is referred to as 'reversion to the mean': overshooting will result in prices falling back towards the mean, undershooting will result in prices rising back towards the mean.

If, on the other hand, higher than average returns this year cause higher than average returns next year, there is a **positive feedback** mechanism at work, resulting in some share prices being persistently 'high'. Positive feedback means that there are reinforcement mechanisms that drive a system increasingly faster in the direction in which it is already going. This could be towards the equilibrium, as assumed by advocates of free markets, but could also be away from it: there is no automatic reversion to the mean. The dot-com bubble is an example of the second case, a 'vicious circle' moving prices away from equilibrium rather than a 'virtuous circle' moving them towards it. The eventual crash could be

Positive feedback
A process through which a shock to a system generates further movement in the same direction; also called 'cumulative causation' or 'reinforcement mechanism'.

interpreted as the market correcting itself, but since it took many years to recover, it is hard to justify this with a theory of 'efficiency'.

Investors caught out by phases of positive feedback are not necessarily irrational or 'mad', as implied in our opening quote from *The Economist*. Insights from psychology do not imply that most investors are blindly following the herd, with no minds of their own (though this is sometimes the case). The more usual case is that they are constrained in their rationality. Understanding the form of such constraints brings us into the world of behavioural finance.

7 Behavioural finance

The analysis of share investment in Chapter 2 assumes rational choices, with risk-averse investors seeking the best returns by maximising the net present value of future dividends. The finding that share price movements are not 'justified', when compared to movements in the underlying fundamentals, suggests that other factors may be helping to determine investment behaviour. Do animal spirits have an identifiable psychological foundation when considered in relation to financial investment?

Recent advances in behavioural finance have tried to answer this provocative question, taking issue with the concept of rationality used by economists and finance theorists. **Behavioural finance** applies psychological research on decision making to investment decisions. A core element concerns how investors in the 'real world' form their expectations and beliefs, and hence their valuations (for example of a company's future earnings or the risk-adjusted interest rate).

7.1 Bounded rationality

As you learned in Chapter 2, Section 2.2, the word 'rationality' is used in economic theory to mean that economic agents (consumers, business managers, financial investors) pursue goals in the most efficient way possible. Firms try to maximise their profits and investors their returns. In the preceding chapters, we have assumed that investors have a model through which they can calculate the expected price of a bond or share, and that their decisions on whether (or how much) to invest in a particular asset are based on that model. There may of course be a variety of models, with varying degrees of complexity, but we have assumed that through rational analysis investors can forecast the price of a security, and hence its rate of return, which then guides their investment behaviour. Given a person's level of risk-aversion (recognising, for example, that an old-age pensioner may be more risk-averse than a 20-year-old), they will choose a particular product based on its risk–return relationship, aiming to maximise the return for a particular level of risk.

Rather than assuming rational behaviour from the start, behavioural finance theory asks: 'What do we know about financial decision making from experiment and observation?' Using this approach, behavioural finance researchers have discovered that investors – even professional

Behavioural finance
An approach to investor behaviour that takes account of departures from 'rational' decision making and their impact on financial markets.

Neoclassical economics
A development of classical economics that recognises some demand-side problems but still traces them to price and wage inflexibility, and assumes that decisions are taken as if individuals have full information that they process rationally.

ones – do not base their decisions about bonds, shares, property and other asset allocations on the exact calculations required for maximisation. In so doing, behavioural economics challenges the concepts of rationality at the centre of traditional economics (often called **neoclassical economics**) and portfolio theory, as introduced in Chapter 3.

Behavioural finance theorists often talk about **bounded rationality**. The main idea is that even though investors try to maximise their returns, their ability to do so is greatly constrained by access to information, time and computational ability. Rather than maximising behaviour, they focus on **satisficing**, getting a good-enough result that takes them above a minimum target. Because they don't have the time or ability to find the most optimal (efficient) solution, they simplify their choices by following a set rules. Examples of this in economics include managers who fix a product's price as a conventional mark-up over costs, even though the profit-maximising price might vary over time, and consumers who go to the store that they consider the cheapest overall rather than shopping around for each item.

Bounded rationality
The idea that individuals' rationality is limited by the information that they have access to, available time and cognitive (brain power) limitations.

7.2 Herd behaviour

A core finding of behavioural finance is that when investors are predicting stock prices, they try to anticipate not the fundamental value but *what others think the fundamental value might be*. It could be argued that this is just another type of rationality, but it is not well explained by the definition that economists normally use. Keynes, whose challenge to traditional macroeconomics was reviewed in Chapter 5, described this sort of alternative investment behaviour when he likened investment choices to an old-style beauty contest, where beauty is not in the eyes of the beholder but in the eyes of those who most closely second-guess all the other beholders:

Satisficing
Looking for a satisfactory, sufficient solution rather than the most efficient one.

> Professional investment may be likened to those newspaper competitions in which the competitors have to pick out the six prettiest faces from a hundred photographs, the prize being awarded to the competitor whose choice most nearly corresponds to the average preferences of the competitors as a whole; so that each competitor has to pick, not those faces which he himself finds prettiest, but those which he thinks likeliest to catch the fancy of the other competitors, all of whom are looking at the problem from the same point of view. It is not a case of choosing

those which, to the best of one's judgment, are really the prettiest, or even those which average opinion genuinely, thinks the prettiest. We have reached the third degree where we devote our intelligences to anticipating what average opinion expects the average opinion to be. And there are some, I believe, who practise the fourth, fifth, and higher degrees.

(Keynes, 1936, p. 156)

One of the main insights of behavioural economists is that people who communicate regularly with one another start to think in similar ways – sometimes referred to as herd behaviour or following the herd. This contrasts with the assumption in the efficient markets hypothesis that investors' decisions are independent of one another, so there is no correlation between two people's decisions, or even between one person's decisions today and tomorrow.

Herd effects may occur due to peer pressure or to individuals assuming that because a lot of people are doing something it must be right. Classroom experiments, which behavioural finance theorists use extensively, have shown that pressure of numbers can convince people of choices that would otherwise seem completely wrong. In one well-tried experiment, individuals are shown two lines, one long and one short, and asked which is the longer. If they are told that before them everyone has chosen the shorter one, they tend to choose that one too – apparently changing their perception, convincing themselves that it really is longer. They are not necessarily acting irrationally – just reasoning, from experience, that if so many people made that decision *then it must be right*.

Activity 4

Re-read Box 1. How might this support the idea that investors follow 'herd behaviour'?

The quote in Box 1 by Michael Jackson, the chairman of a venture capital firm, highlights how investment managers tried to rationalise their late 1990s decisions on dot-com firms by citing exactly this type of herd behaviour: 'at the end of the day you are not paid to sit on your hands while others are making money'. These investors may now seem irrational, but their actions at the time reflected a very reasonable fear of being left behind. Shiller (2000) points out that if a fund manager had acted on the 'irrational exuberance' warning issued by Alan Greenspan (then chairman of the Federal Reserve Board) in December 1996, drawing attention to an impending bubble, then he or she would have missed out on another 40 per cent appreciation in high-tech stocks by not holding on until 2001. Fund investors are judged on how well they perform compared to their competitors: so they can escape blame if they stay on a bandwagon that loses money for everyone, while being condemned if they jump off one that others go on to make more money with. Hence to maximise profits, investors should in fact act in this seemingly irrational way – as long as they get out in time.

Herd behaviour can develop when information is passed between individuals so that an initial decision by one person leads to everyone doing the same. An example, based on observation, is the choice of which restaurant to go to. If one person by chance chooses a particular restaurant, a passer-by undecided in their choice may compare the one next door (still empty) to this one, and assume that the one that someone else has entered must be better. If the same reasoning is followed by all those passing by in search of a restaurant, the first restaurant will soon fill up, while the other stays empty: not because the first restaurant is necessarily better, but simply because the first individual decided to go there, even if they did so randomly. The way in which information is created and diffused, leading to what might be an arbitrary initial decision becoming self-reinforcing, is referred to as an

Information cascade
The process of people ignoring their own private information and basing a decision on what others have decided to do (e.g. invest in certain stocks). It can lead to herd behaviour, where many people do the same thing, ignoring a logical course of action.

information cascade. These cascades can lead to many following the same behaviour even if it goes against what might appear (for example to economists) as rational. However, it is not correct to say that information cascades have to be an outcome of irrational behaviour – the agent may be rationally thinking that if many others have made that decision, then it must be right. This is an example of bounded rationality, defined earlier.

Many have highlighted the role of the media in creating information cascades, by not just reporting events but also creating them. In their search for viewers, listeners and readers, the media may encourage herd behaviour by, for example, blowing out of proportion the significance of market rallies and declines. The short-term focus of many stock-market investors (which may reflect other behavioural biases, as detailed shortly) means that expectations are very sensitive to new information, and media reporting may induce an exaggerated response to this, so that price movements overshoot.

7.3 Prospect theory

In 2002, cognitive psychologist Daniel Kahneman received the Nobel Prize for Economics for radical discoveries using classroom experiments, many conducted with Amos Tversky, to study economic decision making under risk and uncertainty (Kahneman and Tversky, 1979). These revealed two aspects of human behaviour that do not conform to the assumptions of rationality discussed earlier. First, emotions often work against the type of self-control that is required for rational decision making. Second, people often do not understand the choices that they are given, so that even if they think that they are acting rationally, they will make choices that suggest otherwise. These 'cognitive difficulties' are the reason why behavioural theory relies on bounded rationality, not the full rationality that economists traditionally assume.

Kahneman and Tversky devised an approach called prospect theory to account for the observed strong asymmetry between the way in which we make decisions involving gains and the way in which we make decisions involving losses. This describes how people make choices, including financial decisions, featuring alternatives that involve risk. It is called *prospect* theory because of the way in which people view their prospects of winning or losing. Behavioural research revealed that choices using the same information can vary with the way it is presented or 'framed'. In particular, people will generally exhibit risk-aversion when a choice is framed one way and risk-seeking behaviour when the same choice is re-framed another way. This framing effect means that decisions on an investment opportunity will depend on whether the opportunity is framed in terms of a loss or in terms of a gain – even if the underlying information is exactly the same. This challenges the conventional assumption, used in Chapter 2, that investors have a given level of risk-aversion when seeking to maximise returns. An individual's degree of risk-aversion changes depending on how a situation is presented. Box 3 looks at different classroom experiments that Kahneman and Tversky made to illustrate the framing effect.

Box 3 Are you risk-averse?

The asymmetry between the way in which we make decisions involving gains and decisions involving losses is one of the most striking findings of prospect theory. It is also one of the most useful for understanding investment. Where significant sums are involved, most people will reject a fair gamble in favour of a certain gain: getting $100,000 for certain is preferred to a 50–50 possibility of getting $200,000 or nothing. When the options are framed as gains, people are risk-averse. But what about losses? Kahneman and Tversky's first (1979) paper on prospect theory described an experiment showing that our choices between negative outcomes are mirror images of our choices between positive outcomes. In one of their experiments they first asked the subjects to choose between (a) an 80 per cent chance of winning $4000 and a 20 per cent chance of winning nothing, and (b) a 100 per cent chance of receiving $3000. Even though the risky choice (a) has a higher mathematical expectation (expected return), $3200, it was found that 80 per cent of the subjects chose (b), the certainty of $3000. Under this framing they were risk-averse.

Then Kahneman and Tversky offered a choice between (a) the risk of an 80 per cent chance of losing $4000 and a 20 per cent chance of breaking even, and (b) a 100 per cent chance of losing $3000. Now 92 per cent of the respondents chose (a), the gamble, even though its mathematically expected loss of $3200 was again larger than the certain loss in (b) of $3000. When the choice is re-framed to involve losses, people are risk-seekers, not risk-averse.

(Adapted from Bernstein, 1998, p. 272)

Some other general features of 'irrational' investment behaviour, highlighted by behavioural finance, are listed here. As you read them, consider how each poses problems for the assumptions of informational efficiency in the EMH, as well as the assumptions of investor rationality made in portfolio theory.

- *Retrievability.* Investors often give too much weight to the most recent events. Headlines on a recent fall in the stock market will provoke a large reaction, which should not happen if people adopt a longer time horizon. Shiller (2000) even claims that the rise of speculative bubbles, with the 1630s tulip mania, began with the rise of newspapers. The media help to make information publicly available, but they can also cause large groups of people to think in similar ways, creating information cascades that lead to self-fulfilling prophecy. Reports of financial disaster can *become* a disaster due to reactions to the reports.

- *Excessive discounting.* Closely related to the overweighting of current or immediately past events is a tendency to attach little weight to events that occur some time in the future. This often seems to make sense, when the future is very uncertain. But it means that many investors, if they make present-value calculations at all, do so with a higher discount rate than is featured in the valuation models of Chapter 2. This excessive discounting, assigning the future a low weight compared with the present, could account for the many surveys suggesting that people are on average not saving enough for their retirement, even if they are competently handling their money from day to day (see Chapter 8).

- *Loss-aversion.* Investors tend (as recounted in Box 3) to react more to the possibility of a loss than to the possibility of a gain; laboratory tests suggest 2 to 2.5 times as much. This can give rise to panic-selling behaviour and overreaction to stock market volatility.

- *Representativeness.* Investors may wrongly believe certain events to be interdependent, so that the recent sequence of outcomes gives a basis for predicting the next one. Supporters of the EMH argue that this is what afflicts investors when they try using charts or technical analysis to predict share price movements using past price data, not realising that (according to the hypothesis) prices move at random. Two opposite tendencies have been observed in relation to random, unconnected events. Some investors may start to believe that a long run of a particular outcome makes that outcome more likely next time (the 'hot hand fallacy'), others that the long sequence makes a *different* outcome more likely next time (the 'gambler's fallacy'). Investors committing both types of error may be present in the market, but there is no guarantee that their effects will cancel out.

- *Narrow framing.* Also related to representativeness, investors tend to focus on the short term even when their investments are long term. Someone who is 30 years old should not worry too much about how short-term price movements affect their pension plan, but evidence suggests that they often do. Daily and monthly volatility figures are given more importance than annual volatility figures, even when the latter are simple averages of the former (presenting the same data in a different way). This suggests that many people do not understand **time diversification** as a rational investor should.

Time diversification
The practice of investing and/or cashing in investments in a series of lump sums spread over time, in order to remove the risk of choosing a bad time to invest (when prices are high) or disinvest (when prices are low).

Investors who don't understand this may react to short-term losses, taking money out of the stock market during bad times, and so miss out on longer-term gains. Many people fear investing in shares due to their higher volatility (compared to bonds), even though their long-run returns have historically been higher.

- *Overconfidence*. Investors, especially those who believe in active management, are often unjustifiably overconfident in their own abilities to pick winners. They reinforce this by ascribing gains to their own expertise and talent, while blaming losses on the economy, bad luck or someone else. This has the effect of encouraging too much investment during good times (since rising asset values are viewed as a product of personal skill, not benign conditions), and too little in bad times (which are linked to malign conditions beyond the individual's control). Overconfidence has been used to explain why some people hold portfolios that seem far from rational, for example not well diversified. It can also explain irrational acts, such as frequent trading, whose gains are wiped out by transaction costs. And it can help to account for the 'greater fool hypothesis', followed by some traders, who believe that it is always possible to resell an asset at profit, even if bought when already overvalued, because there will always be a greater fool who is willing to pay the higher price.

Activity 5

Re-read Box 1 on Dotcombustion, and use the article to provide examples of the behavioural biases outlined here.

The description of dot-com investors in Box 1 shows them committing an error of representativeness: many thought that the boom would go on forever, causing them to ignore their own normal ways of conducting business. Dot-com entrepreneurs, many of whom had no relevant experience, were also overconfident of their likelihood of success, and managed to transmit this overconfidence to many of their investors.

The behavioural finance critique of efficient markets is thus based less on the availability of information than on how that information is interpreted and applied. Lack of access to information can inhibit market efficiency, and give rise to the mis-selling of financial products discussed in Chapter 7. But the behavioural approach reveals problems even when information is perfect and complete, due to the different ways in which people understand and process it. This is why behavioural economists often do experiments in a closed environment where relevant information can be specified fully. For example, role-playing investors are shown fundamental data on a company, and asked to decide whether to invest in its shares. Sometimes real-world conditions come close to a controlled experimental environment, as when investors are asked to value a security (such as a government bond) with very little uncertainty, whose fundamental value is actually observable. Experiments suggest that even in these 'controlled' environments, investment behaviour can be quite irrational, showing biases like overconfidence and representativeness that work against maximisation.

7.4 Back to fat tails?

Another critique of the EMH has arisen not from classroom experiments on investor behaviour, but from studying the statistical distributions of investment returns. Here, empirical evidence is used to question the assumption that returns follow a normal distribution, with major implications for finance theory when this assumption is dropped (Mandelbrot and Taleb, 2005). Remember that a basic implication of the Capital Asset Pricing Model (CAPM), introduced in Chapter 3, is that only systematic risk (beta) can bring increased return, because all unsystematic risk can in theory be diversified away. As the standard deviation of returns is used to proxy the degree of risk, this theory relies on a particular distribution of returns, based on the normal distribution (also referred to as the bell curve) introduced in Chapter 2, Section 4.4. If the mean is the expected value, then the standard deviation from that mean is taken to be the risk of the investment, showing the probability of returns differing by a particular amount from the expected value. In a normal distribution, most events cluster around the mean, so that those that lie 2.5 (or more) standard deviations from the mean are essentially ignored. Such events are deemed almost impossible, or so rare that they don't matter.

Critics of this assumption draw attention to the role of **high sigma events**, which have proved to be much less rare than the bell curve assumes – such as the sudden fall of major stock markets on 'Black Monday', 19 October 1987. They argue that the actual distribution of returns appears to be much 'fatter' than the normal distribution implies. A distribution with fat tails (as in Chapter 2, Figure 15) means that high

High sigma event
An event that, if normally distributed, should be very unlikely, as shown by its large standard deviation (sigma) from the mean.

sigma events are not so unusual, and have a higher probability of occurring than the normal distribution allows.

The implication is that investors not only have cognitive limitations as revealed by behavioural finance, but also have been wrongly trained to disregard large market moves as near impossible. In a provocative *Fortune* magazine article called 'How the finance gurus get risk all wrong', Mandelbrot and Taleb (2005) claim that while the bell curve works well for the study of physical variables like height and weight, it works terribly for finance:

> Your mutual fund's annual report, for example, may contain a measure of risk (usually something called beta). It would indeed be useful to know just how risky your fund is, but this number won't tell you. Nor will any of the other quantities spewed out by the pseudoscience of finance: standard deviation, the Sharpe ratio, variance, correlation, alpha, value at risk, even the Black–Scholes option pricing model. The problem with all these measures is that they are built upon the statistical device known as the bell curve. This means they disregard big market moves: they focus on the grass and miss out on the (gigantic) trees. Rare and unpredictably large deviations like the collapse of Enron's stock price in 2001 or the spectacular rise of Cisco's in the 1990s have a dramatic impact on long-term returns – but 'risk' and 'variance' disregard them. … The German mark's move from four per dollar to four trillion per dollar after World War I should have taught economists to beware the bell curve.
>
> (Mandelbrot and Taleb, 2005, p. 99)

While the EMH assumes that share prices follow a random walk, making unpredictable and uncorrelated steps, these authors argue that it ignores giant leaps (high sigma events), which are far from rare, are often correlated with one another, and have major effects on market outcomes. Mandelbrot and Taleb interpret different types of financial crises, including the crash of 1929 and the more recent crisis that began in 2007, as direct results of investors assuming that the risk of market returns is the same as that in lottery-type games, whose outcomes do approximate to a normal probability distribution. If these critics are right, the assumption of normally distributed returns undermines the conventional analysis of risk, leaving it unable to account for major events such as the collapse of Lehman Brothers in 2008.

This emphasis on the 'non-normal distribution' of investment returns complements the findings of behavioural finance. This is because one of the main reasons that 'extreme' events occur quite regularly is the occurrence of positive feedback, also central to the behavioural approach. Where, for example, one person's decision influences another person's decisions, any error by the first person will cause correlated errors by the second. Average returns are important only in situations where the dynamic is one of reversion to the mean with no positive feedback. Positive feedback can cause the types of important, and less rare, events that constitute fat tails.

8 Implications for personal investment strategies

You may rightly be asking yourself what the implications are of all these different theories of investment behaviour for your personal investment decisions. The answer is not so simple.

In Chapter 4, Section 4, you saw that the EMH argues against active management, which attempts to 'beat the market' by selecting undervalued stocks and timing their purchase. This is because if markets are informationally efficient, there should be no opportunity for bargain deals. Although assets will be priced differently, with different rates of return, these differences will be solely due to differences in risk, not any failure to capture the potential future gains. So if the EMH is correct, it is impossible to gain excess returns through arbitrage that is based on seeking differences between a security's price and its intrinsic value.

Behavioural finance, with its focus on the impact of emotions, cognitive errors, irrational preferences and group dynamics, leading to predictable patterns (such as buying shares when prices have already risen), is more compatible with active management. This is why some argue that behavioural finance is the theoretical foundation to technical analysis (see Chapter 4), which focuses on discovering arbitrage opportunities by studying past market trends (on prices and trading volume). From this perspective, the repetition of cognitive errors, because of the persistent biases revealed by prospect theory, may give rise to market inefficiencies that allow arbitrage opportunities.

The only way in which one can make more money, according to the EMH, is by taking on more risk, since there are no bargain deals. Hence evidence that some fund managers are in fact able consistently to 'pick winners' would be possible evidence against the EMH. As noted in Chapter 4, it appears that the long-run returns on most index funds are no worse than those on actively managed ones, once adjustment is made for active managers' higher fees. This result provides some support for the EMH. In the UK, investor returns from index funds tended to be in the top quartile of unit trusts ranked by return in the ten years to 2008 (Howells and Bain, 2008, p. 577). Yet even though index funds perform well, many investors still use actively managed ones or run their own portfolio – doubtless due to a belief that they can do a better job, but possibly reflecting irrational biases in their behaviour.

Even though active investment might be driven by fad and hence exacerbate a bubble, due to the presence of information cascades, index tracker funds might also reinforce fads and aggravate the market's tendency to overshoot or undershoot. This is because if a share is popular amongst investors, it becomes a bigger percentage of the index, whose 'trackers' must then buy more of it (see Chapter 4). Fund managers, whose main objective is to outperform their peers (as reputation and bonuses depend on relative performance rather than absolute performance), may in many cases amplify rather than correct irrational behaviour in the market. It is for this reason that technical analysis, by focusing on past trends and using these to predict future movements, can be responsible for momentum trading where fund managers ride the trend rather than counteracting it.

The fact that index funds are subject to informational cascades was one of the reasons why John Maynard Keynes became a 'value' investor. His stock-picking method was similar to that used, in the present day, by Warren Buffett, who became one of the world's most successful and famous investors with a strategy based on selecting only value shares. These are identified when their price becomes very different from the fundamental value, precisely due to the trend behaviour of investors, who may be buying and selling based on informational cascades even when there are no visible bubbles in the market. Keynes described his investment strategy as one that:

> assumes the ability to pick specialties which have, on the average, prospects of rising enormously more than an index of market leaders … It is largely the fluctuations which throw up the bargains and the uncertainty due to fluctuations which prevents other people from taking advantage of them.
>
> (Keynes, cited in Walsh, 2008, p. 80)

The value-based approaches of Keynes and Buffett assume that most investors have little knowledge about the companies whose shares they are buying or selling and so are susceptible to information cascades. Buffett has made his millions by focusing on shares in companies of which he has good knowledge, often acquired by holding sizeable stakes for long periods.

Even though most of us do not have the time to find value shares through stock selection, some simple rules when choosing funds or buying shares directly can help avoid, and even exploit, the pitfalls revealed by behavioural theory (Malkiel, 2007, pp. 239–42):

Avoid herd behaviour

Given the feedback effects that arise from herd behaviour and media hype, often prompting investors to buy when prices are already high and sell after they fall, one logical prescription is to beware of all boom–bust pronouncements. This was in fact Keynes' strategy.

Avoid overtrading

Due to overconfidence, many investors tend to trade too much, moving frequently from one share or fund to another, and so incurring high transaction costs. Buffett's credo 'Lethargy bordering on sloth remains the best investment style' is appropriate, and favours buying to hold long-term. As men appear more routinely overconfident than women in this respect, it is best to ask women for trading advice!

If you do trade, sell losers not winners

Due to loss-aversion, investors are more risk-averse with gains than with losses. This has led to the strange behaviour where investors are less willing to sell losers (admitting their losses), than winners (to cash in on gains). Such a tendency leads to lower returns than when selling losers.

These suggestions from behavioural finance stand in contrast to suggestions from those who highlight the existence of 'fat tail' distributions, even though both groups are critical of the mainstream approach. While the mainstream EMH and CAPM imply that the only smart strategy is to diversify widely via index funds, and behavioural finance suggests that the irrationality of investors allows opportunities for arbitrage, 'fat tail' theorists believe that the frequency of high-impact, unpredictable events means that the only way to protect against them is to diversify as widely as possible. Their prescription is thus similar to the EMH and CAPM theorists, but for very different reasons:

> Diversify as broadly as you can – far more than the supposed experts tell you … Long-run market returns are dominated by a small number of investments, hence the risk of missing them must be mitigated by investing as broadly as possible. Passive indexing is far more effective than active selection – but you need to go well

beyond an S&P 500 fund to do yourself much good. And wherever you put your money, understand that conventional measures of risk severely underestimate potential losses – and gains. For better or for worse, your exposure is larger than you think.

(Mandelbrot and Taleb, 2005, p. 100)

The fact that different theories reach very different prescriptions and conflict over reasons, even where they agree on conclusions, shows that knowing 'what to do' can be less important than understanding *why*. It is essential, in making investment decisions, to understand the assumptions underlying different theories of investment behaviour. Armed with this understanding, you can decide whether you agree with the assumptions underpinning these theories.

9 Conclusion

You have started this chapter by examining the recurrence of financial bubbles over the last 200 years, and seen how different theories have interpreted them. You were then encouraged to question the concepts of normal or rational behaviour that underlie conventional theory, which have led to bubble episodes being classed as anomalies. Do investors behave in a calculating manner, well described by the assumptions of optimisation/maximisation in economics? Why is it that, notwithstanding the existence of very sophisticated investment models, investors often seem simply to follow the crowd? Does this mean that they are 'irrational'? Finally, the chapter ended by considering how alternative theories, which have different answers to these questions, also have different implications for how you might approach your own long-term investments.

Underlying this discussion has been the degree to which investors can make rational 'calculations' about the risk–return relationship, one of the core themes developed in the book. Knight (1921) argued that the use of probability distributions is only pertinent when the underlying phenomenon is not one of 'true uncertainty'. You have seen that periods of technological change are often characterised by such true uncertainty, since its commercial impact and the firms that will profit from it are wholly unpredictable. Taleb and others have emphasised that even when probability distributions are relevant, their form should not be restricted to that assumed by the normal curve. High sigma events are less rare than this curve assumes and so should stay on the investor's radar.

Institutional change has also been increasingly emphasised by economists and financial theorists. Financial regulations are a major institutional enablement and constraint for investment behaviour. Financial crises, which are usually accompanied by financial innovations, tend to be followed by the imposition of new regulations designed to contain their effects. The dynamic tension between these changes, and emergent developments in the regulatory environment, are a further source of uncertainty, which you will consider in the next chapter.

References

Barker, T. (2001) 'Dotcombustion', *Financial Times*, 10 March, p. 16.

Bernstein, P. (1998) *Against The Gods: The Remarkable Story of Risk*, New York, John Wiley and Sons.

Economist, The (2009) 'Wild-animal spirits', A special report on the future of finance, 22 January.

Global Research (2009) *The Great Crash Not Over, Stocks Bear Market Rally Built on Sand* [online], www.marketoracle.co.uk/Article11150.html (Accessed 12 January 2010).

Howells, P. and Bain, K. (2008) *The Economics of Money, Banking and Finance* (4th edn), Harlow, Essex, Pearson Education.

Kahneman, D. and Tversky, A. (1979) 'Prospect theory: an analysis of decision under risk', *Econometrica*, vol. 47, no. 2, pp. 263–91.

Keynes, J.M. (1936) *The General Theory of Employment, Interest and Money*, London, Macmillan.

Kindleberger, C.P. (1989) *Manias, Panics, and Crashes: A History of Financial Crises* (2nd edn), London, Macmillan.

Knight, F.H. (1921) *Risk, Uncertainty and Profit*, Boston, MA, Houghton Mifflin.

NASDAQ Composite (^IXIC) Historical series 1994–2008 [online],http://uk. finance.yahoo.com/q/hp?s=%5EIXIC (Accessed 1 October 2009).

Mackay, C. (1841) *Memoirs of Extraordinary Popular Delusions and the Madness of Crowds*, London, Bentley.

Malkiel, B. (2007) *A Random Walk Down Wall Street* (9th edn), New York, Norton.

Mandelbrot, B. and Taleb, N.N. (2005) 'How the finance gurus get risk all wrong', *Fortune* (Retirement Guide), 11 July.

Mazzucato, M. (2002) 'The PC industry: new economy or early life-cycle?', *Review of Economic Dynamics*, vol. 5, pp. 318–345.

Montier, J. (2007) *Behavioral Investing*, Chichester, John Wiley and Sons.

Moskowitz, E. (2000) *Is Biotech Flaming Out? After Months of Scorching Returns, Biotechnology Investors Have Been Badly Burned. Here's a Smart Way to Play the Most Volatile Sector of All* (1 May) [online], http://money.cnn.com/magazines/ moneymag/moneymag_archive/2000/05/01/278208/index.htm (Accessed 30 November 2009).

Pisano, G. (2006) *Science Business*, Boston, MA, Harvard University Press.

Shapiro, R.J. (2002) 'The American economy following the information technology bubble and terrorist attacks', *Fujitsu Research Institute Economic Review*, vol. 6, no. 1 [online], www.fri.fujitsu.com/open_knlg/review/rev061/08forlam-english.pdf (Accessed 2 May 2009).

Shiller, R.J. (1981) 'Do stock prices move too much to be justified by subsequent changes in dividends?', *American Economic Review*, vol. 71, pp. 421–35.

Shiller, R.J. (2000) *Irrational Exuberance*, Princeton, NJ, Princeton University Press.

Sutliff, T.J. (1925) 'Revival in all industries exceeds most sanguine hopes', *New York Herald Tribune*, 6 April.

Walsh, J. (2008) *Keynes and the Market*, Hoboken, NJ, John Wiley and Sons.

Further reading

Kindleberger, C.P. (1989) *Manias, Panics, and Crashes: A History of Financial Crises* (2nd edn), London, Macmillan.

Shiller, R.J. (2005) *Irrational Exuberance* (2nd edn), Princeton, NJ, Princeton University Press.

PART FOUR: REGULATION AND THE LONG TERM

We are here today to learn lessons from the Enron debacle so that we can strengthen America's pension system and protect America's workers.

At Enron, executives cashed out more than $1 billion of stock while Enron workers lost more than $1 billion from their ... retirement plans. Thousands of Enron workers lost virtually all of their retirement savings. Enron executives got rich off stock options even as they drove the company into the ground and systematically misled workers about the true financial condition of the company.

Sadly, Enron is not just an isolated tale of corporate greed. Instead, the Enron debacle reveals a crisis of corporate values. In America, people who work hard all their lives deserve retirement security in their golden years. It is wrong – dead wrong – to expect Americans to face poverty in retirement after decades of working and saving. Enron has shown us that workers today do not have true retirement security ...

In the wake of Enron's collapse, Americans across the spectrum now recognize that a successful free enterprise economy depends on a framework of laws and institutions to make it work.

Senator Edward Kennedy in the US Senate (2002) 'Hearing before the Committee on Health, Education, Labor, and Pensions, United States Senate', Washington, US Government Printing Office

Thought-provoking questions for Chapters 7 and 8:

- Why, even in an era of financial liberalisation, does an economy need a framework of laws and regulations?

- Is the economic security of individuals, for example in retirement, just a concern for workers and their employers, or is this an issue for the whole of society?

Chapter 7
Regulating the financial system

George Callaghan

1 Introduction

Learning outcomes

After reading this chapter, you will:

- understand the relationship between financial markets and financial regulation
- understand how financial liberalisation does not remove the need for financial regulation
- understand the development of contemporary UK financial regulation
- have an awareness of the issues surrounding international financial regulation.

> This kindness will I show –
> Go with me to a notary, seal me there
> Your single bond, and, in a merry sport,
> If you repay me not on such a day,
> In such a place, such sum or sums as are
> Expressed in the condition, let the forfeit
> Be nominated for an equal pound
> Of your fair flesh, to be cut off and taken
> In what part of your body pleaseth me.
>
> (Shylock, *The Merchant of Venice*, in Shakespeare, 1972)

This quote from the central character in Shakespeare's famous play illustrates some of the passions and drama that can surround financial transactions. Contemporary regulators may not have to officiate over the morality of extracting a pound of flesh for failing to repay a bond but, as the 2007 financial crisis demonstrated, they have an essential role to play in influencing the behaviour of financial services providers more generally.

'Regulation and ethics' is one of the themes that runs through this book. In Chapter 5 you were introduced to the idea of regulation at the level of macroeconomic policy, where a government would use economic levers such as interest rates and taxation to influence the economic system. This chapter deals explicitly with the regulation of financial markets and players, with a focus on the UK's regulatory structure and the regulatory issues that policymakers face. It begins by introducing and analysing the interrelationship between financial markets and financial regulation. Sections 3 and 4 outline the modern history of financial regulation in the UK, starting with financial liberalisation and tracing the development of self-regulation and emergence of the Financial Services Authority. Section 5 looks at the challenges involved in regulating for systemic stability and consumer protection. Section 6 widens the perspective to consider the issues involved in international regulation of increasingly global markets, taking the example of banking supervision.

2 Financial markets and financial regulation

This section sets the context of financial regulation by exploring the relationship between the marketplace within which financial products are bought and sold, and the regulatory framework that attempts to shape and influence market behaviour.

2.1 The power of financial markets

We start by exploring in a little more detail the case for maximising the freedom of financial markets. Free-market theory draws on the work of academics such as the political philosopher Frederick Hayek (1945) and economists such as Milton Friedman (1980). These thinkers, from the **neoliberal** school of thought, argue that individual freedom stimulates energy, entrepreneurialism and economic growth. This implies minimum government intervention and minimum regulation.

Neoliberal
Favouring reduction of taxes and state provision wherever private provision can be argued to be a viable alternative.

Within the sphere of financial markets the argument would be that free markets foster a competitive environment. Competition between firms then leads to product innovation and greater levels of customer service and satisfaction. Box 1 contains an extract from the blog of two distinguished economists in which they argue that minimising financial regulation might be associated with higher rates of economic growth.

Box 1 Market ups and downs

In evaluating the need for greater financial regulation, one should also not forget that the American economy greatly outperformed the European and Japanese economies during the past 25 years. Might that not be related in part to the fact that the United States led the way with major financial innovations like investment banks, hedge funds, futures and derivative markets, and private equity funds that were only lightly regulated? An infrequent period of financial turmoil may be the price that has to be paid for more rapid growth in income and low unemployment. Rapid income and employment growth might be worth an occasional period of turmoil especially if they do not lead to prolonged slowdowns …

(Becker and Posner, 2008)

At the extreme, some economists argue that the most efficient financial system would be one characterised by 'free banking'. In such an environment the financial system would have no central bank, no regulatory body and no government intervention. Financial institutions could borrow, lend and generally act freely. Under the rule of market forces, competitive and well-run firms would succeed while poorly managed firms would fail.

Activity 1

In a country with free banking, what would happen to the bank's shareholders and its depositors if it went bust?

The answer is quite simple: they would lose their money. In such a system the bank and its customers would have to fend for themselves. Theoretically, the possibility of failure would constrain poor and risky decisions.

While there are only a few who would advocate such an extreme position, there are many who have argued that financial markets should be as free and deregulated as possible. Indeed, as you know from discussions in Chapter 4, the turn towards liberalisation that began in the UK and the USA in the early 1980s gathered particular force and momentum in the financial services industry. The pressure to liberalise, innovate and generate increasingly sophisticated and complex financial products grew through the 1990s and into the new millennium. It was only towards the end of the first decade that the forces of liberalisation were once again being challenged.

2.2 Financial regulation

While free financial markets are often associated with economic growth, there are countervailing arguments for financial regulation. Two specific issues raised by those who argue for financial regulation are that:

- free financial markets might threaten the economic system
- free financial markets might harm individual citizens who buy financial products.

Figure 1 summarises these main elements of financial regulation.

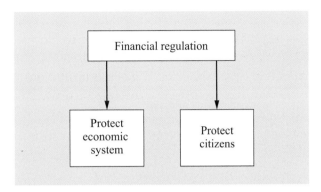

Figure 1 The main elements of financial regulation

Threat to the whole economic system

There is a great deal of interdependence between the financial services industry and the rest of the economy. To take just one example, if a major high-street bank collapses, then the bank clearing system might also fail, or at least be temporarily disrupted. The clearing system, which includes mechanisms such as the Bankers' Automated Clearing Service (BACS), is responsible for (usually electronic) flows of money around the economic system. This includes not just large payments and transfers between banks, companies and public bodies such as central and local government, but also the movement of pay into the current accounts of employees. If workers stopped being paid, cashpoint machines stopped dispensing and shops stopped accepting switch and credit-card payments, the whole economic and social system would come under tremendous pressure.

Chapter 7 Regulating the financial system

How might citizens respond to a threat to the money supply?

Financial journalists use the phrase 'contagion' to describe the idea of financial failure spreading from one firm to others. This links back to the idea of systemic risk that you first encountered in Chapter 1. That is the danger that problems in one institution will spread through the whole economic and financial system. Box 2 contains a summary description from the UK Treasury of how contagion and systemic risk would affect the broader economy.

Box 2 Aggregate costs of financial crises

If multiple banks, representing a significant part of the banking sector, fail or become severely weakened at the same time, there will be additional effects on the economy.

If the banking sector lacks capital, and is unable or unwilling to raise more, it may choose to cut back on lending to firms and households in order to rebuild capital ratios. Similar cutbacks may follow if deposits and other lending to banks are withdrawn due to a loss of confidence in the banking system. Such a loss of confidence is also likely to make it harder for banks to raise additional capital, and may affect even banks with little exposure to the original cause of the crisis if they are unable to prove their soundness to investors.

These reductions in bank lending in turn may affect the economy by limiting the ability of firms and households to make new investments or smooth shocks to their income and consumption.

The effect on output of these and other costs can be very large. One estimate puts the average cumulative output loss (relative to trend) in a sample of 47 banking crises at 15 to 20 per cent of GDP (depending on the measurement method), and found that crises in developed countries are as severe as those in developing countries. Crises can also be long-lasting: in the same study the average length of crises in developed countries was 5.5 years.

These costs are not shared equally across the economy. There is evidence that industrial sectors which have more small firms, or which are more dependent on external financing, are more severely affected by crises. One study finds that the bulk of the fall in output in the first two years of a crisis is accounted for by a fall in investment, although consumption and inventories also fall, offset by a rise in net exports.

(HM Treasury, 2008)

One outcome of a situation in which failure in the financial sector spreads to other parts of the economic system is that the total costs to society are greater than the cost to individual financial firms. This is an example of negative **externalities**, with social costs outweighing private costs. What this means in a practical sense is that if a single bank such as RBS fails, the loss to the broader economy and society is greater

Externality
A situation in which social costs are greater than private costs, or social benefits greater than private benefits.

than the loss to RBS shareholders, employees and (depending on the level of government support) depositors.

Activity 2

Can you think of other examples of negative externalities?

One example of a negative externality could be a coal-fired power station, whose productive activity adds to CO_2 emissions and global warming, the costs of which are not reflected in the price of electricity.

The threat of such systemic risk to the broader economy and society is such that many call for strong regulation of the financial services industry. This is known as **systemic regulation**, in which the responsibility of the regulator is to minimise the threat to the economic system of one or more financial institutions failing.

Systemic regulation
Regulation to avoid a threat to the whole economic system.

Protecting citizens

The second main problem, which will be considered later in the chapter, is that very free financial markets could lead to the exploitation and abuse of citizens in their role as consumers of financial products. Of particular concern is that a mismatch in information resources exists between financial institutions and the individual citizen making a financial choice.

For example, financial institutions employ teams of financial statisticians, economists, lawyers, accountants, and marketing and advertising agents. Moreover, this process of manufacturing and selling financial products is ongoing; it flows like a car production line. This can be contrasted with individual citizens who have limited resources for gathering information and infrequently make large financial decisions such as buying a house or choosing a particular personal pension scheme. This disparity in access to and quality of resources is known as asymmetric information (see Chapter 1, Section 4.4). The idea of asymmetric information is often associated with insurance, and describes the situation in which one party knows something that the other cannot or does not know.

One outcome of this concern about the disparity of information
between industry and individuals is what is known as 'conduct of
business regulation'. Broadly speaking, this means that financial services
firms and financial advisers provide appropriate product knowledge,
avoid misleading marketing campaigns, recommend suitable products
and generally deal with customers in a fair and honest manner. Conduct
of business regulation is particularly important in the retail sector of
financial services, which is the part of the financial services industry
that sells products to individuals. This can be contrasted with business
that takes place between professionals operating in the wholesale sector
of the financial services industry.

Let us take one example, related to the temporal aspect of financial
decisions, to illustrate why individual purchasers of financial products
are particularly vulnerable. A saver or depositor might be recommended
to take out an investment at a particular time when the investment
outlook seems good, and then suffer when, in the months and years
after the initial financial transaction, market conditions worsen. Only
then may it become apparent that the investment was subject to risks

that the individual would not have accepted had they understood the product fully.

2.3 Dynamic tension between markets and regulation

Politicians and policymakers are trying simultaneously to capture the product innovation and economic growth associated with free markets while minimising the risks to the economy and individual households. This has led to what could be described as a permanent relationship of dynamic tension between free financial markets and financial regulation.

On the one side is a belief that markets deliver efficiency and economic growth, and that to maximise this potential, markets must be as free as possible. On the other side is a concern that free markets must be regulated because they might lead to exploitation and inequality, and threaten economic stability.

This idea of dynamic tension implies that the regulator and the regulated are interrelated and often pulling in opposite directions. What this means in practice is that each party – government and the financial services industry – is having to respond continually to changes instigated by the other. So, for example, a government might introduce regulatory policy A in response to a systemic threat to the economy. The financial services industry might innovate to produce product B, which allows them to get around these regulations and make more profit. Government might then introduce regulatory policy C, which seeks to address new threats associated with this product. Industry then develops innovatory product D, and so on. Indeed, the Chancellor Alistair Darling commented in 2009 that:

> We need to ensure that innovation and the complexity it sometimes involves is not an excuse for a lack of transparency or for avoiding regulation.

(Grice, 2009)

Like two clumsy dancers, mismatched and poorly coordinated but cemented together at the hand and hip, regulators and the regulated have continued to stagger across the floor of financial markets. Figure 2 demonstrates this interrelationship, with the arrows indicating a continuous cycle of change.

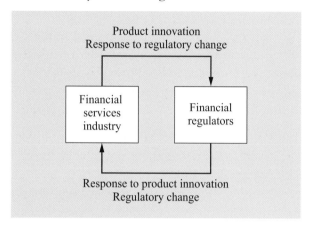

Figure 2 Dynamic tension

3 Financial liberalisation in the UK

The relationship of dynamic tension between financial regulation and financial markets exists within an economic and political context. Indeed, political philosophy and ideology directly affect this relationship. As described in the Introduction to this book, the political and economic policies that have prevailed in the UK since 1980 have been characterised by liberalisation (an example of which is the financial deregulation described in Chapter 1, Section 3.1). That is, there has been an emphasis on market forces and competition to deliver economic growth and efficiency. The emphasis on liberalisation has had a particularly significant impact on the financial services industry. The purpose of this section is to briefly highlight the major elements of financial liberalisation in the UK.

3.1 Thatcherism

There is a long history of politicians, mainly on the right of the political spectrum, arguing that free markets should have a greater role in economic policy. But it was only with the election of Margaret Thatcher in the UK and Ronald Reagan in the USA, in 1979 and 1980 respectively, that the ideology of free-market liberalisation gained particular prominence and power.

Thatcher's first two chancellors, Geoffrey Howe and Nigel Lawson, set about systematically liberalising financial markets. These policies include:

- the ending, virtually as soon as the new government took office in May 1979, of the restrictive guidelines on building-society lending for home purchase
- the abolition of exchange controls in October 1979, which had previously restricted the ability of UK firms to invest overseas and even set limits on the amount of foreign currency UK citizens could take on holiday
- the abolition of the Reserve Assets Ratio requirement in August 1981, under which banks had to hold at least 12.5 per cent of their deposits in a specified range of liquid assets
- the abolition of hire-purchase restrictions in July 1982.

(Lawson, 1992, p. 626)

Policies directed at financial liberalisation were introduced rapidly. Building societies were allowed to move beyond traditional mortgage business, banks were required to hold less capital, and the financial services industry in general was encouraged to grow and compete.

Perhaps the most dramatic symbol of the new liberalised era was the so-called 'Big Bang' of October 1986. This ended restrictive practices such as fixed commissions on purchases and sales of shares. It also marked a move away from transactions being done on a trading floor to electronic dealing and an increase in international equity deals.

This deregulation of financial markets was part of an ongoing political process that saw the privatisation of previously state-owned businesses and the introduction of free markets into many areas of the public sector.

1997 saw the election of a Labour government with Tony Blair as prime minister. While there were changes to the regulatory structure (which will be covered in the next section), there was consistency with the earlier period of Thatcherism through a continued political commitment to liberalised financial markets. This ideological commitment to free markets, therefore, continued through the 1980s and 1990s, and into the new century.

The process of financial liberalisation also became especially strong in the USA and led to repeated calls from the financial services industry and free-market politicians for the Glass–Steagall Act to be repealed. You'll recall from Chapter 1 that this Act, passed on 16 June 1933, split commercial from investment banks. It was felt that single banking institutions that both took deposits from customers and engaged in speculative stock-market trading were inherently risky, and that the existence and behaviour of such institutions helped lead to the Wall Street Crash.

The Act began to lose its effectiveness from 1986 onwards as the US Federal Bank approved the circumvention of restrictions, and it was formally repealed on 12 November 1999. This meant that deposit-taking institutions could once again also engage in speculative investing. It could be argued that this helped to popularise the financial products (mortgage-backed securities, collateralised debt obligations and structured investment vehicles) associated with the global financial crisis that began in 2007. Consequently, this led to calls from many city commentators for a new Glass–Steagall Act that would once again separate deposit-taking institutions from those engaged in more speculative investment activity (Jagger, 2009).

Old and new stock exchanges

This section has sketched out the story of liberalisation, the freeing-up of financial markets and the encouragement of competition. But, as you know from Section 2.3, financial markets are in a constant state of dynamic tension with financial regulation, so liberalisation did not signal the introduction of free markets. Rather, it led to different types of regulation. We now turn to the regulatory structure that emerged in the UK.

4 UK financial regulation

The previous section introduced the political policies behind the financial liberalisation that has taken place in the UK since 1979. But the focus on liberalisation did not mean an absence of financial regulation. Indeed, as this section demonstrates, policies directed towards financial regulation were continually present. This section concentrates on the nuts and bolts of UK financial regulation, starting with a description of financial regulation in the 1980s and 1990s before moving on to examine the regulatory structure introduced by New Labour in 1997.

4.1 Regulation since the 1980s

As you might remember from Section 1, financial regulation has two important aims: to protect the economic system and to protect citizens. In the early 1980s and until the creation of the Financial Services Authority in 1997 (which is covered in the next section), the Bank of England and HM Treasury had, broadly speaking, responsibility for protecting the economic system against failing financial institutions.

The protection of citizens who might be consumers of financial products was scant and mainly reliant on self-regulation from within the industry. This focus on self-regulation began to change following a review of financial regulation by Laurence Gower in the early 1980s. His discussion document favoured a move from pure self-regulation to a system of recognised self-regulatory agencies subject to governmental supervision (Gower, 1984). This led to the Financial Services Act 1986, which required those carrying on investment business in the UK to be authorised by the new self-regulatory agencies.

A government department (at that time, the Department for Trade and Industry, though later this responsibility would be passed to the Treasury) was responsible for the new system but could transfer its functions to a 'designated agency'. At the time, there was debate about whether there should be two designated agencies, one for wholesale markets and another for retail. However, in the event, just one agency – the Securities and Investments Board (SIB) – was established to regulate all types of investment business. A key function of the designated agency was to recognise a number of self-regulating organisations (SROs) responsible for different areas of investment. Anyone carrying on investment business was then required to be authorised by joining the relevant SRO, directly by the SIB or, if investments were peripheral to their main line of work, through membership of a recognised professional body (RPB), which included the existing professional bodies for accountants, solicitors and actuaries. The SROs and RPBs developed detailed handbooks of rules with which their members had to comply. Figure 3 summarises the structure of the system.

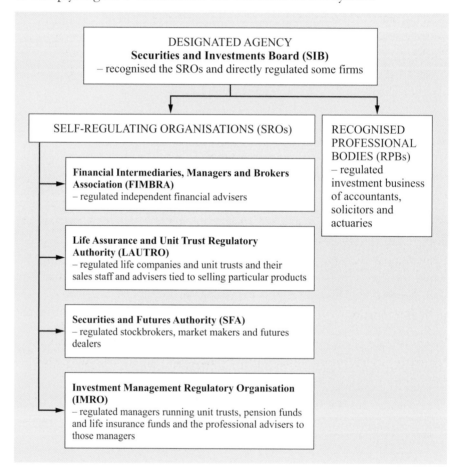

Figure 3 Structure of regulation under the Financial Services Act 1986

The Securities and Futures Authority (SFA) was formed by the amalgamation of two separate SROs, which briefly existed at the start of the 1986 regime. In 1994, the Personal Investment Authority (PIA) replaced FIMBRA and LAUTRO (see Figure 3), which meant that there was now one self-regulating organisation for the whole retail investment industry. As you will see, the whole 1986 system was then absorbed into a single new regulator. One important theme that emerges is this consolidation of regulators. One way of looking at this, which draws on the idea of dynamic tension, is that as financial firms become larger, more diverse and more interdependent, so too does the regulatory structure. In other words, changes in the structure of financial markets cause changes in the structure of regulation.

4.2 Financial Services Authority

The biggest consolidation took place in 1997 when the Labour government began the process of setting up the Financial Services Authority (FSA). This body had enhanced statutory powers and replaced the earlier, more fragmented, self-regulatory system that had attempted to ensure that citizens were protected.

Importantly, however, the FSA also took over responsibility for supervising banks and other financial institutions from the Bank of England. This meant that a single financial regulator had responsibility for protecting citizens and (shared) responsibility for protecting the economic system.

The Bank of England still had a role in protecting the economic system and, under what became known as the tripartite agreement, had responsibility for the overall financial stability of the monetary system, while the Treasury had responsibility for the overall regulatory structure and the FSA had responsibility for ensuring the financial soundness of individual institutions.

With the aim of minimising confusion over regulatory responsibilities, the three organisations signed a memorandum of understanding (see Box 3).

Box 3 Memorandum of Understanding between HM Treasury, the Bank of England and the Financial Services Authority

The Bank's responsibilities

The Bank contributes to the maintenance of the stability of the financial system as a whole. This involves:

- Ensuring the stability of the monetary system.
- Overseeing financial system infrastructure systemically significant to the UK.
- Maintaining a broad overview of the system as a whole.

- Undertaking, in exceptional circumstances, official financial operations.

The FSA's responsibilities

The FSA's powers and responsibilities were set out in the Financial Services and Markets Act 2000. Within the scope of the Act, it is responsible for:

- The authorisation and prudential supervision of banks, building societies, investment firms, insurance companies and brokers, credit unions and friendly societies.

- The supervision of financial markets, securities listings and clearing and settlement systems.

- The conduct of operations in response to problem cases affecting firms, markets and clearing and settlements systems.

- Regulatory policy in these areas, including that intended to promote the resilience to operational disruption of authorised firms and Recognised Bodies.

The Treasury's responsibilities

The Treasury is responsible for:

- The overall institutional structure of financial regulation and the legislation which governs it.

- Informing, and accounting to Parliament for the management of serious problems in the financial system and any measures used to resolve them.

- Accounting for financial sector resilience to operational disruption within government.

(Bank of England, 1997)

This memorandum of understanding went beyond paper agreements and included physical representation on the various management structures. For example, the Bank's deputy governor was to be a member of the FSA board, and the FSA chair sat in the Court of the Bank of England. In addition, there were to be monthly meetings of a standing committee involving representatives from each institution (FSA, 1997).

The FSA initially took on the responsibilities of the SIB and, following the Financial Services and Markets Act 2000, took over the powers and functions of the SROs and several other bodies. These included the Building Societies Commission, Friendly Societies Commission and Register of Friendly Societies. This made the FSA the main UK financial regulator. It has since been given powers over other areas, such as general insurance, mortgages and equity release.

Together, these changes represented a substantial upheaval in organisational structure and institutional culture. Workers moved, lines of managerial responsibility changed and new methods of cooperation had to be established.

Box 4 FSA statutory objectives

FSA statutory objectives:

- Maintaining confidence in the financial system;
- Promoting public understanding of the financial system;
- Securing the appropriate degree of protection for consumers;
- Fighting financial crime.

(Financial Services and Markets Act, 2000, Sections 3 to 6)

Activity 3

What immediate challenges to operational integration might the FSA have faced in its early days?

The FSA was bringing together staff from different working environments, for example taking civil servants from the Department of Trade and Industry, career bankers from the Bank of England and finance professionals from organisations that were used to self-regulation. The FSA would have had to establish common employment terms and conditions, work with the self-regulating authorities up to the time of merger, and bring staff together in one physical office space. In addition, each of the component organisations whose staff went to the FSA would have developed unique work cultures and values, a situation that might have led to conflict and confusion as well as cooperation.

FSA: what it meant for the financial services industry

Instead of regulation to protect citizens being provided by a number of bodies, the financial services industry became coordinated and controlled by one organisation. With thousands of firms and hundreds of thousands of employees, the UK financial services industry was large and complex. Faced with such a substantial and sophisticated industry, the FSA's initial strategy was to establish a system in which regulatory principles would shape company behaviour. As the FSA wrote: 'We want to give firms the responsibility to decide how best to align their business objectives and processes with the regulatory outcomes we have specified' (FSA, 2007, p. 4). These regulatory principles were supported by a rules handbook.

Another element of the FSA's initial strategy was to develop what it described as a risk-based approach. Here the FSA would allocate organisational resources according to what it saw as the riskiest firms. At the heart of this approach, the FSA built its ARROW system, used to identify risks to its statutory objectives based on information gathered through its supervision of firms and other regulatory activities. Risk probability was split into ten high-level 'risk groups' which, in turn, were subdivided into 52 'risk elements'.

FSA: what it meant for citizens

As you may remember from Section 2.2, the problem of asymmetric information meant that financial regulation should try to ensure that firms adhered to an appropriate standard of business conduct. With the FSA's establishment, this responsibility was enhanced and strengthened through its statutory commitment to 'promoting public understanding of the financial system'.

Howard Davies, the first FSA chair, commented that information offered to individuals was frequently very poor and in some cases positively designed to mislead:

> I saw an advert for a with-profits bond, detailing its performance over 5, 10 and 15 years, even though it was launched last summer. The small print said these are 'hypothetical' returns which should not be used as a guide to the future. We certainly have a mission to improve that.

(Hughes, 2001)

The FSA supported financial education through its website, publications and roadshows, through schools and in conjunction with the Institute of Financial Services, through universities (including The Open University) and through initiatives with individual banks and other bodies.

Building on the work of previous financial regulatory bodies, in particular the 'key features' documents established under LAUTRO rules, the FSA adopted a 'key facts' system. Customers, whether buying direct or through a financial adviser, who are arranging a mortgage, buying insurance or purchasing other financial products, receive information in an FSA-required format and branded with the FSA's key facts registered trademark (see Figure 4).

Figure 4 The FSA key facts logo

Deciding on the level of detail provided by these key facts documents represents another form of dynamic tension. The regulator has to overcome the problem of asymmetric information without overwhelming those purchasing financial products. What can customers understand? How much time might consumers be willing or able to give to taking in the information? How might those selling financial products judge whether customers understand the key facts? How might the regulator ensure that both the buyer and the seller of financial products fully understand each other?

While the FSA became the pre-eminent body in the UK regulating for consumer protection, there are a number of other regulatory agencies, which the next section briefly introduces.

4.3 Other regulatory agencies

First, consider where customers go with complaints and for compensation. Those who are not satisfied with the service they receive from an FSA-authorised firm can first complain to that firm; if not satisfied, they can take their complaint to the Financial Ombudsman Service (FOS). The FOS acts independently, but its chair and directors were appointed directly by the FSA. If customers suffer a loss because of the actions of a firm but it has gone into liquidation, they can seek redress, up to certain limits, through the Financial Services Compensation Scheme (FSCS). More details on particular examples of redress are given in Section 5.

Responsibility for regulating the important area of work-based pension schemes (which you will look at in Chapter 8) was in 2009 shared between the Pensions Regulator and the FSA. For example, the Pensions Regulator focused on employers, concentrating on efficient administration and the payment of employer contributions. The FSA regulated the firms managing pension funds. Members of work-based pension schemes normally take complaints to the pension-scheme organiser; if unhappy with the outcome, they can take their case first to an advice-and-mediation body, the Pensions Advisory Service, and, if necessary, to a more formal complaints body, the Pensions Ombudsman. Compensation arrangements exist that may replace part or all of pensions lost through fraud or the insolvency of a sponsoring employer.

Another area of shared regulatory responsibility for consumer protection is in consumer credit. Here another government department, the Office of Fair Trading (OFT), has a broad level of responsibility for consumer protection, but in 2009 some aspects fell within the FSA's remit of the promotion of public understanding. See Box 5 for a practical example of joint working.

One outcome of this dual responsibility was that the FSA and the OFT signed a Concordat that set out how they would work together (FSA, 2006a). They also wrote a series of Joint Action Plans.

Box 5 Joint working between the FSA and the OFT

Credit card interest calculation

The consumer body *Which?* made a super-complaint to the OFT about credit card interest calculation methods. Which? considered that methods should be standardised to enable easier comparison. The OFT responded that it agreed consumers did not understand interest calculations, but thought the key problem was that most consumers do not compare credit cards effectively at all.

The OFT worked on establishing how to help consumers make effective comparisons. In consultation with the FSA, the OFT recommended that the FSA create a price comparison website as

---

part of its 'Moneymadeclear' consumer site. The central proposition, discussed between the FSA and the OFT, is a comparison table which would allow consumers to sort products by the actual cost of the card based on their predicted usage.

(FSA/OFT, 2008)

5 Regulatory challenges

The previous section provided an account of the UK's regulatory structure. You have seen how this is a dynamic system, responding to the tension between regulator and regulated, and to the underlying changes in the industry. This is not just a matter of history; regulatory change is likely to continue. For example, at the time of writing, the Conservative shadow chancellor, prompted by the financial crisis that started in 2007, advocated transferring the FSA's prudential bank supervision responsibilities back to the Bank of England. However, no matter what changes might be made to the regulatory structure, the two main underlying reasons for financial regulation – protecting the economic system and protecting consumers – remain.

In this section, we will examine a set of regulatory challenges that flow from these two reasons and which were brought into particular relief by the financial crisis.

5.1 Insolvency

One particularly important issue is the possibility of a financial institution becoming insolvent, for example, a bank going bust. An obvious sign of impending insolvency is a 'run on the bank'. As you learned in Chapter 1, this happened in August 2007 when Northern Rock faced queues of customers waiting to withdraw their money. This event marked the point at which the financial crisis entered into the UK public consciousness.

Many commentators have been critical of the way in which regulators handled the collapse of Northern Rock. For example, David Llewellyn, Professor of Money and Banking at Loughborough University, has written that Northern Rock:

> was a multi-dimensional problem, revealing several fault-lines in the institutional architecture of financial regulation and supervision. Basically everything that could go wrong, did.

> (Llewellyn, 2008, p. 37)

But it was not just Northern Rock that became threatened with insolvency during 2007–08. Smaller financial institutions, such as the Bradford & Bingley and the Dunfermline Building Society, and large financial conglomerates, such as HBOS and RBS, were also on the verge of collapsing.

As Llewellyn (2008) and others have commented, these events highlighted issues to do with the legal mechanisms behind bank insolvency. Historically, banks had to follow the same procedures as other companies, which meant a potentially long-drawn-out process with delays for creditors. In the case of banks, these creditors include savers and those with money in current accounts, meaning the prospect of delays in gaining access to their accounts. Any such threat is likely to have an impact on bank customers' behaviour, making people nervous and more likely to move funds or close accounts at the hint of bank failure.

This threat neatly brings together systemic and consumer risk. For, if savers have asymmetric information on the safety of a particular financial institution, their actions might lead to bank runs elsewhere and increase the risk of insolvency spreading to other banks and through the economic system more generally.

The financial crisis that started in 2007 highlighted the more general problem of insolvency and led to UK policymakers rethinking their approach. One particular issue was the speed and efficiency of the insolvency process. To tackle this, the Banking Act 2009 established a 'special resolution regime' to allow for the partial transfer of ownership of failing banks to another body. This measure aimed to create greater legal certainty, ensuring that customers retain continued instant access to funds. The associated liquidity and confidence should, the argument runs, help to protect financial stability.

Communication

When there is a threat of insolvency hanging over an institution, or, even more seriously, when the entire financial system is under threat (as it was in 2007 and 2008), communication between all parties is important. This includes communication between regulatory bodies (where there is more than one) and between regulators, the financial markets and the general public.

During the 2007 crisis, the mechanisms for allocating responsibility between the FSA, the Bank of England and the Treasury were flawed. For example, the House of Commons Treasury Committee wrote in their report *The Run on the Rock* that the tripartite authorities did not prepare adequately for the support operation:

Those authorities and Northern Rock ought to have strained every sinew to finalise the [rescue] operation and announce it within hours rather than days of the decision to proceed with the operation. The tripartite authorities at deputies level failed to plan in advance for the announcement of the government guarantee on Northern Rock deposits that proved necessary to stop the run.

(House of Commons Treasury Committee, 2008, p. 64)

Northern Rock's boss gives evidence

Of particular concern was the fact that the FSA had responsibility for the prudential supervision of individual institutions while the Bank of England had responsibility for the stability of the financial system as a whole. As Willem Buiter of the London School of Economics said in comments to the Committee:

The notion that the institution that has the knowledge of the individual banks that may or may not be in trouble would be a different institution from the one that has the money, the resources to act upon the observation that a particular bank needs lender of last resort support, is risky.

(House of Commons Treasury Committee, 2008, p. 105)

Clearly the memorandum of understanding between the Bank of England and the FSA (described in Section 4.2) was meant to ensure efficient and trusted lines of communication; these were severely tested throughout 2007 and 2008.

In addition to the problem of communication between different regulators, another vital issue is communications between the regulators, the financial markets and the public more generally. During the financial crisis there were perceived problems with the way in which communications with the public at large were conducted. For example, using language such as 'emergency lending' to describe support operations was thought to increase public concern, and using industry-specific words like 'solvent' was seen as confusing.

5.2 Deposit protection

Closely linked to insolvency is the need to protect savings. The mechanism that decides the level at which citizens get their deposits back should a bank fail is an important part of any regulatory regime. As Box 6 on Bradford & Bingley shows, later rebranded by its new owner Santander, it is a very real worry for savers.

Box 6 Savers react to Bradford and Bingley rescue

First it was Northern Rock, now it's Bradford and Bingley

It has become the second British bank to be rescued from collapse by the Government.

At a branch of Bradford and Bingley on the high street in Redruth in Cornwall, a small queue of people waited patiently for the doors to open on Monday morning.

As well as worries about mortgages, many were concerned about their savings and banks accounts too.

Nick's a student and all the money he owns is in Bradford and Bingley.

Current accounts

He said: 'It's the only account I could open because of my bad credit rating. Now I'm worried if all of my degree funding and everything else is going to be safe and whether I'm still going to have an account or not.'

The Government insists people's savings and current accounts will be safe.

> The Spanish banking giant Santander, which now owns Abbey, has bought B&B's £20bn savings.
>
> The rest of it, the mortgages and loans, have been taken over by the Government.
>
> This deal is designed to keep your money safe. The only people who'll lose out immediately are those who have got shares in the bank.
>
> They've lost much of the value of those shares.
>
> (Ford, 2008)

By placing a limit on the amount of deposit protection, the government is attempting to share some responsibility. So if, for example, Dodgy Bank plc offers 10 per cent interest and Steady Bank plc 5 per cent, customers might think further about the risk profile of the competing banks. What policymakers hope is that such customer behaviour will constrain risky banking practices.

Until the Northern Rock collapse, 100 per cent of the first £2000 of deposits and 90 per cent of the next £33,000 were protected, through redress from the Financial Services Compensation Scheme (which you met in Section 4.3 of this chapter). From 1 October 2007, changes took place so that £35,000 of deposits was 100 per cent protected. Then, from 7 October 2008, the threshold was raised again so that the first £50,000 is fully protected. Around this time, finance ministers throughout the European Union agreed to raise bank deposit guarantees to at least €50,000.

Activity 4

What might be a problem with guaranteeing 100 per cent of all deposits?

From the short-term perspective, you might think there is no problem; in fact, if you were fortunate enough to have £100,000 in a high-street bank that was about to collapse, you would be very pleased. But from the perspective of the economic system, important issues arise. The most obvious is that individual savers and investors are less likely to pay attention to the riskiness and general financial soundness of the bank in which they are depositing money.

The problem for policymakers is that if they do insist on a limit on deposit protection, so the depositors share some of the risk, then at the first hint of trouble depositors might withdraw all their funds, or at least those above the deposit protection maximum. What is true of individual investors is equally true of institutional investors. If these organisations, who constantly move millions of pounds between different banks, believe that the solvency of a particular bank is in doubt, they might quickly withdraw funds.

Whether a government protects 50 per cent, 75 per cent or 100 per cent of deposits, the very fact of covering savings invites what economists call moral hazard. You'll recall from Chapter 1, Section 3.1, that this is where risk is displaced onto a third party, in this case the risk of a bank's collapsing being displaced onto the government. The obvious danger is that if government covers risks, it removes the incentive for customers to think about where they should save their money.

During the 2007 financial crisis it could be argued that moral hazard applied not only to depositors but also to institutions themselves. The government ensured that individual depositors would not lose any savings and also ensured that no financial institution would collapse. Therefore, regardless of the quality of individual or institutional decisions, the government took over responsibility for financial loss and presumably would stand willing to do the same in a future crisis. Clearly this decreases the incentive for individual savers, banks and other financial institutions to act prudently.

5.3 Conflicts of interest

Another important regulatory issue is the need to be aware of the potential for conflicts of interest between different parties (see Chapter 4). This section investigates such conflicts, including the role of commission payments in the mis-selling of financial products to individual customers, the potential for institutional investors to put short-term bonus rewards ahead of long-term business rewards, and the possible dangers of staff switching between regulators and the financial services industry.

Mis-selling

One area where conflict of interest appears is the need in a capitalist economy for those selling financial service products to make a profit and the regulatory requirement to give appropriate customer advice. For example, financial advisers who describe themselves as 'independent' might in reality be acting more like the agents of the life insurance industry if they are paid almost entirely on commission.

One industry insider, Andrew Fisher, chief executive of Towry Law Wealth Managers, commented thus on commission-driven selling:

> It is a gravy train that accounts for much of the retail financial services mis-selling over the past generation and it must be stopped in its tracks.

> (Fisher, 2009)

A good example of this is what became known as the pensions mis-selling scandal, which took place between the late 1980s and the early 1990s. It involved workers being encouraged to opt out of occupational schemes and take out a personal pension. Indeed, the government of the day sponsored a marketing campaign describing how people could be 'freed' from the 'constraints' of occupational pensions and could choose their own personal pension.

The financial services sector identified personal pensions as a way to increase profits and, often through commission-driven sales staff, advised up to 2 million people to shift from relatively safe occupational to relatively risky personal pension schemes. The subsequent harm to people who would have been better off under their occupational pension scheme led to £11.8 billion in compensation payments being paid out to over 1 million customers (BBC, 2002).

The quality of information provided to potential customers is vital to understanding the pensions mis-selling scandal. A particular issue related to projections of future returns. While there were some regulatory requirements relating to these, many financial institutions projected unrealistic patterns of return with no comparable estimate of the occupational pension being given up.

To take one example, investment regulator IMRO (see Figure 3) reported that, in advising customers about transferring pensions from occupational to personal schemes, Lloyds Bank had two main failings. The first is that they did not obtain relevant information about customers' personal and financial circumstances. The second is that they did not always provide adequate illustrations of the personal pension returns that could be compared with employer pension schemes. The result was that many individuals transferred their pensions and lost money. Lloyds Bank were subsequently fined £325,000 (Treanor, 1997).

When you realise that this example of Lloyds Bank is typical of the way in which many in the financial services industry treated their customers, the size and scale of the subsequent compensation becomes clear. Regulators were concerned with the way these financial services firms conducted their business with customers. They felt that banks and their intermediaries and financial advisers had unfairly exposed customers to risking their future pension returns. The fines illustrate why the conduct of business regulation, which you were introduced to in Section 2.2, is seen as an important element in protecting citizens who purchase financial products.

Activity 5

Have a look at the questions contained in the pension checklist given below. Are these questions familiar to you or to someone in your household?

Pension checklist

- Were you advised to take out a personal pension when you were a member of an employer's pension scheme or could have joined such a scheme?
- Was this pension plan taken out between 29 April 1988 and 30 June 1994?
- Were you under 35 at the time?

If the answers are 'yes', you may qualify for compensation, but your case must be reviewed by your pension provider.

If these questions in the pension checklist are familiar, it is likely that you are one of the many people who were alerted to the possibility that they may have been mis-sold a pension. Starting in 1999 there was a substantial advertising campaign, using checklists similar to the one above, to try to identify such people. This re-emphasises the importance of information: many people were themselves unable to work out whether they had been the victims of mis-selling.

While pensions mis-selling probably affected the largest number of people, it was not the only scandal to affect the financial services industry, as Box 7 shows.

Box 7 Mis-selling

Equitable Life: this company had promised thousands of its members guaranteed annuity rates. However, Equitable failed to set aside sufficient reserves to meet these guarantees, which became increasingly valuable in a falling annuity market. A legal ruling by the House of Lords that the guarantees should be honoured meant that other policyholders would lose money, and the very survival of Equitable was in question.

Mortgage endowments: here customers were sold interest-only mortgages without adequate explanation that the investment vehicle set up to pay off the capital was linked to stock-market operations and therefore might prove insufficient.

Split-cap investments: this involved a type of investment trust that contains different varieties of shares. There was substantial cross-holding of shares between investment trust companies, and the riskiness of products was insufficiently explained to customers.

Precipice bonds: these are examples of structured products (see Chapter 3), typically with three- to five-year terms, that offer high flows of income and seem to protect the initial capital investment. But the protection evaporates if the stock market falls by more than a specified amount. Advertising and marketing literature was developed that emphasised the high income and targeted retired people, many of whom were looking for a safe home for their retirement savings. Many lost money when the stock market slumped.

Payment protection insurance: this was sold alongside financial products such as personal loans. However, there were substantial exclusions and complex charging patterns, which made the cover expensive and inappropriate for many people.

Over the years, a number of regulatory measures were designed to counter the possible effects of commission-led bias. But the problem was only finally tackled head-on when the FSA initiated the Retail Distribution Review in 2006 (see Chapter 4). After a variety of proposals, in 2009 the review finally advocated the total abolition of commission as a way of paying for investment advice from 2012 onwards. The review also set out measures to improve the clarity of distinction between the advice services on offer and to raise the professional standards of financial advisers. The idea was to create a more obviously professional class of financial advisers where recognised qualifications and career structure are clearly apparent.

Whether the abolition of commission will mark the end of investment mis-selling will become clear only over the next decade or so. But creating a cultural change in the market for financial services products will face challenges. One of these is the cynicism of customers towards an industry that has a history of using exploitative sales techniques to make substantial profits.

Bonus culture and investment decisions

Another potential problem is with the financial brokers and traders working within financial institutions. Many of these individual traders deal with large sums of money and can earn substantial bonuses. A conflict of interest arises when decisions are made that maximise short-term individual or departmental bonuses but harm the long-term interests of the firm.

As Box 8 describes, this is certainly an accusation that many commentators have made about UK and international banks.

Box 8 Bankers' £16 billion bonus bonanza

Official statistics reveal that, in the financial year to April 2008, City workers took home £16bn, almost exactly the same as in 2007. The period covers the Northern Rock nationalisation and the UK employees hit by the Bear Stearns implosion. During the period, banks across the world were forced to make huge write-downs on investments linked to US subprime mortgages.

Bonus payments in the UK financial sector have more than trebled in just over five years, from £5bn in 2003, according to the Office for National Statistics (ONS). This is shared among just over one million employees in the sector, but that is heavily skewed towards the high-powered executives, who are routinely handed seven-figure packages …

Vince Cable, the Liberal Democrat Treasury spokesman, said: 'It is deeply alarming that, after what has happened in financial markets,

---

> no lessons have been learnt. The bonus culture was deeply destabilising and contributed to the crisis.'
>
> (Clark, 2008)

Part of the culture of working in the City of London is that financial traders are incentivised by earning lots of money. While such a culture dates back many years, it was greatly strengthened and enhanced during the financial liberalisation and 'Big Bang' of the 1980s. As financial services became increasingly globalised through the 1990s and into the 2000s, competitive pressure grew. This type of highly charged, highly competitive market environment was an ideal breeding ground for the growth of new investment products that offered immediate profits. The development of securitisation and originate-and-distribute strategies that you read about in Chapter 1 was a consequence of this culture. While huge short-term profits and bonuses were earned, the associated financial crisis ended up destroying large financial institutions and threatening entire economic systems.

The challenge for financial regulators is to try to ensure that those who manage financial institutions develop strategies and organisational cultures based on longer-term returns. This is dynamic tension again – balancing the power of the market to innovate against the risk to the economy and individuals.

Industry capture

A third potential conflict of interest is associated with the staffing of a financial regulator. Such a regulator will need to recruit those who understand the financial products and general operational practices of the financial services industry. One obvious source of such people is the financial sector. But might such individuals be too committed to market orthodoxy to genuinely challenge financial markets? Another problem is the commitment of regulatory staff drawn from the financial services industry who, at some point in the future, might hope to return to the private sector.

Such a situation can be described as 'industry capture', that is, a situation in which the commitment, culture and values of regulators are overly influenced by the industry.

While any regulator would face the difficulty of matching current technical knowledge with regulatory objectivity, the FSA encountered a particularly difficult position. This is because it was staffed and funded by the regulated industry. On the issue of staffing the FSA said:

> Staff are drawn from (and, indeed, return to) regulated firms and the professional services firms that advise them. More than half our staff comes from the industry and at any one time around 100 people are seconded to or from the industry and other bodies.
>
> (FSA, 2006b)

The potential for such conflicts of interest was underlined on 11 February 2009 when Sir James Crosby, who was deputy chair of the FSA as well as being chief executive of HBOS, resigned from the FSA following allegations about his conduct when he led HBOS (see Box 9 for an example of the media comment on this story). The fact that the same person can hold a senior position in both a regulated institution and a regulatory body illustrates the potential for conflict of interest.

Box 9 A financial elite in disarray

Sir James [Crosby] clearly believed that staying on would damage the FSA, either reputationally or hamper it practically: that is the import of his statement. But it goes to the heart of the problem: the FSA, many in the finance industry believe, was 'captured' by the banks it was supposed to regulate …

There was systemic failure and the role of the regulator is now right in the spotlight. How can you have a policing body overseen by those who are to be policed? How can you have the deputy chairman of the FSA being the same person who designed the strategy that, arguably, crashed a major bank?

This is the essential conundrum of UK financial regulation.

(Mason, 2009)

The act of balancing effective regulation with appropriate industry knowledge is another example of dynamic tension.

6 International financial regulation

So far we have mainly focused on the UK, but at an economic, social and cultural level the UK is part of a global system. Indeed, when it comes to financial services, the policies of financial liberalisation have meant that the City of London was not just part of a global system of finance; rather, with New York, it was the driver of innovation and strategy. Together, London and New York became the heart and head of global financial services.

As we have seen in earlier sections, while the UK has devoted substantial resources to creating and recreating sophisticated structures, the emphasis has continued to be on 'light-touch' financial regulation. Indeed, it could be argued that giving financial firms the freedom to innovate was a deliberate part of economic policy, as these companies would then be better placed to compete successfully with those from other countries.

One contextual feature of the international scene is, then, the commitment of the UK and the USA to open and free wholesale financial markets. Another is the existence of the European single market, with certain regulatory powers centralised in the European Parliament and Commission. Yet another is the complexity of international financial transactions. These include not just banks but also stock markets and hedge funds, which are often located in offshore financial centres. Through all of these, however, there runs a common thread. This is the desire for individual nations to retain autonomy over the economic activity that takes place within their boundaries. One consequence of this has been a historical reliance on voluntary agreements and a complex, sectorally based, regulatory structure.

We will now use the development of the Basel Committees on banking supervision (which you met briefly in Chapter 1) to demonstrate how this context makes it difficult for national regulatory bodies to reach shared and meaningful agreements.

Basel Committee on Banking Supervision

Historically, central bank governors and supervisory agencies met in Basel in Switzerland (hence the Committee's name). These meetings were informal, but with increasingly liberalised financial markets there were calls for a more concrete agreement. This crystallised in 1974 following the collapse of a German commercial Bank, Bankhaus Herstatt, in West Germany in the early 1970s.

The collapse of the German bank forced regulators to consider the question of who has regulatory responsibility when a bank based in one country, but with branches in another, fails. As we know from the failure of Icelandic banks operating in the UK and the consequent diplomatic tension between Iceland and the UK, this issue still has the potential to cause problems.

This led to a 1975 'Concordat' being signed by banking supervisors, which focused on minimum supervisory standards and capital amounts.

Activity 6

What kind of national competitive advantage might be gained by having lower minimum capital requirements?

As you saw in Chapter 1, capital ratios affect the amount of lending that a bank can do. The lower the amount of minimum capital, the more business and, theoretically, profit a bank can generate. Therefore, if national regulators set low capital ratios, it may mean that certain banks can become powerful and adopt a predatory attitude to businesses in other countries. International agreement aims to avoid this situation.

Three countries, the UK, the USA and Japan, took a lead in negotiations that led to the Basel Accord (Basel I) of 1988. But there were major areas of disagreement and debate, including what counted as capital and a desire to keep sovereignty over the regulatory systems of nation state territories. Rosa Lastra, Professor of International Financial and Monetary Law at the University of London, described the problem of this national focus in the following way:

> Sovereignty as a supreme power is typically exerted over the territory of the state: the principle of territoriality. Sovereignty has a territorial dimension. The demise of the national frontiers in today's global financial markets shows the limitations and inadequacies of this principle (territoriality = sovereignty) to deal

with financial conglomerates, international holding structures and cross-border banking and finance.

(Lastra, 2008, pp. 175–6)

Basel I maintained national sovereignty and instead of legal contracts offered voluntary agreements. One of these was that 8 per cent of a bank's overall capital should be kept in reserve. As Davies and Green (2008, p. 38) commented: 'The Agreement in 1988 was not binding because, like other agreements of this kind, no regulator was in a position to commit their national parliament to go along with what was agreed.'

Although not legally binding, Basel I's reserve capital recommendation was seen by some in the financial marketplace as a constraint. This led to product and process innovations that got round these capital requirements and increased profit. This, in turn, led to pressure for further regulatory reform.

Basel II

The second agreement, signed in 2004, was to link capital requirements to market-related risk assessments (see Box 10). Basel II was based on three pillars as shown in Table 1.

Box 10 Basel II: the regulators strike back

The principles underpinning Basel II are a reaction to the failings of the 1988 capital adequacy rules that are now frequently circumvented by clever financial innovators. Future capital requirements are to be far more flexible, and more closely aligned to free market forces. ... The core idea of Basel II is that market disciplines, whether direct or mediated through banks' own risk-modelling, should be placed at the heart of financial regulation.

(Eatwell, 2002)

Table 1 Basel II

Pillar I	Minimum capital requirements, based on the application of risk weights to the bank's assets. The Pillar I requirement includes capital to back credit, market and operational risks.
Pillar II	Supervisory review, which includes an assessment of the quality of a bank's systems and controls and risk management, and may result in an adjustment of the Pillar I capital requirement, either up or down.
Pillar III	Market discipline, including more stringent and detailed rules on disclosure and transparency.

Source: Davies and Green, 2008, p. 43

Basel II meant that banks' own internal ratings systems could be used in the calculation of risk-weighted assets. This judgement then informed the amount of capital required to be held by a financial institution. This gave banks more power and freedom.

The Basel Committee on Banking Supervision explains the choice faced by banks under the Internal Ratings-Based Approach to the management of credit risk:

> The Committee has made available two broad approaches: a foundation and an advanced. Under the foundation approach, as a general rule, banks provide their own estimates of PD (probability of default) and rely on supervisory estimates for other risk components. Under the advanced approach, banks provide more of their own estimates of PD (probability of default), LGD (loss given default) and EAD (exposure at default), and their own calculation of M (effective maturity), subject to meeting minimum standards.
>
> (Marciniak, 2005)

Banks that wish to adopt an 'advanced approach' must obtain a Basel II waiver from the FSA and, once adopted, this can mean that they are required to keep lower levels of capital.

On 29 June 2007, Northern Rock was told by the FSA that its application for a Basel II waiver had been approved. This meant a drop in capital requirements and an increase in dividends.

Owing to this approval, Northern Rock felt able to announce on 25 July 2007 an increase in its interim dividend of 30.3 per cent. This was because the waiver and other asset realisations meant that Northern Rock had an 'anticipated regulatory capital surplus over the next three to four years'. Mr Applegarth, Northern Rock's chair, explained that the waiver had led to a dividend increase because:

> When you get your Basel II approval, the relative risk weighting of certain assets in your balance sheet changes. So what we had, because of the quality of the loan book, was you saw our risk weighting for residential mortgages come down from 50% to 15%. That clearly required less capital behind it, so that links to why we were able to increase the dividend.

> (House of Commons Treasury Committee, 2008, p. 25)

Here we can see how the UK's national commitment to competition and deregulation combined with Basel II's emphasis on market-influenced capital requirements to create a very risky situation. In fact, it could be argued that Basel II hastened Northern Rock's demise.

The collapse of financial institutions such as Northern Rock, HBOS and RBS in the UK and Lehman Bothers and Bear Stearns in the USA has prompted new debate about international financial regulation. As Box 11 shows, policymakers have made some efforts to establish new guidelines.

Box 11 European Commission consultation on potential changes to the Capital Requirements Directive

The Capital Requirements Directive (CRD) implements the Basel II accord into EU law and came into force on 1 January 2008. Through its negotiation in the EU, a number of issues were set aside pending a more detailed review.

The review now under way aims to strengthen financial stability, simplify and clarify elements of the Directive and learn lessons from the recent financial market disruption, covering, among other issues, four key areas:

large exposures: regarding the maximum exposure a financial institution can have to a single entity, including exposures within a group and between banks;

definition of capital: clarifying the type and quality of the capital financial institutions are required to hold as a buffer against potential losses;

supervisory arrangements: aiming to strengthen supervisory coordination by improving cooperation and information exchange and reinforce the efficiency and effectiveness of supervision of cross border banking groups; and

securitisation: changes concerning the way that institutions should manage credit risk and liquidity risk in the context of securitisation transactions and the capital treatment of liquidity facilities for securitisations.

The European Commission has been consulting on these potential changes. The Commission will submit its revised proposal to the Council of Member States and the European Parliament for discussion. The Treasury will represent the UK in these discussions, working with the FSA and the Bank of England, and is engaging actively with stakeholders to develop its position.

(European Commission, 2009)

But the core contradiction of trying to establish meaningful international regulation in a world dominated by territorial nation states remains. Committees such as Basel can sign memorandums of understanding, attend coordinating dinners and amend voluntary agreements, but legal powers remain with national governments.

The UK's commitment to financial liberalisation, 'light-touch' regulation and open financial markets both domestically and internationally meant that when a crisis hit the UK in 2007, it was acutely exposed. While globalisation meant that the financial crisis affected many countries, the financial services sectors of Spain, Germany and other European economies suffered less than those of the UK and the USA. As the Governor of the Bank of England commented at the 2009 G20 meeting in London, 'global banks are global in life, but national in death' (BBC, 2009). Because of the City of London's prominent global position, promoted by government policy, the threat of bank failure is particularly pronounced.

The internationalisation of financial services and the accompanying desire for national sovereignty over economic affairs provides another example of dynamic tension. This is because UK financial regulators and the UK government must try to balance the economic growth and consequent tax revenues that they believe will flow from free international financial markets with the need to protect the UK economy and citizens.

7 Conclusion

This chapter opened by linking financial regulation to the theme of regulation that runs through the book. While Chapter 5 spoke of the government using interest rates and taxation to regulate general economic behaviour, this chapter has focused on the need to regulate financial markets.

It opened by describing the capacity of markets to innovate and stimulate economic growth. It was a belief in these powers that led to socio-economic change and the development of the UK's liberalised financial services sector. This sector is characterised by profit-seeking firms and bonus-seeking employees who continually produce innovatory financial products that maximise return. However, policymakers have also had to use financial regulation to guard against systemic risk and protect citizens who purchase financial products. This led to what has been described as a situation of dynamic tension, where there is continual interaction between financial regulators and the markets that they regulate. In this situation one side changes its policies, practices and business models in response to developments from the other side; these changes then cause another cycle to begin.

One of these changes led to UK financial regulation moving from being a mix of the Bank of England and mainly self-regulated industry bodies to a tripartite system with a newly established Financial Services Authority at its heart. This is one structure in a pattern of constantly shifting regulation but, regardless of structure, the issues that regulators must deal with remain – specifically threats to the economic system and the need to protect individuals in a market characterised by imperfect information. From these a number of related issues arise, which will also have to be addressed regardless of who is in government. These include how to protect against bank insolvency, the level of deposit protection, the need to avoid conflicts of interest, and the dynamic tension associated with marrying globalisation with a demand for national sovereignty.

It is to be hoped that after reading this chapter, you will have gained knowledge and insight that will help you to follow the regulatory debate whenever regulatory structures shift – as inevitably they will continue to do. A particularly important idea is that of dynamic tension. Often in economics, there are opposing forces drawing on and responding to particular political viewpoints. Financial regulation offers a good example of these tensions working through into policy, a process that generates passionate debate. In the next chapter, you will see how these tensions are also present in social policy.

References

Bank of England (1997) 'Memorandum of understanding between HM Treasury, the Bank of England and the Financial Services Authority' [online], www.bankofengland.co.uk/about/legislation/mou.pdf (Accessed 28 January 2010).

BBC (2002) *Pensions Scandal Costs £11.8bn* [online], http://news.bbc.co.uk/1/hi/business/2070271.stm (Accessed 17 June 2009).

BBC (2009) *Can Banking Regulation Go Global?* [online], http://news.bbc.co.uk/go/pr/fr/-/1/hi/business/7950758.stm (Accessed 17 June 2009).

Becker, G. and Posner, R. (2008) *Match Making through the Internet* [online], www.becker-posner-blog.com/index.html (Accessed 24 March 2009).

Clark, N. (2008) 'Bankers' £16bn bonus bonanza', *The Independent*, 18 October [online], www.independent.co.uk/news/uk/home-news/bankers-16316bn-bonus-bonanza-965445.html (Accessed 2 December 2009).

Davies, H. and Green, D. (2008) *Global Financial Regulation: The Essential Guide*, Cambridge, Polity Press.

Eatwell, J. (2002) 'Basel II: the regulators strike back', *The Observer*, 9 June [online], www.guardian.co.uk/business/2002/jun/09/theobserver.observerbusiness9/print (Accessed 26 March 2009).

European Commission (2009) *Regulatory capital* [online], http://ec.europa.eu.internal_market/bank/regcapital/index_en.htm (Accessed 2 December 2009).

Fisher, A. (2009) 'Question of the week: do we really need a change to the way financial advisors operate?', *The Observer*, 21 June [online], www.guardian.co.uk/money/2009/jun/21/financial-advisers-fsa-reform (Accessed 2 December 2009).

Ford, T. (2008) *Savers React to Bradford and Bingley Rescue*, BBC Radio 1 Newsbeat [online], http://news.bbc.co.uk/newsbeat/hi/the_p_word/newsid_7642000/7642992.stm (Accessed 2 December 2009).

Friedman, M. and Friedman, R.D. (1980) *Free to Choose: A Personal Statement*, Orlando, FL, Harcourt.

Financial Services Authority (FSA) (1997) *Financial Services Authority: An Outline*, London, FSA.

Financial Services Authority (FSA) (2006a) *A Concordat Between the Office of Fair Trading (OFT) and the Financial Service Authority (FSA)* [online], www.fsa.gov.uk/pubs/other/concordat_fsa_off.pdf (Accessed 18 February 2009).

Financial Services Authority (FSA) (2006b) *Essential Facts about the Financial Services Authority*, London, FSA.

Financial Services Authority (FSA) (2007) *Principles-based Regulation*, London, FSA.

Financial Services Authority (FSA) and Office of Fair Trading (OFT) (2008) *Delivering Better Regulatory Outcomes – May 2008 update: A Joint FSA and OFT Action Plan*, London, FSA/OFT.

Gower, L.C.B. (1984) *Review of Investor Protection*, Cmnd 9125, London, HMSO.

Grice, A. (2009) 'Confidence returning – but Darling gets no credit in poll', *The Independent*, 17 June.

Hayek, F. (1945) 'The use of knowledge in society', *American Economic Review*, vol. 35, no. 4, pp. 519–30 [online], www.econlib.org/library/Essays/hykKnw1.html (Accessed 17 September 2009).

HM Treasury (2008) *Financial Stability and Depositor Protection: Further Consultation*, M 7436, London, HM Treasury.

House of Commons Treasury Committee (2008) *The Run on the Rock*, London, The Stationery Office.

Hughes, C. (2001) 'The buck stops here: the most powerful financial regulator in the world', *The Independent*, 3 October [online], www.independent.co.uk/news/business/analysis-and-features/the-buck-stops-here-the-most-powerful-financial-regulator-in-the-world-630040.html (Accessed 15 April 2009).

Jagger, S. (2009) 'MPs look at the possibility of breaking up the banks', *The Times*, 10 April [online], http://business.timesonline.co.uk/tol/business/industry_sectors/banking_and_finance/article6070045.ece (Accessed 22 April 2009).

Lastra, R.M. (2008) 'Northern Rock, UK bank insolvency and cross-border bank insolvency', *Journal of Banking Regulation*, vol. 9, no. 3, pp. 165–86.

Lawson, N. (1992) *The View from No. 11*, London, Bantam Press.

Llewellyn, D. (2008) 'The crisis Britain had to have?', *Financial Regulator*, vol. 13, no. 2, pp. 37–46.

Marciniak, Z. (2005) *Risk Management* [online], www.marciniak.waw.pl/NEW/635202/RI13.pdf (Accessed 18 October 2009).

Mason, P. (2009) *A Financial Elite in Disarray* [online], www.bbc.co.uk/blogs/newsnight/paulmason/2009/02/a_financial_elite_in_disarray.html (Accessed 26 March 2009).

Shakespeare, W. (1972) *The Complete Works of Shakespeare*, London, Spring Books.

Treanor, J. (1997) 'Lloyds fined over pensions mis-selling', *The Independent*, 9 January [online], www.independent.co.uk/news/business/lloyds-fined-over-pensions-misselling-1282338.html (Accessed 17 June 2009).

Further reading

Davies, H. and Green, D. (2008) *Global Financial Regulation: The Essential Guide*, Cambridge, Polity Press.

Financial Services Authority (FSA) (2009) *The Turner Review: A Regulatory Response to the Global Banking Crisis*, London, FSA.

Chapter 8
Conclusion: investing for the long term

Andrew Trigg

1 Introduction

Learning outcomes

After reading this chapter, you will:

- see how the main theories and techniques considered in the book fit together
- understand how portfolio theory is applied to the issue of investing for the long term
- have an awareness of the issues surrounding state versus private pension systems
- understand some of the limitations of personal investment.

Everyone has the right to a standard of living adequate for the health and well-being of himself and of his family, including food, clothing, housing, medical care and necessary social services, and the right to security in the event of unemployment, sickness, disability, widowhood, old age or other lack of livelihood in circumstances beyond his control.

(United Nations, 2009)

This statement, from Article 25 of the 1948 UN Universal Declaration of Human Rights, requires all governments to take ultimate responsibility for the standard of living and security of their populations. How these human rights are pursued has varied between countries and at different points in time. At one extreme, the Soviet-era regimes of Eastern Europe took responsibility for many aspects of daily life. State welfare systems were also introduced in Western countries, as for example by the formation in the UK of the National Health Service by the 1945–51 Attlee government. More recently, the neoliberal agenda, pioneered by Ronald Reagan in the USA and Margaret Thatcher in the UK (see Chapter 7), has pointed to private, market-based solutions. In many economies, a mix of private and public sector funding is found in areas as diverse as education, health and business financing.

In a market-based approach, individuals are encouraged to take responsibility for their own standard of living and security. A key challenge here is to devise structures that create the right incentives. For example, if the state provides free health care, this could create a lack of incentive for private individuals to take care of themselves. Unemployment benefit might similarly result in people not looking for employment. The main function of the state is to ensure that there are efficient markets in which individuals exercise their claim, as stated in the United Nations declaration, to rights such as health care and employment. Critics of this approach argue that it places much risk on the shoulders of individuals, many of whom are not able to find adequately paid work or finance their own health care. The state has to intervene if poverty and destitution are to be prevented.

The shots fired in this debate ricochet into the field of personal investment. Proponents of a market-based approach argue that individuals should be encouraged to have their own private savings, investment and insurance; critics point to the limitations of any system in which the state does not protect individuals from the damages caused by market failure. To explore these issues in more detail, this chapter will look at a striking example that most of us will at some point in our lives be concerned with: security in retirement and old age.

The key vehicle for retirement planning is the provision of pensions. Most individuals in developed countries receive some form of state pension. But even where state pensions remain relatively generous, governments have reacted to an anticipated 'retirement boom' – more people than ever living longer in retirement – by encouraging an expansion of private pensions. These take the form of personal pensions taken out by individuals, or work-based pensions delivered through an employer. With many people lacking access to a work-based pension, and many employers forced to make their pension schemes less generous, personal pensions have become one of the most lucrative products recommended and sold by the financial services sector.

In private pension systems, people channel savings, either directly or via their employer, into a pension fund. By using such a fund, directly or indirectly, each individual has a pension portfolio, which includes a mix of assets such as cash, bonds and shares. In introducing personal investment, this book has provided some of the nuts and bolts required for designing a pension portfolio. Investors are faced with great uncertainty about the prospects for investment: whether a particular company or sector of the economy will grow, whether a particular bank or building society – or the whole financial sector – will lose profitability; and whether government will continue to offer financial incentives for particular types of investments. Key tools and techniques used in personal investment have been introduced, while at the same time highlighting their limitations.

In portfolio theory, the individual investor is assumed to make efficient decisions about how much to save and invest, operating on an efficient frontier between risk and return. Of particular relevance in this chapter is people's capacity to plan ahead, distributing resources across time to ensure that retirement is catered for as efficiently as possible. Section 2 will assess the main decisions faced by the individual investor, drawing on the early chapters of the book. Should, for example, an active or passive approach to portfolio building be followed? And could residential property be a viable alternative to investment in shares?

Section 3 will use private pensions as a case study for asking a key question: 'What are the limitations of personal investment?' The book has steered a path through some of the decisions that have to be made as a personal investor, but we have not pretended that investing is always feasible for everybody, or for society as a whole. To fully evaluate the limitations of personal investment, a further step back is required to look at the social and economic context. With respect to pensions, a key aspect is the role of government regulation and policy. In France and Germany, for example, the bulk of pension provision is provided directly by the state. But governments that offer higher state pensions and welfare benefits tend also to impose higher tax rates, which critics argue erode market incentives. In the UK, much more emphasis is placed on individuals having private pensions. The wider context for personal investment will be explored in this final part of the chapter by comparing private and state-run pension systems.

2 Retirement planning for the individual investor

This section starts by describing some of the basic choices and issues faced by the individual investor.

2.1 The individual investor

Whether acting alone or seeking help from an adviser, the first stage in a retirement plan is to consider some key questions. An adviser does this by conducting a 'fact find', which would, among other issues, ask:

- When will you retire?
- What income would you like when you retire?
- What is your attitude to risk?

Implicit in these questions is a particular assumption about how the individual investor will behave. The investor is expected to be forward-looking, making a plan for when they will retire and how much income they intend to live on after finishing work. They are expected to weigh up how their income and wealth is distributed across their lifetime. The question is not 'Do you plan to have any private income on retirement?' On the contrary, it is assumed that some money will be saved when the individual is young, thus postponing some consumption until later in life.

To make this retirement plan, the individual must decide on their attitude to risk. As described in Chapter 2, the individual may be risk-averse or risk-preferring. Portfolio theory is based on the assumption that individuals efficiently balance risk and return, the first main theme of the book. So for a given level of return they will always choose the option with the lowest level of risk. The risk–return spectrum, which has been developed throughout the book, is central to all forms of personal investment, including retirement planning.

By asking 'What is your attitude to risk?' the financial adviser is trying to establish where the client would like to be located on the risk–return spectrum. It is assumed that a high return on investments usually requires incurring a relatively high degree of risk. Potential high returns on shares in a clothing retailer, for example, will also incur high risks since many of these companies fail, or suffer sharp declines in profit, due to the difficulty of responding to changes in fashion. If a client is

willing to take risks and seek high returns, a financial adviser will
suggest an adventurous portfolio in which some high risk/return shares
are included. If, on the other hand, a client is extremely averse to such
risks, then a safer portfolio may be suggested, in which savings are held
in assets that are risk-free or very low in risk. Investors who are close
to retirement are likely to be more risk averse, and wary of long-term or
low-liquidity investments, than investors who have a longer time left to
retirement.

Underlying this financial advice will also be some notion of
diversification. It can be especially dangerous to put all nest eggs into
one basket. Chapter 3 has shown that by adding shares to a portfolio,
higher expected returns can be secured for the same level of risk.
Individuals are usually advised to have a diversified portfolio that
spreads risk across assets and types of investment within each asset
class. Portfolio theory recommends a combination of risky assets (such
as shares) and assets that are close to being risk-free (such as
government bonds, or government-backed cash deposits).

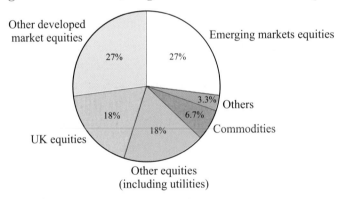

Figure 1 Example of a pension fund portfolio

(Source: Stevenson, 2009)

Activity 1

Figure 1 shows a portfolio recommended by David Stevenson in the
Investors Chronicle. Which type of investor might this portfolio be most
suited to, and what are its limitations?

David Stevenson refers to this as a global growth portfolio with a title
'Target Date 2040'. It is, in his view, ideally suited at the current time as
a long-term investment for someone retiring in 40 or so years. The
portfolio, which diversifies across various equity markets, is 'aimed at

equity investors looking for racy returns built around investing globally'. Higher risks incurred from investment in emerging economies enable the portfolio to 'power ahead' with its returns. There is no room in this aggressive portfolio for bonds, which might be more suitable for someone retiring soon who needs to conserve the value of their investment. However, some investment managers are now including bonds even in aggressive portfolios, believing that the 'cult of equity' is over after a decade of poor performance (Sutcliffe, 2005).

It should also be noted that according to the Capital Asset Pricing Model (CAPM), investors' risk attitude should only affect the proportion of their total portfolio that goes into the risk-free asset, as represented by government bonds. As explained in Chapter 3, no choice is exercised over the equity mix, since each investor is assumed to have the same risk–return diagram, thus choosing the same market portfolio of equities. All that varies is the proportion of the total portfolio that is invested in the market portfolio of shares. When advisers, such as Stevenson, suggest that younger investors should go for more aggressive shares (such as those from emerging markets), or older investors more defensive shares, this is not consistent with the CAPM. The latter implies that an investor nearing retirement, with less appetite for risk, would simply change the mix between the market portfolio and the risk-free asset. As with the CAPM's implication that actively managed portfolios will not consistently outperform the market portfolio, it also produces some strategy ideas that advisers and their clients may find difficult to accept.

A key part of financial advice is also to suggest vehicles for retirement saving that are tax-efficient. Governments tend to offer tax incentives for retirement saving, and investors endeavour to secure a retirement income that minimises the taxation that is paid to the state. The main vehicle, promoted by governments, is to take out a pension scheme. These have a number of advantages for the long-term investor. Employee and employer contributions get tax exemption, and pension funds also grow partially tax-free. There are, of course, other government-designed vehicles for tax-free investment, such as ISAs (see Chapter 3). These have the advantage that they are more flexible than pensions, and may be suitable in particular circumstances. Cash can be withdrawn at any age from an ISA, whereas money is tied up in pensions in the UK until at least age 55. There are, however, stricter limits on ISA savings compared to pensions. Among financial advisers pensions are usually, though not always, regarded as superior on tax grounds.

2.2 Basic issues for the individual investor

Portfolio theory, under the Markowitz refinement outlined in Chapter 3, suggests that most or all of the specific risk associated with investment in company shares can be diversified away by investing in portfolios on the efficient frontier, which include the market portfolio – a basket of shares based on the market as a whole. Using portfolios on the efficient frontier achieves a more effective balance between risk and return than following a naïve diversification in which, say, ten to fifteen shares are held in a portfolio.

The CAPM carries the further implication, by assumption, that individuals can afford to be passive, allowing the market – or an investment fund that tracks the market – to carry out diversification on their behalf. The portfolio in Figure 1 could, on this approach, use tracker funds to follow the different types of equity markets. This passive approach is also suggested by the efficient markets hypothesis, introduced in Chapter 4. Under the strongest version of this hypothesis, all information that helps to predict future earnings is already captured in the share price. Individuals cannot expect to 'beat the market' by picking out particular companies.

The investor may not, however, always be convinced that markets are fully efficient. As discussed in Chapter 4, individuals can and do engage in fundamental analysis, looking at publicly available information about companies. Some use technical analysis, which tries to find information on the future path of prices from their past movements. The widespread use of these strategies suggests that information is not always distributed efficiently, and investors can at times try to beat the market (see Chapter 6). For the individual investor, therefore, there is a deep tension between active and passive approaches to investment. An individual, or the financial adviser on behalf of an individual, has to choose between investment funds and fund managers that to varying degrees operate active and passive approaches.

Activity 2

What are the attractions to an investment fund provider of recommending to clients an actively managed investment fund?

One attraction of recommending an active fund, as demonstrated in Chapter 4, Section 5, is that fund providers can receive higher fees than when recommending a passive fund. But providers can also point to some active funds that have outperformed passive funds over certain periods – though there is evidence that most will fail to do so in the long term.

The discussion thus far has focused on investment in shares as part of a retirement income plan. But this is not the only asset available that can bring high returns. Instead of saving when young, individuals may – and do – decide to borrow to invest in education. In economics, the term human capital (see Chapter 2) is defined as the capacity to produce income through work. There is a working-life earnings premium from being academically or vocationally qualified, which may be preferable to engaging in saving at an early age. Investing in education to enhance human capital may initially incur additional expenditure and restrict wage-earning opportunities, but it may increase future earnings, which can translate into retirement income if saved.

Investors have in large numbers also preferred property as a way of securing income and wealth in retirement, especially in Britain and the USA. As Box 1 of Chapter 3 reported for a 2006/07 survey in the UK, 60 per cent of adults below pension age agreed with the statement 'Investment in property is the best way to save for retirement'. In comparison, only 49 per cent considered pensions, in which shares are the main vehicle for obtaining high returns. Investors take out mortgages on properties using leverage (see Chapter 1), which allows a much larger investment to be carried out than if limited to cash savings. On retirement, the plan is to have paid the mortgage off, eliminating housing cost and enabling the resale value to be used through trading down or **equity release** for retirement income.

Equity release
Withdrawing capital (as income and/or a lump sum) from a paid-for property, often by remortgaging.

Activity 3

What problems might there be in using property as a basis for retirement income?

One problem is that investing in property may lead to less diversification. Property is so expensive that it is very difficult to put together a diversified portfolio. It is easier for an established landlord to obtain mortgage approval than it is for a newcomer. Relying on just one property for retirement income would certainly amount to putting all your eggs in one basket. Property is also relatively illiquid, and any number of problems relating to the resale value of a property could derail its function as a retirement plan. It might be possible to invest in a residential property fund. But since property prices may move together as part of more general housing market trends, correlation between prices may be too strong and positive for diversification to work. Investing in funds may also not have the same appeal as buying actual properties. As argued in 2007 by Melanie Bien of Savills Private Finance mortgage brokers: 'People like property because it is more tangible than a pension: instead of a piece of paper listing details of your investment, you can see bricks and mortar' (Bien and Sodha, 2007).

Property could furthermore be regarded as a high-risk proposition since its purchase usually requires leverage. The returns are high, but so are the risks, placing it high up on the risk–return spectrum. Property price falls in 1991–93 and 2007–08 left many UK homebuyers in **negative equity**, owing more than their houses were worth and at risk of losing capital if forced to sell at that time. Investors in the UK also have to pay capital gains tax on the sale of any property that is additional to their main home. This has, however, at times been lower than the top rate of income tax, providing tax advantages that have to be weighed up against the tax incentives available from private pension schemes.

Negative equity
The excess of a mortgage over the value of the property that it is secured against.

Property, like other assets, is subject to uncertainty and change, a second main theme of this book. The main problem with investment in property is that it is subject to the same uncertainties as the rest of the economy. Property prices in the UK have enjoyed four major booms in the past 40 years: 1970–73, 1978–79, 1985–89 and 2000–07. But each has been followed by a crash in property prices, the last two of these being the most severe. We saw in Chapter 5 how the Lawson boom in the UK economy in the late 1980s, and its associated boom in property prices, was choked off by high interest rates. The consequence was a crash in house prices in the early 1990s, as mortgages became unaffordable, with around 500,000 repossessions (Hamnett, 2009, p. 4). The end of the 2000–07 boom in property prices took a different form, as a result of the freezing up of the supply of mortgages. UK banks had been financing new loans by securitising old ones, a trade that suddenly ended when the purchasing banks realised that falling house prices and borrower defaults were causing securitised debt to go bad. As shown in Chapter 1, the financial crisis that started in 2007 was so pronounced that major mortgage providers such as Halifax–Bank of Scotland and Northern Rock had to be bailed out by the government and stronger banks. The subsequent 'credit crunch' sent the economy into recession, worsening the fall in prices of housing and other assets, for reasons explored in Chapter 5.

Box 1 Property versus shares

Celebrity Amanda Holden gives her views to *The Sunday Times* about money and investing.

Do you own a property?

I have a house in Richmond and a cottage in Norfolk which we go to about once a month. We bought for £2.1m, and bizarrely, given what has happened to the housing market, were recently offered £2.5m for it. We don't want to move, though.

The cottage is near Burnham Market. I've had it for 12 years or so and have no mortgage on it. It was £69,000 when I bought it but was valued at £275,000 recently.

Do you invest in shares?

I bought shares in Carlton Television because someone suggested it to me in the late 1990s. I managed to sell them at a profit just before the stock market crashed and made something like £5000 on a £10,000 investment. Other than that, I've steered clear of the stock market. I just think it's too risky.

What's better – property or pension?

Property, for sure. With property, at least I can see where the money has gone rather than some obscure fund that is subject to the whims of whatever government is in power.

(*The Sunday Times*, 2009, p. 8)

For those who invest in residential property as a retirement plan, short-term fluctuations in prices can be of great concern. A strategy for the individual investor with a long time to go before retirement is to buy and hold, offsetting periods of falling property prices with periods of boom. For the individual nearing retirement (less than ten years), however, a plan to use property as a nest egg will be threatened by uncertainty in the property market. This problem also applies to individuals holding private pensions, as you will see in the analysis that follows.

3 Retirement as a social challenge: the case of pensions

Earlier in this chapter we asked: what are the limitations of personal investment? Thus far we have considered some of the specific choice decisions made by individual investors, for example, between active and passive approaches, and between shares and property. The discussion now turns to the wider social and economic system in which personal investors operate. Problems that face the individual investor are also a problem for society as a whole. Poverty in old age is not just a potential challenge for each individual; it is also a social problem that governments cannot ignore. And the personal investment approach to planning for old age arises from a particular political and social context. In the discussion that follows, we will look at pension systems as a case study for exploring the limitations of the personal investment approach.

3.1 Two types of pension system

There are two main types of system for arranging the payment of pension income in old age. In the first, private savings are placed in pension funds and invested in assets such as shares and bonds, out of which payments are made to the retired. In the second, pension payments to the retired are provided by the state, funded by revenue from taxation and National Insurance. The first is a private, savings-based system, the second a state-run, tax-based system. Figure 2 provides a simplified summary of these two systems.

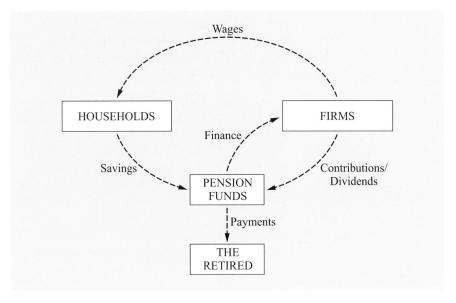

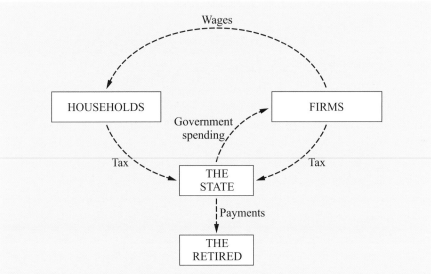

Figure 2 Two types of pension system: the private system (top; 2a) and the state system (bottom; 2b)

Activity 4

Can you spot any similarities between Figure 2 and the circular flow of income diagram (Figure 5) introduced in Chapter 5?

Common to both parts of Figure 2 is an assumption that people work through most of their adult life, and then retire from work at a particular point in time. Figure 2 therefore includes part of the circular flow of income that was introduced in Chapter 5, Section 3. The circular flow is based on the relationship between firms and households, with firms paying wages in return for the labour provided by households. The key question, in looking at pension systems, is how these households can afford to live once they cease to provide labour and earn wages, on retirement. To examine this issue, members of households are divided into two types: employees and the retired.

The private system is based on the idea, shown in Figure 2a, that employees save part of their wages in a pension fund. This saving can be through a work-based scheme, operated by an employer, or through a personal pension that is taken out by each individual. In a work-based (occupational) scheme, the firm also usually makes a contribution to the fund (which can be thought of as deferred pay or employer-directed saving out of pay). In both schemes, pension funds usually invest in shares, which entitle them to payments of dividends from firms, as shown in Figure 2a. The assets accumulated in pension funds provide the basis for payments that are made to the retired. Because funds are built up in individuals' names before they retire, this private arrangement is often referred to as a 'funded' system.

Transfer payment

A tax-funded welfare benefit, such as a state pension or jobseeker's allowance.

In the state pensions system, taxes are charged on the wage income (and consumption) of all individuals, and on the profits of firms. This money is used by the state to make payments to the retired (Figure 2b). Money is transferred entirely through the state sector, its allocation decided by politicians, who are usually elected. Instead of each individual deciding how much to save, electorates affect the level of tax rates and **transfer payments** through their choice of government. There are no assets held in a fund, just a promise by the state to pay pensions to current workers when they reach retirement, in return for current contributions. The state system is usually referred to as a 'pay-as-you-go' (PAYG) system.

3.2 State or private?

Dependency ratio

The ratio of non-working to working-age population.

There is a general consensus that state pension systems are faced with a demographic challenge. Not only are people living longer, and retiring earlier, they are also having fewer children. This means that in the future there will be fewer workers paying taxes, and more retirees to provide for. The old-age **dependency ratio**, of retired people to working-age people, is now rising in most countries: in the UK it is projected to rise from 30 per cent in 2006 to 35 per cent by 2030 – and would have risen to over 45 per cent by 2030 in the absence of planned rises in the state pension age (ONS, 2008).

In response to these fears, the last 30 or so years have seen a neoliberal push by governments to seek private solutions to the problem of pension provision. Employees have been encouraged, for example, to contract out of state-run pensions into private, individual pension schemes. As the UK government's Green Paper in 1998 stated:

> Public spending on pensions will decline as a share of GDP, from 5.4 per cent today to 4.5 per cent in 2050. By 2050, the proportion of pensioner incomes coming from the State, now 60 per cent, will have fallen to 40 per cent, and the proportion coming from private pension provision will have increased from 40 to 60 per cent. This will ensure that the pension system remains both fair and affordable.
>
> (Department of Social Security, 1998)

This move towards private pensions has gained momentum throughout the world. The most radical neoliberal response has been in Latin America. Chile, for example, replaced its state-based system with a system of individual funded accounts. Private firms were brought in to manage a suite of five different portfolios, each with a different mix of shares and bonds (Barr and Diamond, 2008, p. 228). Individual funded accounts have been promoted widely by the World Bank (1994) as a response to the perceived crisis in global pensions.

The core themes explored in this book can be used to compare some strengths and weaknesses of state and private pensions systems. We will now consider each in turn.

Risk and return

The main strength of the private system of pension provision is that decisions can be based on the reasoned choices of individual investors. When taking out personal pensions, individual investors are in principle free to choose the most efficient solutions to their own problem of how to prepare for retirement. They can decide their own balance between consumption and saving, and their own balance between risk and return when this saving is invested. It is not assumed that the state can somehow plan a portfolio for each individual. Economic theory suggests that this can raise the *rate* of saving – because the personalisation of the pension pot gives people an incentive to pay into it – and the *return* on saving, because people can channel it to the most productive uses in a low-tax environment. So long as individuals are allowed to invest efficiently, this will result in the most efficient outcome for society as a whole. As Adam Smith argued, in a way revived by neoliberals, individual self-interest leads to a promotion of the public interest, as if by an invisible hand (see Chapter 5).

Figure 2a shows that this private system can also channel savings to firms, via pension funds. Chapter 2 showed what a sizeable role institutional investors such as pension funds have had in the ownership of UK shares. The World Bank (1994), in particular, has used this argument to promote the development of private pension funds in developing countries. Once a country develops a private pension fund industry, this allows the development of a viable stock market, which can channel savings into firm investment. This is a supply-side approach to pensions, as introduced in Chapter 5.

The logic of the private approach is that individuals should also choose when they retire. If an individual manages to secure a high return from their portfolio, and hence has amassed sufficient savings, then they may retire early, say before the age of 65. But if the individual has been less successful in growing their pension pot, then they may sensibly decide to work longer and retire at a later age. The argument is that this makes it much less likely that there will be a future crisis in pension provision.

Such a crisis, in which everyone is living longer and many are retiring earlier, placing too much burden on future generations, will be averted if individuals are allowed to make their own retirement decisions.

A possible weakness of the private approach is the inability or unwillingness of many individuals to save for their retirement. A 2005 survey commissioned by the Financial Services Authority asked a representative sample across the UK if they agreed with the statement 'I would rather have a good standard of living today than plan for retirement' (Atkinson, 2007). Those that agreed with this statement represented 55 per cent of the population. Behavioural economics refers to this as excessive discounting (see Chapter 6, Section 7.3), where there is a tendency to attach little weight to events that occur some time into the future. It is one of a number of anomalous behaviours that, as seen earlier in this book, can affect investors' actions and market outcomes – including herd behaviour, overtrading and loss aversion. As Chapter 6 also shows, these behavioural biases can also be rational, depending on the circumstances. Whichever is the case, those who adopt a behavioural perspective argue that the financial model of an individual investor, efficiently balancing risk and return, is far from realistic.

Proponents of the private approach argue that if individuals lack forward-planning skills or capacities, and other aspects of financial literacy, it is because they are currently too dependent on state support. If the state ceased to provide a cushion to individuals, this would provide an incentive to think more seriously about becoming self-reliant savers and investors. Juurikkala (2008, p. 91), for example, argues that the state should withdraw from pension provision in order to induce 'greater flexibility based on individuals bearing the costs of the retirement decisions they make'. Even a move to 40/60 proportion of state/private provision might introduce more incentives for individuals to become active personal investors.

Uncertainty and change

Proponents of the private approach argue that flexibility on the part of individuals allows them to respond to change. As we have seen, of central importance to pensions is the problem of demographic change. From there being in 1950 seven individuals of working age for each individual of pension age, the OECD (2009) estimates for its 30 member countries that there will be only three for each pensioner in 2023, down to two in 2047. This is another way of looking at the old-age dependency ratio, as noted earlier. The neoliberal argument is that state pension systems will not be able to sustain future generations of retirees without an unacceptable rise in taxation.

Some economists, however, regard these arguments as 'demographic alarmism'. Mullan (2000) shows that if the economy increases by, say, 2.5 per cent each year, the GDP of developed countries could by 2042 actually outstrip the drain on resources provided by projected demographic changes. The same burden on resources, on his projection, could coincide with a doubling of living standards for the elderly (Mullan, 2000, p. 129). The argument is that the labour force, though smaller, gets much more productive, and so can afford to transfer more income to retirees and still live well.

Critics of the attempt to promote private funded over state pay-as-you-go pension arrangements also argue that they are not as dissimilar as the World Bank and other proponents suggest. Any pension system must redistribute income from today's employees to today's non-working retirees. The state system does so by taxing employees (and other taxpayers) to pay the pensioners. The private system does so by channelling the bond interest, share dividends and proceeds of share and bond sales from pension funds to pensioners. Privatising pensions may lighten the tax burden on labour income, but it increases the amount of capital and income that is directed to retirees rather than employees and the firms that they work for. Unless the privatised system raises the rate of saving and the efficiency with which savings are invested, or else reduces the overall level of pensions, it does nothing to reduce the inter-generational income transfer that any pension system represents.

Underlying this debate is deep uncertainty about future economic and demographic change. It is very difficult to know if a smaller working population will be sufficiently productive to pay for an increasing elderly population. Are economies now 'overdeveloped', with little room for increasing productivity? And has the financial crisis that started in 2007 heralded a period of long-term stagnation for the world economy? Or can we reasonably expect economies to continue on their previous growth path? If the UK economy has a steady growth path, it may also continue to attract working-age migrants who would help to support the retired. Policymakers need to make a judgement about whether economic growth will override or be dominated by demographic change. They will not, of course, enjoy the luxury of being passive observers. It will be their responsibility if the world economy is allowed to stagnate.

This uncertainty is relevant to the viability of private pension systems. They also face the problem of more retirees living longer and having to be supported from funds with fewer subscribers. Moreover, policymakers have conspicuously failed to predict the future growth path of the stock market, on which such funds rely. Their consensus, for example, that burgeoning stock-market performance in the 1980s and 1990s would continue into the future led them to change the UK tax rules regarding occupational pension funds. The Thatcher government in the 1980s encouraged companies to take 'holidays' from paying into their funds; the Blair government in the 1990s increased the amount of tax levied on pension funds. Stock markets, as we now know, did not continue to grow, with severe corrections taking place in 2000–01 and 2008. Deficits opened up in many **defined benefit** occupational pension funds, forcing major companies such as British Gas and British Airways to reduce benefits available to new members.

There has been a growing trend to move away from defined benefit schemes, where the employer guarantees a proportion of working income on retirement, to **defined contribution** schemes, in which benefits are dependent on the health of the stock market. A survey of UK companies by consultants Watson Wyatt Worldwide (2009) found that 75 per cent of defined benefit schemes were already closed to new members. These developments have transferred the risk from companies to individuals, a key reason, in addition to demographic pressures, being the failure to anticipate stock-market performance.

People who invest in private pensions need to be able to rely on stable economic growth. Those who retired just after the worldwide stock market crash of 2008, for example, found that their pension pots had suddenly shrunk. In addition, **annuity rates**, the rate of fixed income paid during retirement on a pension pot, also collapsed since interest rates were so low and pensioners were living longer. Pensioners were trapped in a position where they could not afford to wait for either the stock market or interest rates to recover.

Defined benefit
A pension payout calculated in accordance with a pre-set formula rather than determined by investment returns and other factors.

Defined contribution
A pension payout determined by a private fund's investment returns and other factors.

Annuity rate
The amount of income payable per unit of lump sum invested in an annuity. Unlike most other investments, the lump sum is not returnable.

Activity 5

What Keynesian levers might government use to generate sufficient tax revenue to pay for pensions?

The Keynesian response to uncertainty, as introduced in Chapter 5, is for governments to actively intervene in the macroeconomy, using levers such as taxation and government spending, as illustrated in Figure 2b. Government spending, for example on infrastructure projects, can secure economic activity for firms in the private sector, leading to more employment and wages, which generates tax revenue to pay for it. Out of this state-sponsored growth, tax revenues can be secured that are then channelled into state pensions. The Keynesian argument is that the state tempers the uncertainty generated in a market economy, ensuring through intervention that economic growth and provision of facilities such as pensions are taken care of.

The supply-side response to these arguments is that state intervention will distort the workings of the market economy. Resources that would have been directed to private entrepreneurial activity are crowded out by the state sector. The higher taxes needed to pay rising state pension costs will reduce incentives to work, invest and innovate, restraining the growth of productivity and GDP. Growth and employment, on this view, requires an efficient price mechanism, in which wages adjust to reconcile demand and supply for labour. All that governments should do is control inflation so that the price mechanism can operate, and so that real wages are high enough to allow employees to save. Increased government spending not matched by higher tax revenues will lead to fiscal deficits, introducing the spectre of inflation, which eats away into the real value of pension funds, and undermines the circulation of funds from savings into investment. Moreover, state intervention may also be unstable, since governments are elected on a four- to five-year cycle, with different priorities about pension policy and how the economy should be managed.

Regulation and ethics

In addition to economic and demographic constraints, privately funded pensions have a recent track record of severe ethical problems. There have been a number of cases in which work-based pension schemes have collapsed because of employer fraud. The death of newspaper tycoon Robert Maxwell in 1991 revealed how he had raided his employees' pension fund, leaving 30,000 pensioners forced to sue for compensation. A similar scandal took place in the USA with the fraud-induced collapse of Enron in 2002, leaving many of its employees with no pension provision. Some schemes have also failed because of actuarial miscalculation. As reported in Chapter 7, the near collapse in 2000 of the life insurance provider Equitable Life resulted in a million people in the UK losing a large part of their personal pension entitlements. The provider had promised to pay its pensioners in the future on the basis of high interest rates that prevailed in the 1970s and 1980s. With interest rates low in the 1990s (uncertainty again), Equitable Life could not afford to honour its commitments.

Even where schemes remain viable and their investments perform well, the cost of private pension schemes can erode their real returns to retirees, especially on the personal pensions taken out by many who cannot enrol in an occupational scheme. The high and often hidden costs of traditional personal pensions have led the UK government to work with the industry on a series of low-cost alternatives, including stakeholder pensions (introduced in 2001) and the proposed national system of personal accounts from 2012.

Finally, as also shown in Chapter 7, individuals have been subject to the problem of pension mis-selling. In the 1980s, some people in the UK were persuaded to transfer out of work-based schemes into personal pensions. Individuals had insufficient knowledge to compare pension products and had to turn to pension advisers. It is estimated that around a million individuals were mis-sold pension products between 1988 and 1994 (Sullivan, 2004, p. 93). Pension advisers were found to have behaved unethically, earning commission from selling products that were not tailored to the needs of these individuals.

These scandals have led to more regulation of private pensions by the UK government. The Pensions Act 2004 set up a pensions regulator to take over from the previous regulatory body in monitoring occupational pension schemes, protecting benefits, promoting good administration, and reducing the risk that members of schemes might make a claim. It has powers, for example, to ensure that companies contribute to schemes. In part to restore consumer confidence in private pension provision, the Pensions Act 2008 provided further regulation of pensions, setting up a framework of personal accounts that is intended to make low-cost pension savings available through the workplace.

There are also wider ethical issues to consider in evaluating private pensions, even if products are sold and pension funds run according to professional standards. It has been argued that the private system is more likely to lead to inequality and poverty than the state system. A TUC PensionWatch survey in 2009 found that directors of the UK's top 103 companies had pensions 30 times larger than the average workplace pension of £8320 per year (TUC, 2009). This is not surprising given the high incomes paid to directors. In the USA, Barry Diller, chief executive of InterActiveCorp received take-home pay in 2006 equivalent to 9.8

per cent of his company's profits (Perelman, 2007). Whereas state pensions and defined benefit occupational pensions may enable a degree of income redistribution between individuals, the increasingly adopted defined contribution scheme links each person's retirement income more closely to the amount that they have been able to earn and save while working, and the vagaries of both the stock market and the annuity market. Each individual gets back only what is put into their retirement fund, so inequalities in income are maintained under privately funded pensions.

Inequalities in income also lead to inequalities in power. Directors of companies have a degree of power over their own pension provision relative to that of employees. The TUC (2009) survey also showed that in the private sector, 61 per cent of top directors continued to enjoy defined benefit pensions in 2009, compared to only 13.5 per cent of employees. Such inequalities in corporate power have been documented by Lazonick (2007) for the new technology sector in the USA.

This issue is also compounded by inequalities in education, which are closely related to income inequalities. The Atkinson (2007) survey, mentioned earlier, found that of those with no formal qualifications, 64 per cent agreed with the statement that they would prefer a good current standard of living to planning for retirement. Compared to a person of high education and income, a person with low income and no qualifications is less able to save and may be less aware of the importance of saving. A private pension system, which leaves these decisions to the individual, can reinforce such inequalities.

Even if an individual is a prudent saver, financially literate, and has sufficient income to save, there is still a risk of poverty in old age if the fund does not perform well. Chapter 3 showed that individuals have to choose between a vast array of investment funds, with a wide variation of performance. Even if people have made an informed choice of fund, its performance may fail for reasons beyond their control, and the outcome may be difficult to defend on ethical grounds. Can society step back and say that it is acceptable for a retiree to live in poverty because her fund performed badly, or interest rates were too low when she bought her annuity?

There is a strong ethical case for society as a whole to take responsibility for poverty in old age. For this reason, all governments spend public money on pension provision. The main issue for policymakers is how much they should spend. Figure 3 shows how public spending varied between countries in 2005.

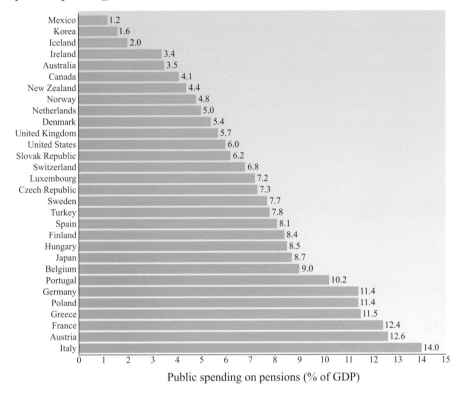

Figure 3 Public pension spending in OECD countries, 2005

(Source: OECD, 2009)

Whereas governments of countries such as France and Germany, which still have largely state pension schemes, spent over 11 per cent of GDP on pensions in 2005, those of other countries such as the UK and the USA, which rely more on private systems, spent around 6 per cent of GDP. Proponents of the state system argue that lower public spending on pensions leads to higher poverty for pensioners. The European Commission has found that the UK has 30 per cent of its population over age 65 living on poverty levels of income (defined as less than 60 per cent of median income). This compares to 13 per cent in France and 17 per cent in Germany (Eurostat, 2009).

A key argument in favour of a state pension system, therefore, is that it can provide a fairer and more equal distribution of income to pensioners than a private system. For society as a whole, this has been used to argue that government should regulate the distribution of income in order to reduce the possibility of poverty in old age.

For proponents of the private approach, however, large-scale regulation and intervention also raise ethical problems. If society rescues pensioners from poverty caused by making inadequate provision, when they could have saved more, are we being unethical towards those who did make such provision (and get no such help, or may even be taxed to help others)? There may be a moral hazard (see Chapter 7) in allowing people to believe that the state will always rescue them from financial deprivation. The strength of the private approach is that it encourages individuals to take responsibility for their own pension provision. Governments accused of allowing pensioner poverty through lack of redistribution in their private pension systems also argue that this is a 'static' argument that ignores the dynamic benefits of privatisation. They claim that lower state spending has allowed lower taxation, which promotes private-sector investment and faster growth, eventually expanding the tax base and the value of pension investments so that present and future pensioners can be lifted out of poverty.

4 Conclusion

The motives and methods of private investing can be fully understood only in a wider context. This chapter's focus on pensions, increasingly central to personal investment strategy, has required further assessment of themes that you have been confronted with throughout the book. You have been shown that investment returns must be balanced against risk. But uncertainty and change mean that the precise forecasts and calculations that are often assumed in portfolio theory can never be made in practice. Even if behavioural anomalies did not disrupt the working of financial markets, there would still be unequal and unpredictable outcomes to many important financial decisions. The state would still be frequently called on to intervene — to correct individual injustices, regulate industry practices, and sometimes rescue the whole financial system from serious instability.

Despite the problems raised, your own view may be that the private approach is preferable to any state-organised system. This could translate into your own personal investment planning; and if you work in the financial services industry, it will inform your role as a practitioner. Even if you recognise potential problems in the private approach, a widespread drive to make people more responsible for their own financial planning is likely to continue, so both financial services providers and their customers must become better informed. Whatever your view, we hope that this book has conveyed the practical relevance of personal investment to our everyday lives, the changing context in which it is pursued, and the interplay of ideas between theorists and practitioners in a constantly developing financial system.

References

Atkinson, A. (2007) *Financial Capability amongst Adults with Literacy and Numeracy Needs*, Bristol, Personal Finance Research Centre.

Barr, N. and Diamond, P. (2008) *Reforming Pensions*, Oxford, Oxford University Press.

Bien, M. and Sodha, S. (2007) 'Head to head: property or pension?' [online], www.news.bbc.co.uk/1/hi/business/6407909.stm (Accessed 6 November 2009).

Department of Social Security (1998) *A New Contract for Welfare: Partnership in Pensions*, Cmnd 4179, London, The Stationery Office.

Eurostat (2009) *Community Statistics on Income and Living Conditions* [online], www.epp.eurostat.eu (Accessed 6 November 2009).

Hamnett, C. (2009) *The Madness of Mortgage Lenders*, London, Institute for Public Policy Research.

Juurikkala, O. (2008) 'Retire early, save little: the ironic disincentives of public pension systems' in Booth, P., Juurikkala, O. and Silver, N. (eds) *Pension Provision: Government Failure Around the World*, London, Institute of Economic Affairs.

Lazonick, W. (2007) 'The US stock market and the governance of innovative enterprise', *Industrial and Corporate Change*, vol. 16, no. 6, pp. 983–1035.

Mullan, P. (2000) *The Imaginary Time Bomb*, New York, I.B. Tauris.

Office for National Statistics (ONS) (2008) *Pension Trends*, London, ONS.

Organisation for Economic Co-operation and Development (OECD) (2009) *Pensions at a Glance 2009*, Paris, OECD.

Perelman, P. (2007) *The Confiscation of American Prosperity*, London, Palgrave Macmillan.

Stevenson, D. (2009) 'Back to basics', *Investors Chronicle*, 16–22 January.

Sullivan, M. (2004) *Understanding Pensions*, Abingdon, Routledge.

Sunday Times, The (2009) 'My pretty woman moments: Amanda Holden talks to Ali Hussain', Section 5, *Money*, 19 April.

Sutcliffe, C. (2005) 'The cult of the equity for pension funds: should it get the boot?', *Journal of Pension Economics and Finance*, vol. 4, no. 1, pp. 57–85.

Trades Union Congress (TUC) (2009) *PensionsWatch 2009* [online], www.tuc.org.uk/extras/PensionsWatch2009.pdf (Accessed 6 November 2009).

United Nations (2009) *Universal Declaration of Human Rights*, www0.un.org/en/documents/udhr/.

Watson Wyatt Worldwide (2009) 'Pension scheme closure: nuclear option becoming the norm', press release, 17 August [online], www.watsonwyatt.com/news (Accessed 6 November 2009).

World Bank (1994) *Averting the Old Age Crisis: Policies to Protect the Old and Promote Growth*, Oxford, Oxford University Press.

Further reading

Barr, N. and Diamond, P. (2008) *Reforming Pensions*, Oxford, Oxford University Press.

Sullivan, M. (2004) *Understanding Pensions*, Abingdon, Routledge.

Glossary

Glossary

This glossary collects some of the key terms you have come across in the book. All terms in italic refer to entries in this glossary.

Absolute return

An investment target expressed as a percentage return, or return above the risk-free rate, rather than a comparison with *peer* or *benchmark* performance. See also *relative return*.

Active investor

An investor who seeks to outperform a specified investment *benchmark*.

Adverse selection

The disappearance of profitable or trustworthy buyers or sellers from a market, due to prices or rules set, leaving only less profitable or less trustworthy participants.

Aggressive shares

Shares in companies with high expected growth but high *risk*, compared to their relative *benchmark* (*beta* higher than 1). See also *defensive shares*.

Allocative efficiency

The allocation of resources to their best possible use.

Alpha

The amount by which a *portfolio* has outperformed (or underperformed) its *benchmark* by taking on *specific risk*.

Alternative investment market

A London-based 'second tier' *stock exchange* that offers simplified listing for *shares* in smaller or newer companies, usually regarded as riskier than those on the main market. See also *London Stock Exchange*.

American-style option

A *share* option that can be exercised any time ahead of the specified expiry date. See also *European-style option*.

Amortisation

The cost of intangible asset acquisition spread across its lifetime. See also *depreciation*.

Animal spirits

Psychological traits and urge for action (or inaction), as motive for investment decisions, largely influenced by perception of the environment and by others' thoughts and actions.

Annual equivalent rate (AER)

The interest rate received for the year on deposits and *savings*, taking into account the frequency as well as the number of payments.

Annual percentage rate (APR)

The interest rate charged for the year for borrowing money, taking into account the frequency as well as the number of payments.

Annuity rate

The amount of income payable per unit of lump sum invested in an annuity. Unlike most other investments, the lump sum is not returnable.

Arbitrage

The pursuit of profit from price misalignment by buying the underpriced asset and/or selling the overpriced asset.

Assets

What a company or an individual owns, or can collect from others who owe them money.

Asymmetric information

One party in a transaction knowing more than the other. Sometimes the one who knows more can get a better deal; but if the other side knows this, they adjust prices to offset their *risk*, so that sharing the information can actually produce a better deal.

Balance sheet

A periodic record of the *assets* and *liabilities* of a bank or non-financial company, showing what it owns and what it owes.

Bank for International Settlements (BIS)

An international organisation that harmonises banking regulations and serves as a bank for *central banks*.

Bank run

A rush by depositors to withdraw their money from a bank because they think it is no longer safe.

Base rate

The official interest rate at which the *central bank* lends to other banks, which sets a baseline for the interest rates available to private borrowers and lenders. See also *repo rate*.

Basel II agreement

Internationally agreed rules setting minimum capital requirements for banks in relation to their risk-adjusted *assets*.

Basis point

One hundredth of a percentage point, used for exact specification of interest rate levels and changes.

Bear market

A market where the majority of investors are selling ('bears'), causing overall *share* prices to fall. See also *bull market*.

Behavioural finance

An approach to investor behaviour that takes account of departures from 'rational' decision making under social, emotional or cognitive influences, and their impact on financial markets.

Bell curve

See *normal curve*.

Benchmark

A performance target: for *active investors*, the return on investment in the *market portfolio*.

Beta

The beta of a *portfolio* (or an individual *share*) measures the sensitivity of its return to changes in the return from the *market portfolio*.

Bid–ask spread

The difference between the bid price received by the seller of an asset and the slightly higher ask or offer price paid by the buyer.

Black Swan event

An unexpected event that has a major impact on the course of history, and can usually be rationalised only after it happens. See also *high sigma event*.

Black–Scholes formula (or model)

A formula (or model) of *share* option pricing, named after its inventors, Fischer Black and Myron Scholes. Based on the *CAPM*, it links the price of a *call option* to its strike price, the time to expiry, the *spot-market* price of the underlying asset, the risk-free rate of interest, and the *volatility* of the underlying asset.

Blue-chip shares

Shares in large, well-established companies that typically pay dividends and are expected to deliver growth in line with the general economy (named after the highest chip in poker).

Bonds

Investments that are loans to a government, company or other body. Typically, a bond has a set repayment date and, in the meantime, pays interest and can be bought and sold on the stock market.

Bounded rationality

The idea that individuals' rationality is limited by the information that they have access to, available time and cognitive (brain power) limitations.

Bretton Woods Agreement

The 1944 agreement between major economies that tied monetary policies to a fixed exchange rate system, and created the International Monetary Fund and the World Bank, with the objective of securing global financial stability and faster economic growth.

Broker

An *intermediary* acting for a buyer or seller of *securities* who may receive a commission for arranging their purchase or sale.

Bubble

The *inflation* of an asset price, eventually reversed by a sudden burst or a prolonged decline.

Building society

A mutually owned financial institution, originally set up to take deposits from members and give them loans with which to build or buy houses.

Bull market

A market where the majority of investors are buying ('bulls'), causing overall *share* prices to rise. See also *bear market*.

CAC40

A Paris Stock Exchange index of the largest 40 French companies, weighted by *market capitalisation*.

Call option

An option to buy an asset at a specified future time and price.

Capital

A resource that can be used to generate income, such as an investment in machinery that generates profit (physical capital) or skills that command a higher salary (*human capital*) or money utilised by an investor (financial capital).

Capital Asset Pricing Model (CAPM)

A financial theory which states that, under certain (restrictive) assumptions about investors' preferences with risk–return opportunities, the *discount rate* used to calculate the net *present value* of a risky investment is the difference between the *market return* and the risk-free rate. It implies that all investors should buy the *market portfolio* and combine it with the *risk-free asset* according to their attitude to *risk*.

Capital market line

A line representing combinations of the *market portfolio* and the *risk-free asset*. See also *efficient frontier*.

Capital ratio

The proportion of a bank's *assets*, recorded on its *balance sheet*, that can reliably hold their value – as distinct from investments that could fall in value, or loans that could be diminished by a wave of defaults.

Capital risk

The possibility that investors may lose some or all of their original capital and returns (if reinvested) made to date.

Central bank

The bank that issues a nation's currency, sets its interest rates, manages its foreign currency and supervises other banks. Examples are the Bank of England (UK), the Federal Reserve System (USA) and the European Central Bank (*eurozone*).

Chartism

Use of past price patterns to predict an asset's future price movements. See also *technical analysis*.

Churn

Turning over the investments in a *portfolio*, incurring *transaction costs*.

Classical economics

Economic theory based on the assumption that prices are fundamentally determined by input costs and will adjust (along with wages and interest rates) to keep the economy at full employment. See also *neoclassical economics, supply-side model*.

Collateralised debt obligations (CDOs)

Bonds secured against a bank's loan books (of which *mortgage-backed securities* are one type).

Commercial bank

A bank that takes deposits from, and makes loans to, households and businesses, engaging in *maturity transformation* to offer longer-term loans. See also *investment bank*.

Complete information

The situation in which all market participants know all the information held by, and strategies available to, all other participants, and know that this information is shared. See also *perfect information*.

Compound interest

Interest earned not just on the amount originally invested but also on the interest previously earned and reinvested.

Confidence indicator

An index measuring optimism about future prospects of the economy and their own situation, among consumers, producers or investors; used to inform investment strategies and economic forecasts.

Consumer Prices Index (CPI)

The average price of a range of goods and services consumed by a typical household; the measure of *inflation* targeted by the Bank of England, and used for comparisons by international organisations such as the OECD and the EU. See also *Retail Prices Index*.

Contract for difference (CFD)

An arrangement where an investor expecting a price rise can 'borrow' a quantity of an asset, in the hope that the profits from the price rise will exceed the interest cost of the loan; or one expecting a price fall, who can 'lend' a quantity of the asset, receiving interest that they hope will outweigh the amount that they must pay out to compensate for the price fall.

Convertible unsecured loan stock (CULS)

Corporate *bonds* that can be converted to ordinary *shares* on set future dates at pre-set prices. As a conversion date gets closer, CULS tends to behave more like the underlying shares than like bonds.

Cooperative bank

A bank that operates comparable loan and savings-account facilities to a *commercial bank* but is owned by its depositors and borrowers, not by external shareholders.

Correlation

The extent to which movements of variables are associated with each other.

Countercyclical

Falling when the state of the economy improves, and vice versa. For example, governments' *fiscal deficits* and *insolvency* practitioners' revenues tend to vary countercyclically. See also *cyclical*.

Counterparty risk

The risk that the counterparty to a transaction or contract will default on their obligations.

Coupon

The interest rate on a bond expressed as a percentage of nominal (par) value.

Credit crunch

A period when banks drastically reduce their lending to companies and individuals, in an attempt to restore their *balance sheet* and cash flows.

Credit default swap (CDS)

An arrangement whereby an investor 'insures' a risky loan through regular payments to a counterparty, which agrees to repay the loan if the borrower defaults.

Credit rating agency (CRA)

An organisation licensed by regulators and paid by government or corporate borrowers to issue *default-risk* assessments on their *bonds*.

Credit union

A financial institution originally set up to take deposits from members, offer them unsecured loans when their ability to repay was deemed adequate, and channel any profits into community improvement, including members' financial education.

Currency risk

Where an investment is denominated in a foreign currency, the *risk* that unexpected changes in the exchange rate will alter the sterling (or other home currency) value.

Cyclical

Rising and falling with the state of the economy. Thus income and profits of a cyclical business will tend to be high at times of fast economic growth, and low or negative when the economy is stagnant or shrinking. See also *countercyclical*.

Default risk

The likelihood that a borrower will fail to repay a loan, or make other due payments, usually because of *insolvency*.

Defensive shares

Shares in companies with lower *risk* than their *benchmark* and more stable returns prospects though lower *beta* (beta less than 1). See also *aggressive shares*.

Defined benefit

A pension payout calculated in accordance with a pre-set formula rather than determined by investment returns and other factors.

Defined contribution

A pension payout determined by a private fund's investment returns and other factors.

Deflation

Falling prices, shown by a negative *inflation* rate.

Demand-side model

An economic model that views the *price mechanism* as insufficient for demand to absorb full-employment supply at all times, with periodic need for government intervention to boost demand upwards. See also *supply-side model*.

Demutualisation

The conversion of a *building society* or other mutual financial institution into a bank, through the issuance of external *shares*, sometimes compensating depositors and borrowers with a bonus paid from reserves.

Department for Work and Pensions (DWP)

The UK government department responsible for welfare, social benefits, pensions and employment.

Dependency ratio

The *ratio* of non-working to working-age population. See also *support ratio*.

Deposit protection

A mechanism for reimbursing savers whose money is lost through the collapse of a financial institution; also termed deposit insurance, as usually funded by a levy on institutions. See also *Financial Services Compensation Scheme*.

Depreciation

The cost of tangible asset acquisition spread across its lifetime. See also *amortisation*.

Depression

A prolonged period of low economic activity and high unemployment that may not be reversible without government intervention. See also *recession*.

Deregulation

The loosening of rules of a particular market or industry.

Derivative

A contract on one or more underlying *assets*, whose price is derived from the *spot-market* price of the assets.

Discount rate

The rate of return that will set a stream of future payments from an investment equal to its *present value*.

Discounting

The process of reducing a future payment to find out how much it is worth today. See also *present value*.

Diversification

Reducing *risk* by combining a variety of investments that are unlikely to all move in the same direction at the same time.

Dividend cover

Earnings per *share* divided by the net dividend per share.

Dividend payout ratio

The percentage of a company's earnings (profits) for a given period paid out to shareholders as dividends.

Dividend valuation model (DVM)

A method of trying to find the intrinsic value of an investment in *shares* by *discounting* an assumed flow of dividends that continues indefinitely; also known as dividend discount model.

Dividend yield

Net dividend per *share* divided by the current share price.

Dow Jones Industrial Average (DJIA)

The earliest US *stock exchange* price index, a price-weighted average of the largest 30 companies in the USA.

Dynamic tension

Continuous interplay between the potential for *free markets* to boost investment returns through innovation and efficiency gain, and the need for regulation to contain risks.

Efficient frontier

A curve representing the most efficient combinations of *risk* and *expected return*, *portfolios* on which are said to be *Markowitz efficient*. They include the *market portfolio*. See also *capital market line*, *CAPM*.

Efficient Markets Hypothesis (EMH)

The theory according to which financial markets present some degree of *informational efficiency*, so that prices reflect the best information available in the market.

Equilibrium

The point at which price and quantity of the demand side meet those of the supply side, and are supposed to remain stable if conditions do not change.

Equities

Shares; also called stocks (in the USA).

Equity release

Withdrawing capital (as income and/or a lump sum) from a paid-for property, often by remortgaging.

Ethical investment

A strategy of focusing on investments that promote the social and natural environment (such as affordable housing and renewable energy), and avoiding those viewed as damaging it (such as tobacco and rainforest logging).

Ethics

Principles for determining appropriate conduct and values in social or commercial situations.

Euronext

An alliance of the Paris, Brussels and Amsterdam *stock exchanges*.

European-style option

A *share* option that can be exercised only on a specified expiry date. See also *American-style option*.

Eurozone

A geographic area that comprises all countries in which the euro has been approved as the official currency by the European Central Bank.

Excess volatility

The degree to which *share* prices are more volatile than the underlying earnings (or other fundamentals).

Excessive discounting

Putting too much weight on present income or value, by *discounting* future income flows at too high a rate.

Exchange rate

The number of units of a foreign currency that exchange for one unit of home currency (or vice versa).

Exchange rate swap

An arrangement whereby a company (or investor) that wants funds in one currency but can borrow more cheaply in another (usually that of its home country) swaps currencies with another that can borrow more cheaply in the target currency.

Exchange-traded fund (ETF)

A fund that typically tracks market indices.

Expected value or return

The average of possible returns from an investment, where each possibility has been weighted by the probability that it will occur.

Externality

A situation in which *social costs* are greater than private costs, or social benefits greater than private benefits.

Fat tail

A distribution of data (such as possible investment returns) where even values that are a long way from the *expected value* have a relatively high probability of occurring. See also *Black Swan event*, *high sigma event*.

Federal Reserve

The US *central bank* (equivalent to the Bank of England).

Financial exclusion

The inability to access mainstream financial services, and employment and market opportunities linked to these. Factors contributing to exclusion may include low income, location, adverse history and inappropriate products.

Financial Ombudsman Service (FOS)

The official independent body appointed to settle consumer complaints against financial services providers.

Financial regulation

The imposition of rules on financial transaction, accounting and investment behaviour, by government or other agencies, designed to uphold professional *ethics* and prevent *systemic* and *prudential* risks. See also *professional regulation*, *systemic regulation*.

Financial Services Authority (FSA)

The UK financial services regulator from 1997.

Financial Services Compensation Scheme (FSCS)

A fund set up to insure UK personal investors against loss if a financial firm fails, owing them money. It covers investments, bank (and similar) deposits, *mortgages* and insurance.

Fiscal deficit

The excess of government spending over the revenue that it receives, usually expressed as a proportion of national income.

Fiscal policy

Decisions by government on public expenditure and taxation.

Fitch

One of the major three *credit rating agencies*.

Fixed capital

Machinery, buildings, communication and transport networks, and other physical installations that sustain many runs of a production process.

Footsie (FTSE) All Share Index

A *London Stock Exchange* weighted index of the largest *market capitalisations* of UK companies; in 2009, included 619 *shares*, weighted by market value, which represented 98–99 per cent of the value of all the shares listed on the market.

Footsie 100 Index (FTSE100)

A *London Stock Exchange* weighted index of the largest 100 *market capitalisations* of UK companies.

Forward market

A market in which the price and quantity of a transaction can be specified in advance, as through a *futures contract* or *option contract*. See also *spot market*.

Free markets

Markets where consumers and producers exchange goods and services at mutually agreed prices, without the intervention of a central coordinating authority.

Friendly society

A mutual insurance association formed to encourage *saving* for old age, sickness, burial expenses or nest eggs for children.

Fundamental analysis

A method of trying to find the *intrinsic value* of an investment by examining factors that may affect it, including the financial and operating situation of the provider, sector conditions, investment markets and the wider economy.

Futures contract

A contractual right to buy or sell a quantity of an asset at a specified price at or before a future date.

Gilts

'Gilt-edged' *bonds*, issued by the UK government.

Glass–Steagall Act

Act passed in the US on 13 June 1933 to formally split *commercial banking* from *investment banking* institutions; repealed in 1999.

Great Depression

Massive shrinking of the world economy which followed the Wall Street and other stock market crashes in October 1929. The Depression lasted until 1933 in many western countries.

Gross Domestic Product (GDP)

The value of all the goods and services produced by a country over a year.

Growth fund

An *investment fund* targeting capital appreciation by selecting companies tipped for above-average earnings growth and reinvesting dividends. See also *income fund*, *value fund*.

Hedge

To invest in a way that protects income or wealth against unpredictable price movements.

Hedge fund

A fund that engages in a wide range of investments, usually pursuing *absolute returns*, and may (but does not necessarily) *hedge* its risks.

Herd behaviour

Behaviour that is influenced by what others think or do, sometimes away from what an individual would do if acting *rationally*.

High sigma event

An event that, if normally distributed, should be very unlikely, as shown by its large *standard deviation* (sigma) from the *mean*. See also *Black Swan event*, *fat tail*.

HM Revenue & Customs (HMRC)

The UK government department responsible for taxation.

HM Treasury

The UK government department responsible for overseeing *financial regulation* and *fiscal policy*.

Human capital

Capacity, based on qualifications, skills and experience, to produce income through working.

Hyperinflation

Very high *inflation*.

Illiquidity

The inability to meet immediate cash demands, including short-term debt repayments, due to unavoidable delays in receiving income or selling off *assets* even if there is still fundamental *solvency*.

Imputed rent

The financial benefit that a homeowner is deemed to receive as a result of not paying rent.

Income fund

An *investment fund* that favours companies with high *dividend yields*. See also *value fund*, *growth fund*.

Income risk

The risk, where payments are variable, that they may fall below the amount the investor had expected, or fail to be paid.

Income statement

An annual accounting report that shows how a bank or non-financial company has made (or lost) money in the past financial year.

Index fund

An index fund is a fund that aims to track rather than outperform a particular stock market index.

Index-linked gilt

A UK government bond whose interest payments and redemption value are increased in line with *inflation* throughout the life of the bond.

Individual Savings Account (ISA)

A *tax wrapper* for *savings* and other investments, subject to maximum annual allowances.

Inflation

A rise in the general level of prices that means that over time a constant sum of money will buy less and less. The rate of inflation is the annual percentage change in the price of a large basket of goods and services that are typical of the way households spend their money. See also *CPI* and *RPI*.

Inflation risk

The risk that the return from an investment will be worth less than expected in real terms because of an unexpected rise in prices.

Infomediary

An *intermediary* who provides information, analysis or forecasts on financial variables of interest (*share* prices, companies' profits, etc.).

Information cascade

The process of people ignoring their own private information and basing a decision on what others have decided to do (e.g. invest in certain stocks). It can lead to *herd behaviour*.

Information ratio

A risk-adjusted performance measure of fund performance: the *alpha* divided by the *tracking error*. It identifies funds that earn consistent, positive alphas, rather than higher but more volatile alphas over time, so is a widely used measure of active fund managers' success.

Informational efficiency

When prices reflect the best information available in the market. See also *perfect information*, *complete information*.

Initial public offering (IPO)

The flotation of new *shares* on a *stock exchange*, when a formerly privately-owned company 'goes public'.

Insolvency

The situation of being unable to repay all debts, owing to *liabilities* exceeding the sum of *assets* and *shareholders' equity*.

Institutional investor

A financial institution that invests large sums of money on behalf of others.

Inter-bank interest rate

See *LIBOR*.

Interest yield

The income that a bond will produce expressed as a percentage of the current market price.

Interest-rate risk

The risk that return on an investment differs from expectation because of unanticipated change in interest rates.

Interest-rate swap

An arrangement whereby two parties borrow on different terms, often one at a fixed rate and one at a variable rate, and then arrange payments of interest to each other.

Intermediary

A financial institution that connects buyers and sellers, or borrowers and lenders.

Intrinsic value

The fundamental, underlying or actual value of an investment as opposed to its market price, which may be out of line with its underlying value.

Investing

Deploying money with the aim of receiving more money, through income or capital appreciation, usually after a period of time and with an element of *risk*. In general, investing puts the initial (principal) sum at risk, whereas *saving* involves risk only to the income earned from the principal, but in practice the terms are often used interchangeably.

Investment bank

A bank that lends to businesses and governments for fixed investment (for example, in new machinery and infrastructure), and trades for profit in financial markets on its own account. It mostly raises capital from individuals or companies that are willing to invest it for a long period, via *shares* or *bonds*, rather than through customer deposits. See also *commercial bank*.

Investment fund

A financial product that invests in a broad range of different *bonds*, *shares* and/or other *assets*.

Investment grade

The highest grade assigned to borrowers and their *bonds* by a *credit rating agency*, signalling low probability of default.

Investment trust

A company that invests in a diversified *portfolio* of *shares* and/or other investments. Investors buy shares in the investment trust.

Investments

Assets that are traded on a *stock exchange*, or products that invest in such assets. More broadly, any item purchased with the intention of generating future financial income and/or growth and eventually recovering the original sum.

Keynesian

Usually describes a policy of pumping money into the economy, in particular by boosting government spending; derives from John Maynard Keynes, who showed that economies could operate with permanently high levels of unemployment. See also *demand-side model*.

Leading indicator

A measure of economic activity that tends to change before other measures change.

Lender of last resort

A *central bank* function under which it lends to banks that are in difficulty and unable to borrow from elsewhere.

Leverage

Technically, the *ratio* of a company's debt to its total capital (which also includes, for example, money raised through issuing *shares*). More generally, it means using borrowed funds to increase the return from an investment (whether made by a business or an investor).

Liabilities

What a company or an individual owes to others, and has to pay back to them.

Liberalisation

A government policy to promote *free markets* and competition.

Liquid assets ratio

The *ratio* of cash and immediately cashable *assets* to total assets. Shows the proportion of what is owed – to creditors and shareholders – that could be paid back today, or in the next few days, from assets with high *liquidity*.

Liquidity

In accountancy, the ability of a business to pay its debts as they fall due.

Liquidity risk

The risk of being unable to cash in an investment rapidly enough, or for a sufficiently high price, to pay debts as they fall due or to take advantage of better investment opportunities.

Liquidity trap

A situation where low or even zero interest rates fail to revive an economy, because investors refuse to buy non-liquid *assets*. See also *Keynesian*.

Logarithmic scale

A scale used for plotting graphs where the values on an axis reflect *ratios* of the underlying quantity, such as a percentage increase.

London Inter-bank Offered Rate (LIBOR)

The rate of interest that sets the cost of borrowing funds (or making deposits) on the inter-bank market in the UK.

London Stock Exchange

The main London stock market, located in the City of London.

Loss-aversion

The tendency of individuals to dislike losses more than they favour equivalent gains. Leads to agents being *risk-averse* when faced with gains and *risk-preferring* when faced with losses.

Macroeconomics

The analysis of whole-economy features such as national output, *inflation* rates, interest rates and growth rates.

Margin trade

A short-term investment made with a loan, intended to be repaid from profits on price movement. A drop in the value of *assets* held relative to the amount borrowed may result in a 'margin call' for additional capital to close this gap.

Market capitalisation

A company's current market value, obtained by multiplying its number of issued *shares* by their current market price.

Market portfolio

A *portfolio* of all the *shares* in the market, in proportion to their market value. Bought by investors or funds that wish to diversify away all *specific risk*; the portfolio recommended for all investors by the *CAPM*.

Market return

The return on the *market portfolio*. See also *beta*.

Market risk

The risk on the *market portfolio*, arising from events that unexpectedly affect asset prices throughout the market and not from those that affect the prices of specific *assets*.

Market timing

An investment strategy that involves buying and selling a particular *portfolio* to try to outperform the alternative strategy of buying the portfolio and holding it.

Marketmaker

An individual or firm that buys and sells *assets* in large amounts, ensuring a liquid market in them.

Markowitz diversification

Combining *portfolio* assets in an effort to lower *risk* without sacrificing *expected return*.

Markowitz efficient

Describes a *portfolio* that has the highest *expected return* for a given level of risk.

Mark-to-market

To put a value on an investment, for balance-sheet purposes, by taking its current market value.

Maturity transformation

Turning short-term, highly liquid *liabilities* (such as households' bank deposits) into longer-term, less liquid *assets* (such as loans to companies for *fixed capital* investment).

Mean

The weighted average of a set of values. Provided all values are equally probable, it is obtained by adding them up and dividing the total by the number of values.

Microeconomics

The analysis of an economy's constituent parts, e.g. firms, consumers and particular markets, and especially the role of prices and wages as incentives for efficiency.

Mis-selling

Inducing personal investors to buy a financial product that is unsuited to their needs and circumstances, and/or that involves them in financial loss, usually after failure to follow an acceptable sales procedure.

Momentum trading

Buying *assets* whose prices are moving, in order to profit from further movement; sometimes termed 'noise trading' because it focuses on (and may amplify) unexplained price movements that other traders call noise.

Monetary policy

The control by *central banks* of money supply and interest rates.

Money market

A market for overnight and very-short-term loans to governments and large companies, in which investments are regarded as highly liquid and low-risk.

Money market fund

An *investment fund* that seeks low-risk returns predominantly in the money markets.

Money multiplier

The *ratio* of banks' deposits to banks' reserves; used in a model that suggests that banks, by channelling deposits/*savings* into investments, inject money into the economy.

Moody's

One of the major three *credit rating agencies*.

Moral hazard

The *risk* that insuring or otherwise protecting someone against a bad outcome will make them less careful about the consequences of their actions and so encourage more risky behaviour.

Mortgage

A long-term loan used to buy a fixed *asset* (such as a house), and secured against the asset.

Mortgage bank

A *commercial bank* specialising in *mortgage* loans to households.

Mortgage-backed securities (MBSs)

Bonds secured against a bank's loan books; a form of *securitisation* used by *commercial banks* and *building societies* to raise capital.

MSCI World Index

The Morgan Stanley Capital International composite index of all major indices of 23 developed countries, weighted by market value.

Naïve diversification

When *shares* are combined without reference to their risk–return characteristics in an effort to lower *portfolio* risk. See also *Markowitz diversification*.

NASDAQ

The National Association of Securities Dealers' Automated Quotation, an *over-the-counter* US *securities* market, specialising in high-technology companies.

National income

The sum of all the income spent in the economy (consumption by households, investment by firms, net government expenditures, and current balance of payments), a close equivalent to the *Gross Domestic*

Product, and functionally equivalent to national output and national expenditure.

Negative equity

The excess of a *mortgage* over the value of the property that it is secured against.

Neoclassical economics

A development of *classical economics* that recognises some *demand-side* problems but still traces them to price and wage inflexibility, and assumes that decisions are taken as if individuals have full information that they process *rationally*.

Neoliberal

Favouring reduction of taxes and state provision wherever private provision can be argued to be a viable alternative.

Net

Usually 'after tax', in contrast to the gross (pre-tax) amount. Can also mean 'after depreciation' (as with net national product), 'after deduction of interest' (as with net profit) or 'after deduction of liabilities' (as with *net asset value*).

Net asset value (NAV)

The market value of the *portfolio* underlying a *unit trust* or *investment trust*. The net asset value per *share* is the net asset value divided by the number of shares or units.

New Deal

A massive programme of government spending (mainly in public infrastructure) launched by US President Roosevelt to combat the *Great Depression* of the 1930s.

New York Stock Exchange (NYSE)

The New York stock market. Also known as Wall Street, where it is located; owner of *Euronext*.

9/11

The terrorist attacks on New York's World Trade Center and other US locations on 11 September 2001, which aroused fears of *systemic risk* and were viewed by many as signalling a new age of financial and geopolitical uncertainty.

Noise trading

See *momentum trading*.

Nominal value

A cash value that takes no account of the buying power of the units in which it is expressed. Also the cash sum repaid on redemption of a conventional bond held to maturity. See also *real value*.

Normal curve

A graph that shows the probability of an outcome taking on different values and which has some specific characteristics: the possible outcomes are distributed symmetrically around the *expected value* (*mean*); a known proportion of the outcomes lies within a specified distance of the expected value. Also known as a normal distribution or *bell curve*.

Occupational pension

A pension scheme offered by an employer (which must contribute at least part of the cost). See also *state pension*.

OECD

The Organisation for Economic Co-operation and Development, which promotes policy cooperation and data-sharing among the world's higher-income nations.

Office of Fair Trading (OFT)

The UK government department responsible for consumer protection.

ONS

The UK Office for National Statistics.

Open-ended investment company (OEIC)

An *investment fund* structured as a limited company (like an *investment trust*) but enabling investors to purchase *shares* in specified types of *portfolio*.

Operating costs

Wages, raw materials and other items that go into creating and delivering a company's goods and services.

Option contract

An optional *futures contract*. See also *put option*, *call option*.

Ordinary shares

Shares whose dividends are not guaranteed to be paid and may vary in amount. Ordinary shareholders are given votes with which they can try to influence the running of the company; if it fails, they can recover *capital* only if there is some left after *assets* are sold to pay off the company's debts.

Originate-and-distribute

A strategy by which a bank *securitises* and sells its customer loans, instead of retaining them for a long-term relationship with the borrower. See also *structured investment vehicle*.

Over-the-counter (OTC)

Trade in a non-standardised contract, away from a *stock exchange* or other organised exchange.

Overtrading

Moving too frequently between one *share* or fund and another. See also *churn*.

Overvaluation

A situation where an asset's market price exceeds the *present value* of its expected payment stream.

Passive investor

An investor who seeks to track, and not outperform, a specified investment *benchmark*.

Pay-as-you-go (PAYG)

A system of financing state (and sometimes other) pensions through taxation, so that today's retirees are financed by today's taxpayers; often contrasted with 'funded' pension schemes, which finance retirement by drawing down an individual's *savings* and investments made while they were working.

Peer group

A group of funds with the same investment objectives.

Perfect competition

The existence of many buyers and sellers in a market, none of which can affect the market price.

Perfect foresight

The accurate prediction of future values: often assumed in economic models featuring *rational* agents.

Perfect information

The situation where all market participants know prices and quantities of all transactions that other agents have entered into. See also *complete information*.

Personal pension

A pension scheme to which individuals can contribute and which is not linked to any employment; treated for tax in the same way as an occupational pension, but usually the employer does not contribute. See also *SIPP*.

Portfolio

A set of financial *assets* held by an individual, bank or other financial institution.

Portfolio theory

An approach that determines the *risk* and return of a *portfolio* given the risk, return and correlation of its *assets*.

Positive feedback

A process through which a shock to a system generates further movement in the same direction; also called 'cumulative causation' or 'reinforcement mechanism'.

Prediction market

A market created to predict outcomes of an event, by inviting people to place bets on it.

Preference shares

Shares that offer a fixed-rate dividend provided that the company's profits are sufficient to cover it. Preference shareholders are paid ahead of ordinary shareholders, and if the company is wound up, they have priority entitlement to any liquidated *assets*.

Present value

The value today of one or more payments due to be received in the future; obtained by applying a *discount rate* to the future payments, to reflect the fact that money in future is generally worth less than money today.

Price mechanism

The adjustment of prices, upwards when there's a shortage and downwards when there's a surplus, so that market supply and demand move into balance.

Price–earnings (P/E) ratio

The *ratio* of the *share* price divided to the company's yearly earnings per share. An approximate indication of the years that it would take to recoup the price paid for the shares, mainly used as a measure of their (and the company's) relative value.

Private equity

An equity investment by individuals or institutions that is not publicly traded; the investment is exited by privately selling the stake, or floating the company through an *initial public offering*. See also *venture capital*.

Private pension

Any non-*state pension* scheme, i.e. an occupational or personal pension.

Professional regulation

Rules that professionals (including bankers and financial advisers) impose on themselves, directly or through a professional institution, to ensure principled and financially sustainable behaviour. See also *ethics*, *financial regulation*.

Prospect theory

A financial theory that argues that individuals' preferences under uncertainty are influenced differently when faced with losses or with gains, and by the framing of the choices available; see *loss-aversion*.

Prudential risk

The risk of a financial institution encountering financial difficulty, including *insolvency* or *illiquidity*, due to inadequate internal financial control.

Public company

A company that has issued *shares* to the general public ('gone public'), the shares being listed and re-traded on a *stock exchange*.

Put option

An option to sell an asset at a specified future time and price.

Random walk

A journey in which the direction of the next step is not influenced by the direction of the previous step; characterises the path of *share* prices, according to the *efficient markets hypothesis*.

Ratio

One amount shown in proportion to another; can be expressed as a percentage or a fraction.

Rationality

In economics, the pursuit by individuals or organisations of goals in the most efficient way possible, usually by maximising financial or material gain subject to constraints of income or wealth. For example, businesses are assumed to maximise profits, and rational investors are assumed to maximise subjective well-being (linked to wealth), given the resources that they have available to invest.

Real economy

The production and trade of goods and services, as opposed to trade in investment products and money (the financial economy).

Real value

The value or price of something after stripping out any change due to *inflation*. For example, if £100 is invested and grows to £110 but the general level of prices goes up 10 per cent, the real value of the investment is still only £100.

Recession

An economic downturn, technically defined as two or more successive quarters of declining national output (or 'negative growth'). See also *depression*, *Keynesian*.

Redemption yield

The total return that a bond will produce expressed as a percentage of the current market price, assuming that the bond is held until redemption. It takes into account both the interest and the redemption value.

Relative return

Investment performance expressed in comparison with the investor's *peer group*, or a *benchmark* such as the *market return*. See also *absolute return*.

Repo rate

The interest rate at which a *central bank* makes short-term loans to *commercial banks* (sometimes called the 'official rate' or 'policy rate').

Retail Prices Index (RPI)

The *inflation* measure that uses a slightly different range of goods and services from the *CPI*, mainly through including housing costs. Used in the UK to adjust state benefits, pensions and interest on index-linked gilts and other index-linked investments.

Return on assets (ROA)

Net income as a percentage of total *assets*.

Return on equity (ROE)

Net income as a percentage of *shareholders' equity*; can be raised above return on income or *assets* if these have been expanded beyond equity through the use of *leverage*.

Return on investment (ROI)

Net discounted income from an investment expressed as a percentage of the initial amount invested.

Risk

The element of uncertainty over an investment's future price or return that can be numerically estimated, through its variability or *volatility*.

Risk premium

The extra return that an investor expects as a reward for choosing a risky investment rather than a risk-free one.

Risk-averse

Tending to choose an investment with a lower level of risk than another comparable investment. See also *risk-preferring*.

Risk-free asset

A *security* whose return must comprise one or more fixed payments on one or more set future dates with no possibility of a different outcome. In the real world, there is no completely risk-free investment, but short-term *bonds* issued by the governments of large, high-income economies such as the USA and the UK are regarded as almost risk-free.

Risk-preferring

Tending to choose an investment that offers a higher level of risk than another comparable investment; the opposite of *risk-averse*, also known as risk-seeking.

Risk–return spectrum

The relationship between the risk of, and return from, investments: usually, lower-risk investments offer lower returns, while investments offering the chance of higher returns involve additional risk.

R-squared (R^2)

The percentage of the total *risk* of a *portfolio* that can be explained by *market risk*. The remainder is the percentage represented by *specific risk*.

S&P500

Standard and Poor's weighted index of the largest 500 *market capitalisations* of US companies on the *NYSE* or *NASDAQ*.

Satisficing

Looking for a satisfactory, sufficient solution rather than the most efficient (maximising or optimising) one. See also *rationality*.

Saving

The flow of money not used for current consumption and which contributes towards an individual's or household's *savings*.

Savings

The total value of all financial *assets*, including investments, that an individual or household has at a particular point in time.

Savings bank

A bank that takes deposits from ordinary households, offering them interest, which is financed mostly by lending to the government, local authorities or other very safe borrowers.

Say's Law

The idea that supply creates its own demand. See also *supply-side model*.

Sectors

Groups of companies listed on a particular *stock exchange* that carry out the same activity (e.g. electrical engineering, property construction or financial services).

Securities and Exchange Commission (SEC)

The US authority that supervises *stock exchanges* and other financial services providers.

Securitisation

Turning an asset that produces a regular flow of income (such as a bundle of bank loans, or properties generating rents) into a tradable investment such as a bond that can be sold to other banks and non-bank investors.

Security

A tradable financial investment such as a *share*, bond or *futures contract*.

Self-invested Personal Pension (SIPP)

A *personal pension* that allows individuals to manage their own investments, giving access to a wide range of investments within the pension *tax wrapper*.

Shareholders' equity

Capital subscribed by shareholders, which gives *public companies* a buffer between *assets* and *liabilities*.

Shares

Also called *equities*, *securities* or stocks. These are investments where each holder becomes part-owner of a company. The return may comprise regular dividends (a share of the company's profits) that are not guaranteed and/or a capital gain or loss when the shares are sold. Shares are often, but not always, traded on the stock market.

Sharpe ratio

An *investment fund*'s return per unit of total *risk*: obtained through dividing its 'excess' return (the *expected return* relative to the risk-free rate) by its *risk*, the *standard deviation* of returns.

Shortfall risk

The risk that a predefined *savings* or investment target will not be met.

Short-selling

Borrowing and selling an asset on the expectation that it will fall in price before the loan is repaid.

Skew

A situation where the data (such as possible investment returns) are not distributed symmetrically around the *expected value*. See also *normal curve*.

Small print

A product's terms and conditions, typically written in small letters and/ or technical jargon.

Social costs

Costs arising from production or consumption that are not paid by the individual or institution concerned, but imposed on the rest of society; e.g. the pollution emitted by a car or factory. See also *externality*.

Solvency

The ability to repay all debts and remain financially viable, usually indicated by *assets* exceeding *liabilities* on the *balance sheet*.

Specific risk

The risk specific to a company, which can be reduced through *diversification*.

Speculative grade

A low grade assigned to a borrower and its *bonds* by a *credit rating agency*, indicating a relatively high *default risk*, thus usually commanding higher interest rates (due to the *risk premium*) compared with *investment grade* bonds.

Spot market

A market in which transactions are agreed for immediate exchange and settlement. See also *forward market*.

Spread betting

An arrangement whereby an investor can place bets on an asset price or index moving above the offer price or below the bid price set by a spread betting firm.

Stagflation

A combination of *inflation* and economic stagnation or negative growth, usually with high unemployment.

Stamp duty

Tax payable on the purchase of a *share* or property (as a proportion of its value at purchase). Not due on share sales.

Standard and Poor's (S&P)

One of the three major *credit rating agencies*; US financial publisher that also provides *share*-price indices such as the *S&P500*.

Standard deviation

A measure of the extent to which outcomes spread out to either side of the *mean*. Commonly used in investment as a measure of *risk*. See also *variance*.

State pension

A pension paid by a government to people who have reached a specified age and meet specified contribution conditions, funded by taxation.

Stock exchange

An organised market on which *shares* and *bonds* are traded.

Stock selection

An investment strategy that involves buying *shares* in different proportions to their weighting in a stock-market index to try to outperform that index, especially by 'overweighting' undervalued stocks and 'underweighting' overvalued stocks.

Structural change

A change in the social, economic, political or technological conditions shaping economic activity; usually slower but less predictable or reversible than *cyclical* change.

Structured investment vehicle (SIV)

An off-balance-sheet subsidiary sometimes established by financial or non-financial companies to buy *assets*, especially *securitisations*, from the company. Also known as special-purpose vehicle; disappeared after the banking crisis that began in 2007.

Structured product

An investment product that guarantees the investor either a minimum capital amount at the end of the product life or a minimum income over the product life, and uses *derivatives* or other complex strategies to deliver the promised amounts.

Supply-side model

An economic model that argues that supply of goods and services creates its own demand, mainly through price adjustments. See also *Say's Law.*

Support ratio

The number of people of working age divided by the number of people over *state pension* age. See also *dependency ratio.*

Swap

A kind of financial *derivative* whereby two investors holding different *assets* agree to exchange the income streams that they generate.

Systematic risk

A *market risk* that cannot be reduced through *diversification.*

Systemic regulation

Regulation to avoid a threat to the whole economic system.

Systemic risk

The danger that problems in one financial institution will spread through the whole system, due to the way in which institutions are financially interconnected. Because of its huge scale and unpredictability, it is not a risk that can be insured against without government help.

Tax wrapper

An administrative structure that shields an investment from either some or all tax.

Tax year

The 12-month period across which, for example, investment and other income is assessed for tax; in the UK this begins on 6 April and ends on 5 April of the next calendar year.

Technical analysis

Use of regularities or trends in past price data to predict future prices. Closely related to *chartism.*

Time diversification

The practice of *investing* and/or cashing in investments in a series of lump sums spread over time, in order to remove the *risk* of choosing a bad time to invest (when prices are high) or disinvest (when prices are low).

Time preference

The tendency of people to prefer 'present goods and services' (those available for consumption now) to 'future goods and services' (those expected to be available for consumption at a future date). See also *discounting, excessive discounting*.

Tobin's q

The value that the stock market puts on a company (measured as the market value of its *shares* and debts) divided by the cost of replacing all the firm's *assets*. A value less than 1 suggests that the company is undervalued.

Total expense ratio

The annual cost to a client of an *investment fund*, including all management fees and charges, but excluding dealing costs.

Tracking error

The *volatility* or *standard deviation* of an *investment fund's alpha* over time. The larger the tracking error, the more likely is a high outperformance or underperformance in any one period.

Transaction cost

The costs incurred when buying or selling an asset, or taking out or closing an investment.

Transfer payment

A tax-funded welfare benefit, such as a *state pension* or jobseeker's allowance.

Treasury Inflation-protected Securities (TIPs)

US government *bonds* where the interest payments and redemption value are increased in line with *inflation* throughout the life of the bond.

Uncertainty

A situation in which the probability of an event cannot be estimated. See also *risk*.

Undervaluation

A situation in which a *share* price is below the *present value* of its fundamentals.

Unit trust

A trust that holds *shares* on behalf of investors. Investors hold units in the unit trust.

Value fund

An *investment fund* that focuses on stocks believed to be undervalued, seeking investment returns through capital gain, when undervaluation is corrected, as well as dividends. See also *growth fund, income fund*.

Value share

A share believed to be undervalued because most investors have ignored or failed to understand the company.

Variance

A measure of the dispersion of a set of values, calculated as the sum of their squared deviations from the *mean*, i.e. the square of the *standard deviation*.

Venture capital

A form of finance used to fund start-up companies; as these are typically riskier than mature companies, and capital cannot usually be retrieved unless the enterprise is later sold to another company or shareholders, venture capital investors expect high average returns.

Volatility

The variability of *share* prices, investment, or any other series of values around their average, usually measured by their *standard deviation* or *variance*.

Warrants

Securities, re-tradable on a *stock exchange*, that give the buyer the right to purchase the company's *shares* on one or more set future dates at pre-set prices. Typically issued to buyers of newly issued shares to make them more attractive. Comparable to a *call option* on the shares.

Weighted average

An average that allows for the relative importance of each component.

Welfare state

A system whereby the government funds or provides public services and redistributes income to provide a 'safety net' for its citizens. See also *transfer payment*.

Working capital

Raw materials, unsold stocks, and other expenditures on production from which money is recovered at the end of the production process when goods or services are sold.

Year-to-date period

The period starting on 1 January of the current year and ending on the current date.

Acknowledgements

Grateful acknowledgement is made to the following sources:

Cover

Copyright © Chris Jackson/Getty Images.

Text

Chapter 6: Box 1: Barker, T (2001) 'Companies & Finance: Dotcombustion', *The Finance Times,* 10 March 2001; Pages 294 and 298: Mandelbrot, B. and Taleb, N.N. (2005) 'How the finance gurus get risk all wrong, Retirement Guide 2005', Fortune, 11 July 2005.

Photos

Page 16: Copyright © Bettman/Corbis; Page 104: Copyright © Joe McDonald/Corbis; Page 121: Copyright © Pictorial Press Ltd/Alamy; Page 137: Copyright © Steve Allen/Brand X/Corbis; Page 153: Copyright © John Giles/PA Wire/Press Association Images; Page 158: Copyright © Brijesh Singh/Reuters/Corbis; Page 184: Copyright © Oliver Eltinger/Corbis; Page 199 left: Copyright © Erik Freeland/ Corbis; Page 199 right: Copyright © Smith Rich/Corbis; Page 225: Copyright © John Struthers; Page 243: Copyright © Bettmann/Corbis; Page 245 left: Copyright © Philimon Bulawayo/Reuters/Corbis; Page 245 right: Courtesy of Everett Collection/Rex Features; Page 316: Copyright © Phil Noble/PA Archive/Press Association Images; Page 336: Copyright © PA/PA Archive/Press Association Images.

Figures

Chapter 1: Figures 3 and 4: Jenkinson, N. (2008) 'Strengthening regimes for controlling liquidity risk: some lessons from the recent turmoil', Bank of England Quarterly Bulletin, vol. 48, no. 2. Copyright © Bank of England; Chapter 2: Figure 4: OECD (2009) OECD Economic Outlook: Interim Report, OECD. Copyright © OECD; Figure 9: Bank of England (2009) 'Markets and Operations', Bank of England Quarterly Bulletin, vol. 49, no. 1. Copyright © Bank of England; Figure 10: Copyright © 2009 Standard & Poor's, a division of The McGraw-Hill Companies, Inc. All rights reserved; Chapter 3: Figure 1: MoneySavingExpert.com; Figure 10: Copyright © Morningstar UK Ltd; Chapter 4: Figure 2: Malkiel, B.G. (2007) *A Random Walk Down Wall Street,* W.W. Norton & Company Inc; Chapter 6: Figure 2: Copyright © Bettmann/Corbis; Figure 4: Montier, J (2007) *Behavioural Investing: A Practitioner's Guide to Applying Behavioural Finance,* John Wiley & Sons Ltd;

Figures 5 and 6: Shiller, R.J. (2005) *Irrational Exuberance*, Princeton University Press Copyright © 2005 Robert J. Shiller.

Tables

Chapter 3: Table 2: www.investmentuk.org/statistics/sector_definitions/fund_class.asp Copyright © IMA; Chapter 4: Table 1: ISDA (2009) Market Survey Results, ISDA; Table 2: SIFMA (2009) ESF Securitisation Data Report: Q4:2008, SIFMA. Copyright © 2008 SIFMA.

Every effort has been made to contact copyright holders. If any have been inadvertently overlooked, the publishers will be pleased to make the necessary arrangements at the first opportunity.

Index

An excellent undergraduate text which links the practical aspects of personal finance and investment with the relevant socio-economic theory in an intellectually stimulating manner guaranteed to engage students.

Dr. Jim Mallon, Lecturer in Financial Services, School of Accounting, Economics & Statistics, Edinburgh Napier University, UK

The Personal Finance Society supports The Open University and Palgrave's aim to improve understanding and inspire confidence in personal investment decision making. This text provides a good introduction to the key theories underlying personal investment planning. The Personal Finance Society is focused on improving trust by setting high technical and ethical standards for those working in the advisory sector. The advent of Chartered status has made a career in financial planning an attractive option for graduates.

Fay Goddard, Chief Executive, The Personal Finance Society

This book not only explains personal finance to those who may be confused, but also helps the reader understand why it can be so confusing. Using a thematic approach to the topic, addressing important and universal issues of risk, uncertainty and ethics, this book is more than just a traditional primer or guide to personal financial issues. It explains simply and clearly a range of concepts from economics and finance that underpin our everyday personal experience of financial services. With a broad range of topical and everyday examples, it thus sets the issue of personal finance in its wider economic and social context, providing a book that is informative and critical as well as being (importantly for this area) an accessible and enjoyable read. A good introductory textbook for universities and colleges, with a wide range of potential application, it will also be a source of guidance for those seeking a better understanding of how to cope with the risks and uncertainties that bedevil all of our personal finances.

Patrick Ring, Senior Lecturer in Financial Services, Programme Leader, Finance, Investment and Risk, Caledonian Business School, Glasgow, Scotland, UK

The authors unlock the doors to the secrets of what every private investor should know – how to secure a more certain tomorrow by embracing the risks and perils of a less-than-certain world today.

David Kuo, Investment Expert, The Motley Fool, www.fool.co.uk

A refreshing, smart, investment book. The recession starkly revealed most economists didn't get it right. This book, drawing from sociology, psychology and institutional economics, shows the challenges real people in real lives face as they increasingly try and fail to manage life's risks through commercial and unstable financial markets.

Teresa Ghilarducci, Schwartz Professor of Economic Analysis, The New School, USA

Explaining the complexities of personal investment is a challenge in itself but to locate these decisions in their political and sociological context is a stunning achievement. This is a remarkable and fascinating book that will appeal equally to finance practitioners and students of social change.

Peter Howells, Professor of Monetary Economics, Centre for Global Finance, Bristol Business School, UK